ON YOUR OWN

Since 1990, when she finished college, Jessica Fein has moved three times (from Ann Arbor, Michigan, to Washington, D.C., to Seattle to Boston), changed jobs (she's not saying how often, but a lot), run out of money, gotten ripped off, and lived with roommates from hell before she got it all together. Now she is here to share her experiences (and those of her friends) to help you avoid the pitfalls of real life. Read this book, and you will save yourself endless headaches and significant time and money. Here are some of the things you will learn:

- How you can move all your stuff short- or long-distance without getting stiffed by moving companies
- How to find an apartment you can afford, in a strange city, in a part of town even your mother approves of
- Ways to make new friends and have dates no matter what city you are in
- How to land a job before you run out of money—and then find a better one (this is the real world, remember)
- 51 ways to cut expenses and save money

All this, and much, much more, including checklists, a sample lease, and a great-looking job resume, in an idea-packed book that tells you everything you need to know to survive on your own like a real adult—now that you are one.

MOVING ON

Jessica Fein is a writer and editor who has moved three times since she graduated from the University of Michigan in 1990. She is currently Marketing Communications Manager for CFO Publishing in Boston.

Jessica Fein

MOVING ON

How to Make the Transition from College to the Real World

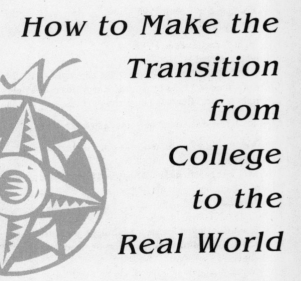

A PLUME BOOK

PLUME
Published by the Penguin Group
Penguin Books USA Inc., 375 Hudson Street, New York, New York 10014, U.S.A.
Penguin Books Ltd, 27 Wrights Lane, London W8 5TZ, England
Penguin Books Australia Ltd, Ringwood, Victoria, Australia
Penguin Books Canada Ltd, 10 Alcorn Avenue, Toronto, Ontario, Canada M4V 3B2
Penguin Books (N.Z.) Ltd, 182–190 Wairau Road, Auckland 10, New Zealand

Penguin Books Ltd, Registered Offices: Harmondsworth, Middlesex, England

First published by Plume, an imprint of Dutton Signet,
a division of Penguin Books USA Inc.

First Printing, September, 1996
10 9 8 7 6 5 4 3 2 1

Ⓟ REGISTERED TRADEMARK—MARCA REGISTRADA

LIBRARY OF CONGRESS CATALOGING-IN-PUBLICATION DATA:
Fein, Jessica.
    Moving on : how to make the transition from college to the real world / Jessica Fein.
        p.   cm.
Includes index.
ISBN 0-452-27603-9
1. Life skills—United States.   2. College graduates—United States—Life skills
guides.   3. School-to-work transition—United States.   I. Title.
HQ2039.U6F45   1996
646.7'0084'2—dc20
                                                                    96-11149
                                                                    CIP

Printed in the United States of America
Set in Times New Roman and Benguiat
Designed by Eve L. Kirch

For Nomi

*How does it feel
to be on your own
with no direction home
like a complete unknown
like a rolling stone?*
—Bob Dylan

CONTENTS

SECTION TWO: YOUR JOB SEARCH

SECTION THREE: REAL-WORLD PRESSURE

ACKNOWLEDGMENTS

Special thanks for their guidance and support to Pam Bernstein, my agent; Jennifer Moore, my editor; and Celeste Sollod, who kickstarted this project.

This book is the product of countless conversations with my friends as we fumbled our way through the post-college transition. Thanks especially to the following people for sharing their stories with me, and consequently with you: Sarah Adler, Lara Bodie, David Chodirker, Kara Dukakis, Karen Flood, Kim Gouin, Kirk Hamill, Wendy Heyman, Sarah Lawrence, Liz Reef, Dhana Rivera, Andy Snyder, Dana Snyder, Jennifer Weisel, Cheryl White, and my sisters, Rachel and Nomi. I am indebted to my parents for their unconditional support of all of my endeavors. My mother, Zelda White, served as a sounding board throughout the writing of this book. Her expertise in career counseling helped me immensely. My father, Leonard Fein, was my partner through each phase of the project; I'm forever grateful for the huge amount of time he devoted to it.

And, for everything, thanks to Rob Flaggert. Without him I certainly would have driven myself—and everyone I know—crazy while I wrote this book. I look forward to returning the favor very soon.

Introduction

The fantasy was clear: I'd finish college and move to a fashionable neighborhood where I'd find a dazzling apartment that was also affordable in a complex where, incidentally, all my friends would also live. I'd scurry to the top of the corporate ladder during the day and at night I'd be wooed by sultry suitors.

What I didn't consider was how to discover that fashionable neighborhood and the dazzling apartment. I didn't consider where my friends would fit if the building were filled with lecherous men, dotty women, and assorted other strangers. I didn't consider how I would get hired by the company whose corporate ladder I was so gracefully and quickly to ascend; I didn't even pause to reflect on the fact that the very idea of a corporate ladder made my stomach churn. And never once did it cross my mind that I might be spending my evenings working a second job just to make ends meet. Sultry suitors? Only if they worked the swing shift.

Two days after graduating from the University of Michigan, I packed myself and the preceding four years of my life into a rented van and drove with two friends to Washington, D.C. None of us had been to D.C. before; we had neither jobs nor housing waiting for us. Our social network consisted entirely of each other.

D.C. was followed a year and a half later by a solo cross-country move to Seattle. Again, no apartment and no job. This time, at least, I had friends to welcome me to town. Actually, "friends" is a bit of an exaggeration. I could count him on the finger of one hand.

Nothing I'd learned during my sixteen years of formal education prepared me to cope with the new circumstances and new challenges that moving and setting up a life involves. Sure, I'd moved to college—but that move had little in common with my postcollege moves. While I managed the college moves with the ease of slipping into a pleasantly warm hot tub, the postcollege ones stung like belly flops into the Bering Sea. My only resource was my friends and they, as it turned out, were just as confused as I.

During my first two years out of college, my phone bill averaged two hundred dollars a month. Most nights I'd talk to at least one college or high-school friend who was living in a different part of the country. For the first several months we commiserated about our problems in finding apartments and roommates and jobs and new friends. Once those were in place, the conversations turned to roommate conflicts or job doldrums or how broke we were or our stagnant social lives.

A good way to spend an hour or three, but not very helpful in solving our problems—especially, obviously, the financial ones. We were all (more or less) bewildered, which meant that we were long on empathy but painfully short on useful advice.

It was out of those conversations that the idea for this book emerged: a book that would provide practical advice and serve as a comprehensive guide for all the different phases of the postcollege transition, a book that would tell the stories of others who have been on the same ride and have survived all its ups and downs, a book written by someone for whom the experience is not just a hazy memory.

Within the pages of this book you'll find information and advice on every phase of your move, from finding an apartment to furnishing it, from balancing your checkbook to balancing your time, from landing a job to leaving one. Though the chapters are organized somewhat chronologically (you can't, for example, furnish your apartment until you have an apartment; you can't leave a job unless you have a job), you may find that its sections work best for you out of sequence. You may also find that you don't need *all* the information that's included. Already have a job? Skip that chapter (but make sure to hold on to the book just in case).

Section One covers all of the aspects of setting up in your new city. What's the best way to move? Do you want to live alone or with roommates? How do you find potential roommates and what should you learn about them before deciding to rent together? How do you find housing? What do you need to find out about an apartment or house before signing a lease? How can you turn an empty space into a place that feels like home? Where can you find affordable furniture? How do you find friends in a new city? These are just some of the questions you're likely to confront; in the first five chapters you'll learn how to set about answering them.

Section Two walks you through your job search. How do you figure out what kind of job you want? What resources can help you with self-assessment, and how do you access them? Once you've chosen a field, how do you find out about job openings? How do you write a successful cover letter? A resume? A thank-you letter? How do you survive a job interview, and how do you succeed at one? What do you do when your new job isn't all you dreamed it would be? Section Two will help you develop a successful job-search strategy by answering all these questions and more.

Section Three covers your general well-being. In Chapter 9 you'll learn how to be financially responsible. How do you construct a livable budget—and live within it? How can you cut costs, and how can you increase income? What do you need to know about saving and taxes and organizing your finances? Chapter 10 covers the emotional aspects of your transition. How do you balance all the new elements in your life? What kinds of new pressures might you encounter, and how can you best cope with them? How do you find medical care in a new city, and how should you take care of yourself?

All this may well seem overwhelming; there are so many questions to answer, so many decisions to make. Keep in mind that there's no right or wrong here, no prior certainty. This story has more than one happy ending. You're not entering a race and you're not taking a test, so don't worry if it takes some time—and some trial and error—to figure out what's right for you. You may start down certain paths and then find that you want to change directions. You might become lost, or feel that you need to visit some rest stops along the way. I hope this book makes your journey less stressful. After all, while this is a time of many decisions, it's also one of endless possibilities.

GETTING STARTED

1. Making Your Move: Planes, Trains, or Automobiles

Moving to a new city when you graduate from college is going to be different—emotionally and practically—from any move you ever made before. Almost all moves create psychological challenges; you have to adjust to a new city, new school, new friends. But, if when you were growing up, you moved from one house to another, chances are that your parents or guardians took care of setting up your new life—like where you'd be living and what school you'd be attending and which room would be yours. And when you moved to college, though you probably felt somewhat insecure, you knew where you were going to live when you got there and what you were going to do on the very first day. Your postgraduation move is going to be different because once you arrive in your new city, you're going to have to create a life for yourself. And knowing that's what lies ahead is going to make this move more complex in every way.

Not to worry. In this chapter, we're going to work through the nitty-gritty, practical aspects of your move. Once we've gotten those taken care of, we'll turn to the other and more amorphous elements of getting started in your new life.

Up until now it's likely that the first time you moved anywhere by yourself was when you went off to college. You packed a trunk and a couple of suitcases, got in your car, or on a bus, or on a plane, and set out for your new "home." When you arrived on campus you found your dormitory, your room, your new roommate(s). That was it. (Aside from fitting all the stuff you brought into the inevitably inadequate closets.) You had successfully completed your move.

The only thing that move has in common with the one you're now undertaking is that you'll again be packing the trunk and suitcases. But this time, odds are you'll also be packing umpteen boxes, plastic bags, and maybe even a milk crate or two. And that's the smallest part of the difference.

The fact is that from now on, every move you make is going to be a hassle. No matter how many times you move throughout your lifetime (the average American moves eleven times*) and regardless of how excited you are about your destination, the move itself is a huge pain. Even without the psychological stress, there are just so very many details to keep track of, so very many decisions to make, that all of us would avoid doing it if only we could.

Think about it: What's the best way to pack your belongings? Should you ship your luggage and fly to your destination or does it make more sense to rent a vehicle—and, if so, a car, a van, or a truck? Should you keep your stuff with you or ship it—and if shipping, have it arrive before you do, or after? (If you don't have an apartment yet, where do you ship it to?) What are the financial implications of shipping vs. schlepping? What about those services you've heard of that provide you with a vehicle on the condition that you drive it to their desired location? How do you find them, and what should you know about them before you make a deal? What details do you need to remember to take care of before leaving your current residence?

These are just some of the components of moving that you need to figure out—and that's what this chapter's about. By the time you've read it, you'll not only know the questions you should be asking, you'll know how to go about answering them or getting them answered with a minimum of fuss. If you start with an understanding of all the elements involved, and work with a checklist that covers all the details, you can pull your move off with only modest discomfort and slight discombobulation. You can avoid the immense waste of

---

*Kathleen Droste, ed., *The Gale Book of Averages* (Detroit: Gale Research, 1994).

time, money, and energy that moving—especially one's first move—so often and so needlessly entails.

Getting There: Relocation vs. Dislocation

The very first thing you need to decide is how you're going to get to your destination. It's impossible to decide on the most appropriate way to pack your things until you figure out how they're going to be transported, and the decision on their transport depends, in turn, on how you yourself will be traveling.

Each mode—driving your own car, driving someone else's car, renting a truck, taking a train, a bus, a plane—has its advantages and its disadvantages. These are spelled out in the next few pages, along with other considerations that will help guide your choice. But bear in mind that in the end, there is no "right" way to travel. One way or another, you'll get where you're going; what follows is a guide to ensuring that "getting there is half the fun." Or, at least, not a misery.

Driving Your Own Car

This one seems easy. If you don't own a car, you can't drive your car. But that doesn't mean that if you do own a car, you necessarily *should* drive it.

Why in the world wouldn't you drive it? If you've got it, drive it, right? You'll almost certainly want it in your new hometown. Moreover, the trip itself can be great fun and even valuable. What better way to see the sights and visit friends along the way? Depending on where you're moving from and where you're going, this may be a chance to see a piece of the country that's worth seeing (as distinguished from seeing an endless string of turnpikes and tollbooths). If you'll be driving with friend(s)—highly recommended if long distances are involved—there's the added pleasure of camaraderie (a less pharmaceutically dependent *Fear and Loathing in Las Vegas*). And if you're driving alone, you can view the trip as an adventure—and also as a useful transition time, a gradual withdrawal from one place and as gradual an arrival at your new home.

Which would seem to be, but isn't, all there is to say, because even if you own your own car, there may be reasons for you *not* to drive it. Maybe you're under a time constraint or are apprehensive about a lengthy solo drive. Maybe your car, much as you adore it, isn't quite up to a long-distance trip, and you're afraid it will collapse somewhere between Oz and Wonderland. Not to worry: There is a way to get your car to your destination without driving it there yourself.

Drive-away Companies

Automobile drive-away companies provide drivers who transport your car to your destination. Prices vary, depending on which company you use, the year and make of your car, and how far the car is being driven. In early 1996, hiring someone to drive your car across the country would have cost around four or five hundred dollars, plus the first tank of gas.* You're responsible for the primary insurance of the vehicle.

But remember—that's the cost for moving your car, not for moving yourself and your belongings. If you want to figure out what your move is going to cost, you've now got to add in the cost of your transportation and the charge for shipping your stuff. So the option of having your car driven for you makes sense only if you can afford top-dollar.

The flip side, of course, is that if you don't own a car but would like to drive to your new city, you can apply to be a driver for a drive-away company. Many companies require that drivers be at least twenty-one years old in order to apply (some have a minimum driver age of twenty-five). You need a valid driver's license and you'll have to provide the company with several references. Most companies require a deposit (anywhere from two to five hundred dollars), which is returned when you deliver the car. You'll be responsible for buying all but the first tank of gas and for your own food and lodging while you travel.

Depending on the distance you're traveling and how much stuff you've got, this option may or may not be financially attractive. On one hand, you can save on shipping costs by packing all or some of your belongings in the car. (Some companies allow the driver to pack his/her things in the trunk; other companies reserve that privilege

*Prices are based on the average rate for national drive-away companies.

for the car's owner.) But on the other hand, if you plan to pack a stereo, six suitcases, and a dining-room table, you'll be in trouble if the car you're given to drive is a Yugo.

Another thing to keep in mind is that when acting as a driver for a drive-away company, you have to be flexible about your date of departure. The way it works is that you go when the company needs a car transported, and the company may not be able to give you the kind of advance warning you want or need—especially if you're headed for a small town, for which there is less demand for drivers.

Once you, the company, and the car are all in synch and you're ready to depart, the company can help you map out a route, allowing a set number of days and miles for your trip. If you like to camp out and you're traveling at a time of the year when sleeping outside is desirable, or if you have friends who will put you up along the way, driving for a drive-away company can save you money.

To find a drive-away company, look in the Yellow Pages under "Automobile Transporters and Drive-Away Companies." Remember to call well in advance of your optimal departure date; it may be some time before a car (or a driver) is available.

Renting a Vehicle

If you don't own a car but want to drive to your new city—whether because it's a good way to see part of the country or because moving to a new city isn't quite enough of an adventure for you or because you're terrified of flying or because you own things that you don't want to ship, or all of the above—renting a vehicle is an option you should consider.

Here's how to think about it: First, decide whether it makes more sense to rent a car or a truck. (Depending on how much stuff you're moving, there's a good chance that you'll actually be renting a ten- or twelve-foot van rather than a truck—so understand that when I use the word "truck" I'm referring to anything ten feet or longer.)

If you're going to be traveling a great distance—say from one coast to the other—there are several reasons a car probably makes more sense than a truck. First, if you've ever driven a truck, you already know that it isn't exactly Indie 500 material. Maneuvering it is going to slow you down; that means that the drive will be more tedious and you'll have to pay for a few extra days rental and a few nights extra lodging.

Moreover, you'll spend additional money on gas. Since trucks generally burn more gas than do automobiles, you can expect to "fill 'er up" a great deal more often in a truck than you would in a car.

Finally, renting a truck to drive across the country costs considerably more than renting a car. In early 1996, for example, you could rent a car for a seven-day drive across the country for about five hundred dollars, whereas a truck, including insurance, would have cost close to a thousand.* When you total the cost of truck rental, extra lodging, and gas, there's a good chance you'll end up paying more to rent a truck than you would to rent a car and ship your belongings.

The advantage of a truck is, of course, the amount of stuff you can pack in it. But that is also its disadvantage, in two respects:

1. If you're setting out for a long journey with a truck full of your belongings, you're inviting misfortune. It will be very difficult to keep the truck in a guarded location at all times, especially if you leave it overnight. Because they are such an easy target for thieves, rental trucks might as well read, "Filled with great stuff, don't let the cheap lock stop you." I know a couple of people who had their belongings stolen from their truck (and one who had his belongings stolen together with his truck) while they were moving across the country; it's not a pleasant way to begin (or end) your move.

2. Regardless of the distance you're traveling, unless you've prearranged your living situation in your new city, you're going to have to figure out what to do with your things while you search for a place to live. Your search might take only a day or two, but it's much more likely to take considerably longer. (Sorry, but that's the way it doesn't go.) So: What do you do with all your things while you're hunting? Dragging them with you around the city is no solution, since that compounds the security problem, forces you to hang on to your (expensive) truck for days/weeks longer than you need to, and generates parking problems. In other words, your "let's pack everything into it and get the whole job done" strategy turns out to be a plague.

*Prices are based on the average rates for major national companies.

When my friends and I moved to D.C. in a fifteen-foot truck stuffed with everything we owned (mostly sweaters, endless sweaters), we made sure to check that the apartment in which we'd be staying during our search for housing had a secure garage. We forgot, however, to ask about the clearance measurements for said garage. In other words, we didn't consider the possibility that our truck would be too high to fit through the garage door. Since we pulled into town after midnight, we had no choice but to leave the truck on the street and hope that it (and the endless sweaters) would be there in the morning. We awoke at first light to find that we still had our truck. But we still had our truck problem.

We knew we'd be pushing our luck if we left our truck on the street the next night, so we called Joel and Bernice, distant relatives in not-so-distant Maryland and asked if they had space in their driveway for a fifteen-foot truck. They did, and that was good for a few nights. But when we realized that our apartment search wasn't going to conclude as swiftly as we'd hoped, we couldn't afford to continue paying the daily fee for the truck rental. Thank heaven for Joel and Bernice. They allowed us to unpack all our belongings into their garage. (They even had enough room for the sweaters.)

We returned the truck, but that left us without a vehicle with which to pursue our apartment search. And three weeks later, when we finally found an apartment, we had to rent another truck to transport our belongings. I don't even want to calculate the amount of money we could have saved if we had used a little forethought.

Even if you know someone in your new city who doesn't mind you unpacking your truck and dumping everything you own in the world on their living-room floor (or in their unused garage), a day of reckoning will come: Once you've found a place to live, you'll have to rent and load and unload a truck all over again. That's not necessarily intolerable—but it is a cost, and you should figure it in. Unless, that is, your circumstances and the nature of your stuff permit you to borrow a car and make multiple back-and-forth trips.

On the other hand, if you're going to be traveling a straight door-to-door shot (say, up to about a twenty-hour drive), are moving not only clothing, books, and your stereo but also furniture, and you have some place to unload the truck when you get where you're going, a truck can be ideal. You won't have to worry about the cost of lodging during your trip, and the money you'll save by not having to ship your things separately will more than make up—by far—for the extra money you'll spend on gas.

How to Go About Renting a Vehicle

After you make the choice between truck and car, it's time to take out your trusty Yellow Pages and start comparison shopping. You'll find cars under "Automobile Rentals" and trucks and vans under "Truck Rentals." You should contact several companies to compare rates. Here's a list of questions you should ask:

- What's the age requirement to rent? Many companies have a service charge if you are between twenty-one and twenty-five and others won't rent to you at all if you're under twenty-one. Make this the first question you ask so you don't waste your time getting information from a company that won't rent to you.
- How much will it cost to rent the least expensive automobile (or a ten-foot van or whatever you need) to drive from X to Y? If it's a truck you're renting, do not succumb to the temptation to rent a larger one than you think you need, "just in case." That will just leave more room for your belongings to shift around while you're driving. Most rental companies (all the big ones) can tell you roughly how large a truck you're going to need if you tell them roughly what you'll be bringing.
- Is there a drop-off charge for returning the vehicle in a different city from the one in which it was rented?
- Does the cost include unlimited mileage? If the answer to this question is "no," look for another company. You don't want to get stuck at the end of your trip with a large extra fee for mileage.
- How much extra is insurance? Usually, the basic price includes a minimum amount of insurance—but this is one area in which

you don't want to skimp. Make sure to get the maximum insurance for both the vehicle and for your belongings. The extra cost will be far less than the cost of replacing a vehicle and/or replacing irreplaceable possessions. That, after all, is what insurance is about. The good news is that many credit/charge-card companies include automobile insurance automatically if you use their card to rent the vehicle. So check with your credit-card company to find out what you have coming, and then make sure that the rental company accepts that card. Note, however, that your possessions are not covered by the credit/charge-card company. They may be covered under your parents' homeowners policy. A quick call to the family insurance agent will tell you. Your things may also be covered by your renter's insurance policy, if you already have one. (See Chapter 9 for a discussion of renter's insurance.)

- Are nonsmoking vehicles available? If this question pertains to you, you are a nonsmoker and know how irritating it can be to travel in a vehicle that reeks of stale cigarette smoke. More and more companies are designating cars for nonsmokers only.

Note: If you're traveling at peak travel times—between June and September—you should make your arrangements a few weeks in advance in order to ensure the best availability and price.

Leave the Driving to Them

If you don't have a car and are looking for the most economical mode to get where you're going, you might want to consider taking a train. And, if you're willing to sacrifice comfort in order to save even more money, take a bus. Contrary to popular belief, the bus does not necessarily take longer than the train and it will generally be much less expensive. Train or bus, you can save still more money by bringing a cooler full of food so you don't have to pay for your meals during the trip.

If you go by bus you'll be allowed two pieces of luggage stowed in the luggage compartment and two pieces to carry on with you. You can take up to three additional bags or boxes for ten dollars each. Trains also permit two bags on board but you are allowed to check three pieces of luggage for free, and three more beyond that will cost you only ten dollars apiece. (That is, until you get to your destination city with all that luggage and have to get from the bus or train station to wherever you're going. Think ahead.)

If you're traveling from one coast to another, the trip will take three days whether you travel by train or bus. If you have some time, however, you might want to buy a nonexpress ticket, which allows you to get off along the way and see some sights. Here's how it works:

- *Bus:* Depending on when you purchase your bus ticket and if there are any special promotions, you will be given a set number of days in which to complete your trip. You can get on and off the bus whenever and wherever you want (it's best to wait until the bus has stopped moving), and you can obtain a reboarding pass from the bus driver. You don't have to bother with the luggage you've checked; it'll be waiting for you at your final destination. The storage fee for your luggage depends on your destination, but it is generally very inexpensive.
- *Train:* The kind of train ticket that you purchase will determine how many days you have to complete your trip, but—here's the crucial difference—you have to prearrange the locations and dates of your stops before you begin the trip. In other words, despite any romantic notions about train travel that *Before Sunrise* gave you, spontaneity is out. You can check your luggage all the way through to your final destination and you will be charged a nominal storage fee.

Both the train and the bus are virtually worry-free modes of transportation (crashes and bandits and weird fellow-travelers aside); your only concerns are missing the departure and finding a way to sleep comfortably—or, for that matter, even uncomfortably—in a sitting position. (Alternatively, make friends with the person in the next seat. *Very good* friends.) Bus and train can both be relaxing ways to travel and seem, somehow, an appropriate way to mark the transition to a new place/life.

The Wild Blue Yonder

If you can afford the airline fare and want to get to your new city as quickly as possible, fly. You should compare the price of a round-trip ticket to the one-way fare. It's often the case that the round-trip fare is no more—and sometimes it's even less—than the one-way, in which case you should buy the round-trip, with a return scheduled for a few months down the road. By that time you might be ready for a trip; if not, you may be able to sell your ticket. (Having a return ticket might also make you feel less "trapped" if things aren't working out in your new city.)

Extra Credit: Prepare to Be Floored

If you can, make arrangements for a place to stay during your search for housing before you make your move. You don't know how long the search will take and you probably can't afford to spend money on temporary accommodations. So rack your brain to think of anyone you know in the city you're moving to who might be able to help. If there is an obvious choice, a good friend or relative, then you're set. If not, ask your friends and family if they have any connections. You may feel awkward calling someone you've never even met and asking to impose on them. Relax. Everyone has camped on a stranger's floor at one time or another and most people will be more than happy to help out the friend/relative of a friend. (Well, maybe not really *more* than happy, but not horrified, either. Not until, say, the third week.)

Pack It Up

After you've decided how you're going to get to your new city, you'll be able to figure out the best way to transport your belongings. Basically you have three choices: (1) move yourself first and have your stuff shipped to you after you've found a place to live; (2) bring your things with you when you move; or (3) pack up and send all of your belongings to your new city before you move there. Your decision is going to depend heavily on the mode of transportation you've

decided to use for your move. If you're renting a truck, you're probably planning on filling it with your belongings and taking them with
you when you move; if you're traveling via the friendly skies, you
can forget about bringing your stereo, computer, and double bed
with you; if you haven't prearranged your living situation, you won't
want to lug your assortment of suitcases, footlockers, duffel bags,
boxes, and shopping bags with you while you look for a place to
live. The decision on how to transport your belongings will, in turn,
have an effect on how you should pack them. So: Even though it
sounds backward, we'll do the part about transporting first, and then
turn to packing.

Moving Before Your Stuff

Unless you've already arranged your living situation, it doesn't
make much sense to take all your stuff with you. The last problem
you need to worry about while you're looking for a place to live and
trying to learn your way around a new city is where to leave all your
belongings. It's therefore a good idea to take just one or two suitcases with you and to pack up the rest of your things and leave them
with someone who will send them to you once you have an address.

Make sure, however, to take a towel and bedding with you, since
once you find a place to live it will take a few days for your things to
reach you. (If you have one, a sleeping bag is an even better idea than
bedding; it takes less room and it can do double service, in case you're
camping out on someone's floor during your apartment search.)

Moving with Your Stuff

If you already have an address in your new city or you know
someone who's agreed to let you stash your belongings while you
look for housing, you can move yourself and your stuff simultaneously. Once you've decided to get the whole move done in one fell
swoop you have three choices:

1. Do-It-Yourself. Obviously this option is, by far, the most economical. But it's only possible if you're traveling in a vehicle that's

big enough to hold all your things. (True, most airplanes would quali-fy according to that standard, but not everything that's true is also use-ful. You'd have to purchase all the seats.) If you're renting a truck, make sure to comparison shop—Hertz-Penske at (800) 222-0277, Ryder at (800) 467-9337, Budget at (800) 367-0522, and U-Haul at (800) 468-4285 are some names to get you started. (For additional companies, look under "Truck Rental" in the Yellow Pages.) Any one of these companies will be able to help you figure out what size truck you'll need. They'll also be able to provide you, either free or for a small price, moving devices such as hand trucks or dollies. If you're going to be moving heavy items—a console TV, for ex-ample—it's worth having one at hand. (Use the list of questions on pages 14–15 to find out what you need to know about renting a vehicle.)

Plan on getting as much help as you can to load and unload your truck on moving day. At the very least you need to have one helper so that one of you can guard the truck while the other makes trips back and forth carrying loads of stuff. (Otherwise you might find that you're unloading considerably less than you loaded.)

I have a friend who didn't want to bother anyone by asking for help on moving day. He worked out, he was strong, he knew he could handle packing a truck all by himself. He made trip after trip between apartment and truck, paying no attention to the kids playing nearby in the street. When his apartment was finally empty he was surprised at how much room he had left in the truck; he could have gone with the smaller size truck after all. Twenty hours and three states later, he unloaded the truck. Funny, he thought, it took much less time to unload the truck than it had taken to load it. It wasn't until the following day, when he set about unpacking, that he realized he'd been ripped off. Each time he'd gone inside to grab another armful of belongings, the kids had stolen half of what he'd just loaded. (Smart kids: If they'd taken everything, he might have noticed.) When he contacted the police he learned that this kind of thing happens frequently and was advised to forget about ever seeing his stuff again.

So for the sake of the security problem, make sure to get at least one friend to help out. But if at all possible, for the sake of the "oh my poor back" problem, get three or four. The more perhaps the merrier, for sure the easier.

How are you going to convince your friends, who'd really rather be anywhere else, to engage in a day of physical labor? Try any or all of the following tactics:

1. Promise them food. Lots of it. Anything they want.
2. Promise them they'll get such a good workout they can justify skipping the gym for a week.
3. Offer them any of your old stuff you've decided to leave behind. (I once inherited a couch, a small TV, and a three-speed bike in return for a couple hours of helping friends load their truck. I'd do it again in a second.)
4. Assure them a free place to stay anytime they're in your new city. (Warning: Use this method only if it's an incentive. Boulder and Miami Beach are in; Detroit and Waterloo are out.)

If none of these tactics works, or if it's a holiday weekend and no one's around, or if you don't have very many friends and the ones that you do have are all weaklings, try calling the Student Union of any nearby college. You should be able to hire a couple of students for a reasonable price (they'll probably charge you by the hour) to help you move your stuff. If you're moving to a place where you don't have even any weak friends, call ahead to a school in the area and hire some help. After a long drive you're going to be exhausted; physical labor is not going to be high on your list of preferred activities. Make sure you have enough cash with you to pay them; your VISA card won't do it and offering pizza and/or secondhand junk won't work on this end.

Unless you have a secure garage or driveway in which to leave your truck, don't pack it until the morning of your departure. It's no fun to have to pack the truck and move your stuff the same day, but at least that way you're assured you'll *have* stuff to move.

Once all of your friends, or hired helpers, or whoever, have agreed to help, you're ready to load the truck. You don't have to be a space scientist to do it right, but if you'd like to maximize the odds on both you and your things getting to where you're going intact, the following Seven Laws of Loading are basic:

1. Most trucks and even many vans come with a loading ramp. It's tucked under and extends from the rear of the truck, and if you don't know about it you might miss it. Without it, you'll need a pogo stick or a trampoline to bounce in and out of the truck, and neither is recommended when your hands are full. With it, life is a breeze. Relatively. In fact, you'd be wise to check on the ramp's presence before you sign the rental agreement.

2. Lift heavy stuff by keeping your back straight, bending at your knees (and one and two and plié), and getting your arms under the object. I know, I know, you've heard that before, and it seemed counterintuitive then just as it does now. Trust me. Better, trust my chiropractor. You should use your relatively strong leg muscles rather than your fragile back muscles to lift. If you throw your back out now, you're not going to have a very comfortable drive. (Not even if you're driving a flatbed truck, which sounds cozy but which is simply a truck with no sides and no top.)

3. Tie any mattresses, futons, or cushy items to the walls of the truck. (There'll be side rails for just that purpose.) These will provide padding should the ride get bumpy or, more accurately, *when* the ride gets bumpy.

4. Load large or heavy appliances (stereo, computer, TV) next, closest to the cab of the truck. Doing this will keep your truck stable on the road. Make sure to keep your heaviest things on the bottom of the stack.

5. Medium size, medium weight go in next; your light stuff goes in last and on top of stacks. Your overnight bag should be the very last thing you put in the truck so you don't have to search for it when you need it.

6. After you've packed each quarter or third (depending on the truck's size) solid from top to bottom, tie the area with rope or canvas webbing to the side rails of the truck. This will help keep your things from shifting during the trip.

7. If possible, pick up your truck the day before you're planning to move. You're going to want to get an early start and won't want to have to deal with getting the truck in the morning. Having the truck a day in advance will also give you the opportunity to drive it around a little bit. Driving a truck is very different from driving a car or even a minivan. Acceleration is

slower, passing and stopping take longer, and you won't have
the rearview mirror that you're used to. Pay special attention to
the side mirrors and get used to relying on them. If you can
practice driving the truck while it's empty, you'll be one step
ahead on moving day.

If all this sounds like a huge burden and leaves you with a pit of
dread in your stomach *and* if you have either (a) a huge quantity of
belongings to move *or* (b) a huge bank account, you do have a second alternative.

2. Leave It to the Pros. There are several different kinds of service you can get from professional movers; here's how it goes:

1. They take care of everything—pack all your things, load the
   truck, drive to your destination, and unpack for you.
2. You pack some of your stuff and leave some for the movers to
   pack. (Depending on the amount of trust you have in your
   packing abilities, you'll leave either your most precious or
   your least for the movers to take care of.) They load the truck
   and drive it to your destination; they unpack either everything
   or only those boxes they packed.
3. You pack everything, the movers load the truck and drive it to
   your destination, they unload all your stuff and put it in the
   rooms to which you direct them, and you unpack at your
   leisure, so to speak.

Your decision on which service to use should depend on how
much money you want to spend (the more they do, the more you
pay) and how much time you have to devote to the packing/unpack-
ing process.

Call a few major moving companies and inquire about rates. It's
okay to ask for the names of past customers you can contact as references; reputable companies will have no problem fulfilling this
kind of request. Companies are also required by the Interstate
Commerce Commission (ICC) to give you, if you ask for it, a copy
of their annual performance report. The ICC puts out a pamphlet
called: *When you Move: Your Rights and Responsibilities*, which

explains your rights as a shipper. Moving companies can provide you with this pamphlet.

For moves within a thirty-five-mile radius, your charges will be based on the number of hours your move takes and the number of movers. Since it's impossible to know precisely how long the move will take before it actually happens, you can't get a *binding estimate* (a guaranteed price) in advance. You can, however, get a *nonbinding estimate* and it will be close to the actual cost. (The actual charge cannot exceed the nonbinding estimate by more than a small percent, which varies from state to state.)

If you're moving more than thirty-five miles away, the price for the move will be based on both the weight of what you're moving and the distance you're traveling. And if you're moving to another state, there will be some price differential between companies, so call around and compare rates.

No matter how far you're moving, before the actual move you'll be given a *bill of lading*, which is your legal contract. The cost and services will be outlined for you and you will be asked to sign it before the movers lift a finger, much less a box of books. Your payment will be required upon delivery, and if you're unable to produce it, your belongings could be placed in storage at your cost.

Make sure to find out in advance what kind of payment the company will accept. Most won't accept personal checks or credit cards, so you'll need to be ready with cash, a certified or cashier's check, or a money order made out to the moving company. (You'll also need to tip each mover and the amount will depend on the nature of the move; use your judgment.)

Another cost that you need to factor in is insurance. Keep in mind that it is possible to purchase extra coverage for especially valuable items. You'll pay a little bit more for this extra protection, but the cost is well worth it. Before you move, document the condition of your belongings. If the moving company is packing for you, they'll put together a detailed inventory of each box they pack. Make sure their descriptions are accurate before you sign. If any damage occurs en route, the inventory will be essential in order to collect insurance.

It's important that you keep the following information about the company with you during your move so you'll know whom to contact in case of an emergency: driver's name, vehicle's license number, telephone number and contact person at the local moving company, and telephone number and contact of the moving company in the city to which you are moving.

3. Shipping Everything. If you're not moving a huge amount of stuff—you've got mostly clothes and books rather than heavy furniture—there's no need for you to deal with renting a truck or hiring professional movers. But you still may have too much for a plane or your car. In that case, the smartest thing is to take just a couple of suitcases with you and ship all the rest—as long, that is, as you have an address to which to ship it all.

Arrange to have your belongings arrive a couple of days after you do in case your trip takes longer than you anticipate. (This precaution is primarily if you plan on driving. If you're flying, it's a reasonably sure bet that you'll arrive not more than one day late. If not—well, let's just say it's not going to matter much when your things get there.) You'll want a day or two in any case to do a little bit of exploring before you turn to unpacking and settling in.

Moving After Your Stuff

Moving after your stuff makes sense only if your lease is ending and you plan on going somewhere temporarily before making your move. Say you're graduating from college, traveling in Europe for a couple of months, and moving halfway across the country in the fall. You'd prefer to pack up now and have your stuff waiting in your new city when you get there.

If you know somebody in your new city who'll store your stuff for you for a couple of months, that's obviously your best option. You'll save a lot of money by going this route (unless of course they charge you); buy this somebody a nice present in Europe.

But even if you don't know anyone who has the space or the heart to let you temporarily stash your things, you can still send them before you yourself move. What you need to do is to find a storage company in the city to which you're moving. (Look under "Storage" in your local phone book and check out the national companies. Otherwise go to the library and look in the Yellow Pages of the city of your destination.) Don't bother calling the self-storage companies; if your self isn't going to be present, it can't be stored, and neither can your things.

Some full-service companies won't let you send stuff to them either; they require that you be there in person in order to have your photo taken and sign the lease. But there are a number of companies that will do all the paperwork over the telephone and be happy to accept a shipment from you and store it themselves. So do the research and keep trying until you find a company that suits your circumstances.

Storage prices depend on the size of the storage area you rent and the location of the company. (Many companies charge more for storage in their inner-city locations than they do for those on the outskirts of town; it's worth driving a few extra miles when you pick up your stuff to get the cheaper price.) Prices vary from company to company but they tend to be very reasonable. Going this route offers you the option of getting your whole packing hassle out of the way before you take your time off. *But be sure that the price you're quoted is comprehensive—remember, they're not just renting you space, they're also putting your things into that space.*

All Packed Up

Packing things for shipping is different from packing things that you'll be moving in your car, or your truck, or even your ship, in that they must meet the regulations of the transporting company. United Parcel Service (UPS), for example, has very strict guidelines for what they will and will not accept—size, weight, and the competence with which the parcel is taped, tied, or otherwise securely sealed are all critical. Make sure to call UPS in advance to check their size and weight limitations. UPS will not ship breakables that you have packed.

When moving from Seattle to Boston, I packed about ten boxes. I spread my picture-frame collection out, packing a couple in each box. When UPS came to pick up the boxes, the driver asked me if I had packed any breakables. "Sure," I naively responded. "I'm sorry," he said, "then I won't be able to take any of these boxes." I had to untape all the boxes, remove all the picture frames, and reseal the boxes. Packing once is a big enough hassle; you don't want to be forced to do it twice.

For any footlockers, duffels, or suitcases that you send, purchase a small lock and keep the key with you while you travel. And, since you're likely to lose the key, consider buying one of the newfangled combination locks—you set your own combination—that are cropping up in luggage stores everywhere.

Use gobs of tape on every box that you're going to ship; remember, more is more.

My sister Nomi once packed up all her belongings to move from Chicago to Boston. When the UPS driver arrived to pick up the boxes—the very same morning that her flight was scheduled to depart—he refused to accept them because they were inadequately taped. He wouldn't even hang around and wait for her to retape them. She had to schedule another pick-up, secure the boxes more tightly, and lug them all to the home of a friend from which UPS would pick them up, since she'd be in Boston by the new pick-up date.

When you call the shipping company to set up the details, they'll ask you how many boxes you're going to ship, how big they are, and how much they weigh. Weighing full boxes may get a little tricky, depending on how big they are. It's going to be difficult to fit the whole box on the scale without covering up the numbers, so here's what to do: Weigh yourself holding the box and then subtract your weight. If the boxes are too heavy for you to lift, call your neighbor, Moose, and ask him to lend a hand.

A second big difference between preparing to transport your stuff by sending it and getting it ready to move by car or truck is that if you're driving your belongings, you don't have to worry as much about the sturdiness of the container (box, suitcase, whatever) or how well your things are packed. You can, for example, use the Hanging Hefty Trick. I learned this method from a college friend of mine who drove from Ohio to Michigan every fall and back again in the spring. (I always sent my stuff UPS and watched with envy as she packed her clothes in half the time it took me.) Here's how it works: Take approximately five hangers, clothes still hanging, and tie them together with a twisty from a box of garbage bags. Then take a Hefty bag—the garbage size, not the sandwich size, unless you happen to be hyper-petite—poke a hole in the bottom, and put the hangers through it. (Alternatively, get some plastic clothing bags from your friendly neighborhood dry cleaner.) Pull the bag down over your clothes and voila! you've got a homemade garment bag. As long as you can hang your clothes in your vehicle or have room to lay them flat, they'll remain unwrinkled and you can put them directly into your new closet.

Moving with your stuff vs. shipping everything also affects your decision on whether to bring your bed with you or to buy a new one after you've moved. (This may seem premature in a chapter about packing, but, getting technical for a minute, we're involved in a feedback loop. See Chapter 4 to learn about buying a bed.) If you've rented a truck or hired professional movers, moving your bed is no problem. (You need those mattresses anyway to cushion the walls of the truck, remember?) But if you're planning on sending your things, it will probably cost you more to ship the bed than it will to purchase a new one (assuming that what we're talking about is a mattress, box spring, and frame, not a brass four-poster).

Whether you're packing just some of your belongings, taking things with you, or leaving most stuff behind to be shipped later, here's how to go about packing:

- Moving is a good time to get rid of things you no longer use. Although it's said that fashion trends are cyclical, it's relatively safe to assume that the purple velour pantsuit that you outgrew in eighth grade is never going to see the outside of your closet again. If you haven't worn something in the last couple of years, get rid of it. Use this opportunity to make a donation to a shelter for the homeless or to a charitable thrift shop.

- Once you've decided on what to bring with you, you'll have a rough idea of how many boxes you need. You can usually get boxes for free from a grocery or liquor store. Many stores break down their boxes for recycling after they receive deliveries, so ask the stores to put the boxes aside for you after they receive their shipment. Used boxes often have the cover removed, however, so you'll have to make your own cover out of a second box or a piece of cardboard. (If you're traveling by car, you can pack some of your belongings in plastic crates. Their handles make them easy to carry and they'll come in handy for storage in your new home.)

If you don't mind spending a few dollars or if you want to get boxes made specifically for the items you're packing, you can buy boxes from the post office or from any local moving or mailing company. *Mirror* boxes are made to hold mirrors and art; *wardrobe* boxes are special boxes that hold your clothes on hangers; *dish* boxes are boxes with dividers for securely packing your dishes. One powerful reason for packing early is that if you run out of boxes, you'll have time to get more.

In general, go for the smallest boxes your things will fit into. Better lots of small boxes than fewer big ones—as you'll learn when you're schlepping them up to your new third-floor walkup.

Remember to buy many, many rolls of tape—strapping, packing, and sealing tape will all do the trick. It's a good idea also to pick up a hand-held tape dispenser made specifically for taping boxes because with each snip your regular scissors become more sticky and less effective. You should be able to get a tape dispenser for under ten dollars at a drugstore, an office-supply store, or, for sure, a hardware store. While you're there pick up some thick magic markers for labeling your boxes.

- Pack your nonbreakables tightly and in small boxes so they don't get too heavy. Breakables, on the other hand, should be packed loosely with a lot of cushioning. (Clothes, towels, and bedding make good padding.) Wrap each breakable individually, like a gift. Newspaper is fine for wrapping but it may smudge, so unless you want to read last May 3rd's weather report every time you use your salad plate, use white paper (available at any moving company) for the first layer. Make sure you mark these boxes "Fragile." Sometimes that helps.

- Don't leave any room in your boxes for things to move around. Fill all the extra space with padding. (Crumpled newspaper works fine.) On the other hand, don't overstuff your boxes. You won't save any money by shipping fewer boxes; you'll end up paying for the replacement of your valuables when the box breaks. If it's bulging, it's overstuffed.

- Stack dishes on end rather than laying them flat. Cushion the bottom of the box and put padding between each layer of dishes. Plates can be wrapped in packs of fours but cups should be stuffed with paper and wrapped individually. Take extra care with your dishes; you can't use too much padding. (I remember helping my father unpack when he moved back to Boston after having spent a year in D.C. A hasty packing job had transformed his box of dishes into a box of dish remnants. Dish parts may have some archaeological value in a few thousand years, but they're not going to do you much good when you want to eat a bowl of soup.)

- Disconnect electronics before packing them. Some items, like CD players and computers, may have a locked position for travel. Try to remember if the item was locked when you first got it. Check the underside for something that looks like it might be called a "set screw." Tighten it. (And remember to loosen it when you're setting up in your new place.) When you take something apart for moving (electronics or furniture) put all of the nuts, bolts, wires, and other small pieces that belong with it in a plastic bag and tape the bag to the something it goes with. There's nothing more frustrating—well, almost nothing—then not being able to listen to music while you unpack because you've lost a connection wire for your stereo.

  If you no longer have the boxes that your computer or stereo or some other valuable item originally came in, kick yourself and then consider getting it professionally packed. Companies like Mailboxes, etc. will pack the object for you and, if you want, they'll ship it for you as well. The charge for packing and shipping won't be insignificant, but you won't have to worry that even though you have all the wires for your stereo, the disc player won't work because it's been jostled during the trip. Make sure to save the boxes so that next time you move you can pack such things on your own. When you've got the right boxes—and, especially, the shaped foam packing materials that came with your whatever when it was new—packing is a piece of cake.

- Books will pack more evenly if you alternate the bindings. If you still have record albums, remember to pack all your albums upright and label the box "phonograph records—fragile."

- Do not pack any of the following in a sealed box: flammables (paint), candles, matches, aerosol sprays (hair sprays), ammunition, cleaning fluids and detergents, nail-polish remover, acids (batteries), lighter. These items are affected by high altitudes or changes in temperature and could cause explosions, spills, or fire. Most movers refuse to transport these items. There's a reason for that.

- Number your boxes and keep a list with you of what's included in each one. If anything should happen to one of your boxes en route you'll know immediately what it contained. And when it comes time to unpack, you can proceed in a more orderly fashion.

- If possible, keep things that you consider particularly valuable with you while you travel.

Go Lightly

I don't mean to put a crimp in your hopes, but until you've truly settled in, it might be smart to move only the things you can't get along without rather than everything you own. It is, after all, possible that things won't work out the way you've hoped, and having to deal with moving everything again will be an enormous burden. So until you settle in, find a job, acclimate to your new home, and decide that you want to stay for at least a year, take with you only those things that you really need and that will make you feel at home in a strange place. ("Need," of course, is relative. Some people "need" every sweater they've ever owned, every record and CD they might conceivably want to listen to, every stuffed bear or hockey stick that makes them feel cozy. I'm not saying that you should abandon all your worldly possessions, or take a vow of even temporary austerity. But in this case, less is less, and less is good.)

Last-Minute Details

Preparing for your move is likely to get chaotic, especially during the final days. With your thoughts focused on leaving the place you're leaving and moving to the place to which you're moving, it's easy to overlook some of the things that need to get done. So take care of as many details as possible in advance. Doing that is a way to alleviate some of the premove hecticity, and also to ensure that you don't forget any transitional musts, such as:

- Give your landlord written notice of your move as soon as the date is set. Many landlords require one month's notice when you move out. Keep in mind that some landlords only rent from the first of the month and won't pro-rate if you move out in the middle of the month; move out on May 9th and you're going to be stuck paying rent for the entire month. A quick check of your lease should tell you what your landlord's policy is.
- Don't forget to ask about having your security deposit returned. If you need to clean your apartment in order to get the entire deposit back, consider hiring professional cleaners. It could take a full day's work for you to get the apartment looking like new. Professionals can do twice the job in half the time.
- Cancel all utilities that are in your name. Electricity, gas, telephone, and cable companies should all be notified a month in advance to ensure that you don't get charged for services after your move.
- Get change-of-address postcards from the post office. If you don't have a new address yet, you can fill out a change-of-address card marked for general delivery. Your post office will be able to give you the address for the post office that accepts general delivery in your new city. Your mail will be rerouted to that address and held there for ten days. As soon as you get a permanent address, all you need to do is fill out a three-way change-of-address card that provides room for your old address, temporary address (in this case, general delivery), and your permanent address. Change your address for any subscriptions and credit cards that you have.
- Notify your gym that you're moving. Find out if they have an affiliate in your new city and whether your membership can be transferred.
- Get a copy of your medical records to bring with you. Dental records, too; no need to get new X rays where you're going if you've just had them where you've been. Fill any regular prescriptions you use and get an extra month's supply in case it takes you some time to find a new doctor. (Many states don't accept prescriptions from out-of-state doctors.)
- Close your bank accounts. The safest thing to do is to move your money in the form of traveler's checks or money orders/bank checks made out to yourself. Remember to keep them with you

when you travel. Alternatively, you may want to wait until you get where you're going and set up a new account before closing your old one. Then you just write a check from old to new for the total you have. You still need to get traveler's checks, however, because it will be some time before the transfer of funds from one bank to the other clears, some weeks before you get permanent checks from your new account, and because many businesses won't accept out-of-state checks.

Moving Checklist

- ☐ Research transportation options and make a decision about which method to use.
- ☐ If necessary, make transportation reservations.
- ☐ Decide if belongings will be shipped or brought with you.
- ☐ Make a guesstimate of how many boxes will be needed and obtain them.
- ☐ Buy packing tape, a tape dispenser, magic markers, twine.
- ☐ Give written notice of move to landlord.
- ☐ Notify all utility companies of disconnection dates.
- ☐ Get change-of-address postcards from post office. Fill them out.
- ☐ Notify credit cards/subscriptions of address change.
- ☐ Stop newspaper delivery.
- ☐ Pick up prescriptions; get medical records.
- ☐ Close bank accounts.
- ☐ Get traveler's checks/money orders.
- ☐ Check with shipping company to make sure your boxes meet their size requirements.
- ☐ Pack all boxes, listing contents as you do.
- ☐ Label boxes.
- ☐ *Make arrangements for staying somewhere upon arrival in your new city.*

2. Roommate Wanted: Two's Company, Three's a Cheaper Rent

Maybe you want to live with a roommate, maybe not. This chapter will help you think through the advantages and disadvantages to roommate living and provide you with issues to discuss with potential roommates; the next chapter discusses various ways to find roommates and housing. There you'll also learn about the questions you need to answer before signing a lease.

If You Want a Roommate

Few things in this world make for so acute a pit in your stomach as not having a place you can call home. Unfortunately, not having the right roommate with whom to share your home comes close—and having the wrong roommate is even worse. Whether you're just beginning the housing search or are trying to fill a vacant spot in your apartment or house, you're under a great deal of pressure to find someone compatible—and to find that person quickly.

These two goals, however, are often conflicting. Though you probably survived a couple of roommate searches in college, your challenge is now intensified in a world where: (1) you are not surrounded by thousands of (at least) semicompatible peers; (2) everybody you know isn't moving every eight to twelve months; and (3) rents are established for professional incomes, not student budgets.

The most important thing to remember during this time is that you *will* find a roommate and you *will* find a place to live. It may take one day, it may take three weeks, and either way it will probably seem like six months, but in the long run this period of uncertainty is really very short.

Living with People You Don't Know

If you've made this move by yourself, you have to decide whether you want to live with people you don't know or if you'd prefer to live by yourself—presuming you can afford to. While the prospect of living with strangers may be disconcerting, it can be a wonderful way to meet new people—and there are precautions you can take to minimize your concerns. Some of the best living situations that I've had have been with people who started out as total strangers.

Since the basis of your relationship when you live with someone you don't already know is that you share living space, you don't have to worry about household tensions affecting your friendship (there being no friendship). If you end up as friends, that's a welcome bonus, but it is not a requirement that the person you share space with also becomes your friend. We're talking roommate, not soulmate. So what's needed is courtesy, responsibility, and basic thoughtfulness. The fact is that you'll probably find that you're each more considerate of the other's space and needs because you know up front that the relationship can easily be ended.

Which, by the way, is another advantage to living with a stranger: If you should find in two weeks or six months that you're unhappy in your new city, or that you picked the wrong neighborhood, or whatever—you're free to move. You will, of course, have a lease to consider but you won't have the same kind of guilt you might if you were abandoning a friend. I know several people who stayed in places they wanted to leave merely because they felt it would not be fair to their housemate-friend if they left. That didn't do much for the friendship.

Choosing the right roommate, however, can be a trying endeavor in itself. Being smart about it means getting into real conversation with those who qualify as prospects. Remember that your discussions are going to be the principal basis for your decision, so you've got to make them count. That means having more than a superficial get-acquainted conversation.

It might feel somewhat awkward to ask personal lifestyle questions of a complete stranger, but the more you learn about this person up front, the less of a stranger s/he will be when you move in together. This is your home we're talking about, so you want to learn as much as possible about the person before deciding to live together. This is also the opportunity for your prospective roommate to learn about you, so be prepared to be open about your habits and needs as well. Remember, there's more than one prospective roommate at the meeting. (If the quasi-interview setting makes you feel as if you're coming across as far too formal a person, explain that you're following a guide and blame me.)

Have a list of questions either memorized or written down. Don't be inhibited; ask many questions and don't worry if your concerns are offbeat or very particular. This is the time to mention your own idiosyncrasies and be prepared for your prospective roommate to fill you in on his strange habits as well. The more open and honest you are at this point, the better the chance you have of making a successful connection.

Bear in mind that you're not looking for a clone; differences in lifestyle can sometimes be enriching. Here's a list of subjects with which to begin the discussion:

First Meeting/Interview

- *Cleanliness.* No issue (not even noise, and that's a big one) can cause more tension between roommates than differences in definition of acceptable mess. If one of you waits to do dishes until there are no more clean plates, while the other insists on cleaning the pots after preparing a meal but before eating it, you're probably not a good match.
- *Significant Others.* While some people accept overnight guests as part of the roommate bargain, others feel intruded upon and resentful when sleep-overs become a regular occurrence. Hash this out now even if neither of you is currently dating anybody,

otherwise you might be irreversibly humiliated when "Jake" and/or "Jennifer" is spending the night yet again and your roommate asks if they intend to contribute to the rent.

- *Schedule/Noise.* If you're a late-nighter who likes to have your friends over often during the week and your roommate awakens to a loud alarm clock at 5:00 A.M. for her morning jog, you are not going to be smiling at each other when you meet in the bathroom.

- *Location of Family.* If your roommate's mother is constantly dropping in to redecorate your living room or pick up your roommate's laundry, it might upset you, particularly if you are far away from your own family. If your roommate's mother is regularly coming over to drop off a precooked dinner for two and to pick up your laundry, it might be agreeable, particularly if you are far away from your own family. (This is a tricky one. It's easy enough to find out where your potential roommate's family is located; it's not so easy to predict which kind of family s/he has.)

- *Peculiarities/Preferences.* It's going to bother you if you come home one day to find that the candle collection you've been working on since junior high has melted because your roommate insists on keeping the heat at eighty-five degrees, or because there was a power outage and your roommate was too lazy to hunt around for a flashlight. It might also grate on your nerves if you are a strict vegetarian and your roommate eats rare prime rib and beef tartar on a regular basis. If one of you is a compulsive talker and the other a clam, careful—unless the clam has big ears.

- *Independence vs. Companionship.* If you've moved to a city in which you don't have many friends, you may think of the roommate relationship as a foundation for a social life. You can go out with your roommate, meet his/her friends, and so forth. But if you already have an established social life or prefer to keep your social life and your home life separate, you might feel pressure living with someone who's looking to you as a social director. I have one friend who moved out of her apartment because her roommate led a totally separate life; she felt that if she and her roommate weren't going to be companions, she might as well live alone. I have another friend who had to sneak out of her apartment whenever she had plans so that her roommate wouldn't see her and ask to come along.

- *Interests/Hobbies.* You both play chess. One of you is a grandmaster while the other has to be reminded the number of spaces a pawn can move. Shared interests don't necessarily make for rich companionship. Also keep in mind that unshared interests can be downright intrusive—e.g., drums, tumbling, taxidermy.

- *Smoking.* Self-explanatory. And remember that an apartment is fairly close quarters in which to designate only one room as a smoking area.

- *Pets.* Any objections, in either direction? Any requirements? Do house pets make your eyes swell and your nose run? If so, is your prospective roommate ready to give his/her pet away? (If s/he says "sure" and proceeds to throw the pet out the window, leave by the nearest exit. Do not walk, run.)

- *Money.* This is surely among the most uncomfortable issues to discuss; it's hard even with people you know well, and can feel invasive with someone you've just met. But you absolutely must know whether this person is capable of paying the rent and the electric bill on time, and there are some reasonably roundabout ways to find out. Most obviously, you'll be talking about employment in any case. Does your prospect have a steady job? If not, and s/he is living off a dwindling savings account while still job-hunting, you may want to wait until s/he is hired before moving in together.

  Use what you learn from a conversation about employment to give you a clue about the individual's financial capability— but bear in mind that there's sometimes more to paying bills in timely fashion than the ability to pay them. Get a sense of whether your prospect is a responsible person. The best way to do that may be to take the initiative by telling the prospect all the things you then hope he or she will tell you. Even if you've just relocated and don't yet have a job, you do have some plan for paying your bills in the interim (or you will once you've read Chapter 9). Try to find out if your prospective roommate has a similar plan.

- *Furniture.* This, too, is a tricky one. If you've just moved from another state, you probably don't have much furniture with you and would be delighted to move into a furnished apartment without spending any extra money. *But:* Remember how tastes may vary. It can be a huge convenience to find a roommate with furniture, but it's wise to take a look at the furniture first.

These are just some examples of issues that arise in a shared living situation. And if, in your situation, sharing means sharing a bedroom, your list of questions will be a great deal more extensive. (Personal differences are much more tolerable when you have the option of retreating to your own room. If your "own" room isn't going to be your own, the subjects of cleanliness, schedule, and sleep-overs will need to be discussed in much greater detail.)

You undoubtedly have developed unique concerns based on your college roommate situations. Add to my list any issues or concerns that are of particular importance to you. And be prepared to live with your mistake, so long as it isn't a horrendous mismatch. (Sometimes, though, even the grossest mismatch can prove to be quite livable.) Also be prepared for a period of adjustment. It'll take some time for you and your roommate to get used to each other.

Remember, even with all the questions, your decision is going to be based largely on intuition. The point of all the preceding is to remind you that an intuitive decision made solely on the basis of appearance and idle chitchat is much riskier than an intuitive decision that follows from an in-depth discussion about issues that are important to you and might cause tension in a living situation. You're taking a gamble by living with someone you don't know, but the risk can be greatly reduced by preparing conscientiously for the initial meeting.

(Information about where to find a roommate is provided in Chapter 3.)

Living with People You Already Know

If you've relocated with a group of friends or if you're lucky enough to already know somebody with whom you want to live in your new city, you don't have to worry about shopping around for a roommate. But no matter how many years you've been friends with the people you're going to room with, it's still a good idea to have some serious "roommate-issue" talks before you sign a rental agreement. Such talks may well feel artificial, but the fact is that best friends don't automatically make best roommates. If it bothers you that you have to sit on the floor when you're at your friend's apartment because all the chairs have clothes piled on them, or if you have to listen to your friend's financial woes on a regular basis, you may be putting your friendship at risk by moving in together.

A friend and I, about to relocate to the same city, decided—what could be more natural?—to live together. I went ahead to scope out the housing situation. I found several places that seemed great, but every time I told her about one of them, she replied that it was too expensive. After an intensive search on my part, countless long-distance telephone calls, and a fair amount of persuasion, we finally settled on an apartment. She signed the lease, sight of the apartment unseen, and moved in a few weeks later.

When she saw the apartment, she felt we had been conned; for what we were paying, she expected a nicer place. (She hadn't conducted the apartment search and therefore didn't realize how expensive rentals were in that city.) For two months she lived in the apartment, stewing each time she wrote a rent or utility check. Finally she moved out, leaving me with the responsibility to sublet her room, deserting not only our lease, but our friendship as well.

Work out a housing budget together before signing a lease to make sure you are both prepared for the same level of expense. Also, unless it's a month-by-month situation, you should never sign a lease without seeing the housing first. Your best friend's taste isn't necessarily your own.

Other issues (e.g., cleanliness, bizarre habits) can usually be worked through in a close friendship; if you're all aware of the potential trouble areas in advance, you'll probably have a healthier living situation as well as a healthier friendship.

Living with People You Know—Once Removed

If you have a friend who knows somebody who's looking for housing in the same city as you, you could be in luck. You know that you have at least one thing, or, more accurately, person, in common and, if it works out, you'll feel more secure than you would moving in with a complete stranger. But it's risky to assume that just because your best friend's third cousin is also moving to Albuquerque, your roommate situation is set. Remember that you might not make a good roommate match with even your very best friend, so don't automatically assume you would be a good match with your friend's third cousin.

Although you'll probably do it in a more casual manner, it's still important to ask all of the "roommate questions" that you'd ask a complete stranger. If you decide that the match just doesn't feel right, listen to your intuition. Don't worry about offending your friend. Better to explain that it seems as though you have a few conflicts in your living styles than to move in together, be miserable, and then not even be able to complain to your best friend about it.

Even if you're moving in with a good friend *and* a friend of his or hers, it's still important to meet the third party before making a commitment. How many times have you met a friend of a friend and thought to yourself: What does he see in her? Now imagine living with that person. If it doesn't work out, you inconvenience everyone and run the risk of damaging your relationship with your friend, who will be stuck right in the middle.

I once found myself in the uncomfortable position of being the middle woman. I moved in with one of my best friends from high school and one of my closest friends from college. All three of us were excited—the two of them had been hearing about each other for years and couldn't wait to meet. Unfortunately, there was no opportunity for them to do so before we moved. (Two of us came straight from college and my high-school friend met us in our new city.) It didn't take long for all of us to realize that the same traits that attracted me to both of them—intense, strong personalities—created deafening personality clashes between them. The two months that we lived together were uncomfortable for all of us and left considerable ill-feeling in their wake.

So, approach living with friends of friends with the same seriousness with which you would living with a stranger; you've got a great deal more to lose if it doesn't work out. And if after a meeting or two you don't think you'd live well together, at least you now know someone who's going to be living in your new city. Just because you're not meant to be roommates doesn't mean you wouldn't make good friends.

Time to Set Some Ground Rules

Once you've figured out with whom you're going to live, it's time to set some ground rules. It's not necessary for you to do it before you move in—you'll be busy enough with the physical aspects of the move—but you should attend to it sooner rather than later. The longer you put off talking about shared expenses, housecleaning, and general household protocol, the greater the potential for misunderstanding and resentment.

When Anne moved in with a woman she had met through a roommate-referral agency (See Chapter 3 for information on roommate-referral agencies), she brought with her twelve rolls of toilet paper for the one shared bathroom. One month later, she explained to me, the toilet paper was used up. (Don't bother to ask why.) She felt, understandably, that her roommate should buy the next batch, and she assumed her roommate would realize it was her turn. But, either because the roommate thought that a toilet-paper-buying precedent had been set with the first twelve rolls, or because she had a secret stash in her bedroom that she used only for herself, or because of possibilities that are best not examined too closely, she didn't buy any toilet paper for the shared bathroom. Anne, meanwhile, grew increasingly agitated and went through countless boxes of Kleenex.

Serious problems can arise when household responsibilities are left undiscussed. You're coming from two different sets of experiences and you probably have some different assumptions about how your home will run. In order to make sure you are both on the same wavelength about what you'll share and the obligations that go along with sharing, talk about the following as soon as possible:

- *Kitchen Supplies.* Even if you've decided not to buy groceries together, chances are you'll identify some kitchen items that it makes sense to share (e.g., aluminum foil, dish soap, sponges, paper toweling). Decide whether you want to: alternate buying the products; each take responsibility for stocking certain items; keep a running list of what you need and, when it's time, do the shopping together; or take the laid-back approach and let whoever happens to be at the store pick up what's needed and figure it'll all even out in the end. (There's no way to know if this last method will work until you try it. If it turns out that one of you is buying everything, it's time to pick another approach.) Running out of paper towels won't cause as much resentment as running out of toilet paper, but it's important nonetheless to figure out how you're going to keep your kitchen stocked.
- *Bathroom Products.* Toilet paper, obviously, but there's also shampoo, toothpaste, soap. And showers: If you're sharing a shower, now's the time to figure out if your work schedules are going to create showering conflicts. (Remember, you have a vested interest in your roommate's hygiene.) Later on, when you learn that there's never enough hot water for two sequential showers, you can hammer that one out as well. (Depending on your roommate, you may consider simultaneous showering.)
- *Housecleaning/Chores.* Your mess is going to increase exponentially with the number of people with whom you live. If you're living with a group, it's a good idea to set aside a specific time during the week for cleaning. If your individual schedules make it too difficult to agree on a time, try a work wheel that designates a different task, or room, as each person's responsibility for the week. If your roommates think you're being anal for suggesting this kind of approach, don't worry. After a month or two of living in the inevitable mess, they'll be embracing both your ideas and your prescience for suggesting them so early on.
- *Shared Services/Belongings.* If you make any apartment purchases together (e.g., dishes, a television, a dog), decide up front who's going to get them when you split up. Some things, obviously, are easier to divide than others.

   It's also a good idea to discuss how you feel about sharing personal belongings. Those who grew up as only children probably feel differently about having someone roam through their closets than those of us who grew up with a houseful of siblings. Even if you're an inherent sharer, you may own some things that are simply off limits and you should make sure your roommate is aware of them.

I had one college roommate who would let all of his housemates wear his clothes, drive his car, even sleep in his bed—which may or may not have been purely altruistic—as long as we didn't use his Special Mug. He told us this on day one and we all made sure to steer clear of it. I have another friend who was once discussing weight with her roommate when her roommate said, "You have nothing to worry about, I wish I were as tiny as you. The only pants of yours I can squeeze into are your white jeans." It turns out that when my friend was out, the roommate was secretly trying on her clothes. Whether this was a sharing problem or an obsession problem we never found out—although the roommate did start styling her hair like my friend.

You also need to figure out what "extras" you want for your apartment: cable TV, daily newspaper, etc. (And is it the collective newspaper or yours alone?) Make sure to put each service in a different person's name so that the ultimate responsibility is shared. Another approach, only to be seriously considered if you know and trust your roommate, is to open a special checking account for shared expenses. You might each put up a certain amount of money when you sign the lease or deposit a designated amount each month. Joint expenditures can be paid for out of this account; you can even arrange to have checks that require both of your signatures.

Troubleshooting

Even the best roommate relationships are periodically tense. Experiencing a problem here and there is natural. But when the strain escalates to the point where you are increasingly resentful of your roommate, or if the problem seems to be ongoing, it's time to intervene. Different problems obviously call for different responses (you're clearly going to react differently when your roommate leaves the cap off the toothpaste than you will when your roommate's rent check bounces).

Generally speaking though, your first course of action should be to approach your roommate with the problem and see if you can work it out together. If you're uncomfortable doing so, or if such a discussion fails to solve the problem, consider getting someone you both know and trust to serve as a mediator. Sometimes an objective person's perspective helps resolve the situation. Such a person, in any case, will probably help soothe a strained confrontation.

If all else fails, or if you simply know that you've made a mistake and you can't live with the roommate you've chosen, check your lease and see what your responsibilities are. If your name is on the lease, you're legally bound to fulfill its terms. But most landlords will allow you to sublet your space—that is, to have someone else move in in your place—as long as you clear it with them first. In that situation, you remain responsible. Therefore sublet only to a person in whom you have total confidence. If, on the other hand, you can find someone who wants to rent your space outright, the landlord might have no objection.

Living Alone

If waiting for the shower or having someone else's dishes cluttering up "your" sink concerns you, you're probably thinking it would be best to live alone. Wait. Before you seek accommodations for one, consider the following advantages to living with other people, at least for now:

ADVANTAGES TO LIVING WITH OTHERS

- *Social Life.* Meeting new people in the Real World is a different game than it was in college. You're no longer surrounded by thousands of people your age with whom you study, don't study, eat, pig-out, sleep, and pull all-nighters. Finding a roommate greatly increases your chances of meeting new people. The simple act of taking a roommate already expands your social circle by one—which may not be much if you already know ten people in your new city, but is a huge number if you know no one else. Plus, now you'll either (1) bump into anybody your roommate knows, or, if your roommate is also new to town, (2) have someone to explore with. And if you don't like your roommate's friends or feel that s/he would cramp your style when you go out, at least you have somebody to whom you can complain about your social life.

- *Finances.* There is no way around it: Two can live almost as cheaply as one, which means that your cost of living will be substantially lower if there are two of you. A two-bedroom apartment of comparable style will never cost twice as much, or even nearly twice as much, as a one-bedroom apartment. The cost of telephone service, electricity, and cable TV is significantly lower if you're only paying half.
- *Food.* If you and your roommate decide to share the cost of groceries, you'll cut your expenses even more. Even if you choose not to share food, there's always the chance that when you're snowed in, it's negative degrees outside, and the contents of your refrigerator consist of one-half of a week-old tomato plus a garlic bulb, your roommate will offer you some of her chicken cordon bleu.
- *Camaraderie.* The next few months are probably going to be a very unsettled period in your life and it may be comforting to have someone to share them with. After you've had your first lousy job interview or become lost riding the public transportation, you might welcome the support of a roommate.

Kim's first postcollege move was solo to San Diego, halfway across the country from anyone she knew. There she rented a studio apartment. One morning, a month after she had arrived, she awoke with an intense stomach flu. She managed to get dressed and stumble out in order to go to the store to buy a bottle of juice and some medicine. She was too preoccupied with her discomfort to notice the shards of glass littering the lot where her car was parked, but when she got to her car she was shocked into awareness: Her car had been broken into during the night, its valuable contents stolen, its ignition wrecked. Dejected (to put it mildly) and feeling sicker than ever, she made her way back to bed, where she remained for the next twenty-four hours. Oh, for a roommate who could go to the store for her and maybe even heat up some chicken soup.

Crises happen, and when they do, a roommate can provide help, security, and chicken soup.

But this is a section on living alone. And if, for whatever reason, you'd prefer living in a small apartment that is completely yours to sharing a slightly bigger place (with a stranger, no less), here are some fairly major advantages to single living:

ADVANTAGES TO LIVING ALONE

- *Social Life.* Taking a roommate creates the potential for seriously hampering your social life. A roommate may do any of the following: Forget to give you vital phone messages; barge in, turn on the lights, and declare, "Oh great, you rented *The Graduate*, my favorite movie. Lucky for us that I didn't have plans tonight!" just as you and your date are getting cozy on the couch; refuse to allow you to throw a party because of the damage potential; or, even worse, show up at your party with ten friends who conspicuously clash with your own; have a hopping social life, which reminds you daily of the absence of your own; have no social life at all, which makes you feel guilty about yours, which is hopping.
- *Finances.* While splitting expenses can save you money, it can also prove to be troublesome, awkward, and a source of friction between you and your roommate. Figuring out long-distance phone bills might require a certified accountant, especially if you live with several people who are far away from their loved ones. The more people with whom you live, the more calls for which no one can account. And then there's electricity—shared electricity bills turn every roommate into a watchdog. Who would have thought you'd be reminding your friends to turn out their lights, encouraging them to take shorter showers, and engaging in temperature wars over the air-conditioning?
- *Food.* After you've had a strenuous day at work and spent the long bus ride home fantasizing about coming home and pop-

ping your last frozen pizza into the microwave, you don't want to return to see your roommate popping the last bite of your last pizza into his mouth. Late-night pilfering is inevitable and leads to retaliation and squabbling. Plus: If you have different eating habits, you run the risk of being revolted by the food your roommates eat and of offending them by your eating habits.

- *Camaraderie.* Even the closest friends need personal space, and if you are the kind of person who would find it awkward to tell a friend that you need her to get lost for an hour or two, you might jeopardize a good relationship by having a roommate. Many wonderful friendships have been destroyed by rooming together. Group living can be suffocating. Sure it's nice to always have someone with whom you can go out or share a meal, but when you are in one of those "I'll kill the first person who asks me how my day was" kind of moods, you'll be wishing you had rented that studio apartment. (Or even a closet, as long as it was empty.) I remember many days when I would repeat a silent prayer over and over again as I walked home from work: "Please let no one be there, please let no one be there."

  Generally speaking, it's better to be with other people when you choose to be with other people, not because they're permanent fixtures in your home.

The preceding is less a list of the advantages of living alone than of the disadvantages of sharing space. Not all the arguments for solitude are negative; here's the positive approach:

- You may feel that it's time to be truly independent.
- You're actually looking forward to fending for yourself during a torrential rainstorm when you've lost all electricity.
- You're ready for a place that is completely your own, that you can mess up at your leisure.
- You like the idea of spending the entire weekend lounging in your flannels on your living-room couch, with no one there to call you a couch potato.
- There's a time and a place for everything, including even camaraderie. "Always" is not a time and "everywhere" is not a place.

3. Coming In out of the Rain: Your Search for Housing

"There's no place like home, there's no place like home, there's no place like home."
—Dorothy

You may think you're just moving to Chicago or to Seattle or to some other new city, but you're not. You're moving to a neighborhood within that city and to a building within that neighborhood and to an apartment within that building. Deciding on a neighborhood and finding a building and determining with whom you want to live are all issues that you're going to confront before getting settled. Here's how to do it:

Choosing a Neighborhood

One of your first challenges is deciding in which neighborhood you'd like to live. The very first step in choosing a neighborhood is to talk to somebody who's familiar with your new city. Find out which neighborhoods are safe and what the relative costs of living are. Try to get a feel for how neighborhood cultures differ. Invest in a detailed street map to help you learn your way around. Take a walk—with a companion—through any potential neighborhoods at night. Notice how many people are about and how well lit the streets are, since these factors play large roles in the safety of the neighborhood. Check the noise level and decide whether it's too high or too low for your taste.

Investigate public transportation in areas that interest you. Different cities have different systems, so if you've never heard of the BART, the El, or the T, call the Department of Transportation, if there is one, or City Hall to get the information that you need. Find out how many stops there are in the neighborhoods you're considering and if they are centrally located. Keep in mind, by the way, that many modes of public transportation offer discounted monthly passes that pay for themselves after twenty or thirty rides; if you're relying on public systems to get around, a pass is a worthwhile investment.

Once you have a few potential neighborhoods in mind, you're ready to begin your housing search.

The Newspaper—"Wanted: A Place to Live"

Billy Crystal, as Harry in *When Harry Met Sally*, suggests that the obituary section of the newspaper be combined with the real estate section. That way, he reasons, when someone dies, the space he's vacated can be listed along with his surviving family members.

Harry has a point, at least in observing that the newspaper is usually the best place to find out about available housing. But remember: The major metropolitan newspaper is not the only paper with listings; community and alternative papers generally have extensive listings for housing and especially for roommates.

If you're just looking for housing and don't need to find a roommate, go straight to the rental section of the newspaper. Listings will most likely be divided by neighborhood so you won't have to read through pages of useless entries. Be aware that listings with real estate agents as the contact may end up costing you more money, since many real estate agencies charge a fee if you rent through them. Their fee is usually significant—often, one month's rent. Once you find a place, you're probably going to be laying out a security deposit (which is usually also a month's rent) as well as your first and last month's rent; you don't need to pay yet another small fortune for an agent's fee.

Some real estate agents, however, charge the owner, not the renter. This distinction is usually clear from the ad; if it's not, call the agent and find out. (There's more on real estate agents in the next section.)

If you're looking for a new roommate as well as housing, the advantage of looking in the "Roommates Needed" section of the paper is that you may be able to find people who already have an apartment or a group house and are looking for one more person to share it. This kind of arrangement can save you from the housing search. You can, in essence, roommate shop and apartment shop simultaneously. And you're able to learn a little bit about potential roommates when you see the sort of place in which they live. (Keep in mind that most people will clean—or, at least, straighten up—their home before inviting a potential roommate over. If, therefore, the apartment/house is messy when you go to check it out, take it as a warning sign: Don't expect it to get any better.)

If you know people in your new city, ask someone to come with you when you visit the advertised space. A second opinion is usually helpful, and you may also feel safer going into a stranger's home if you're not alone.

Responding to a roommate ad in the newspaper can lead to a satisfying living situation and save you a great deal of "hunting hassle." But it's much better to answer a "roommate needed" ad than to place one yourself. That is, it's not wise to find an apartment for two before you have a roommate. It may seem like a great idea to find an apartment that suits your needs and tastes and then advertise for a roommate. That way, you'll be the one conducting the roommate interviews; if there is an advantage in these awkward meetings, you've got it. But to rent a two-person apartment before you have serious roommate prospects is to take a big gamble.

When I moved to Seattle on my own, my first priority was, naturally, to find a place to live. On my very first day in town, I stumbled upon a modern, reasonably priced, safe (a high priority for me), two-bedroom apartment. The apartment manager took a liking to me and, after I explained my situation to her—no roommate yet, but I'd be looking for one right away—offered me the first month at half the regular rent. I grabbed the deal.

Halfway through the month, it became depressingly clear that the hordes of new friends and acquaintances I'd anticipated meeting had chosen Portland or Oshkosh over Seattle. The perfect person? I'd have settled for a whole lot less than perfect. So I had to begin advertising for a roommate.

Which, I quickly learned, was neither cheap nor productive; I received very, very few responses. Of the few people who did answer my ad, at least half made appointments they didn't keep. I soon realized that my apartment, though inexpensive relative to the East-Coast rents I was used to, was on Seattle's pricier side. And, to make matters worse, none of the few people I did end up meeting via the ad had anything in common with me—or I with them, for that matter.

With just two weeks left, I had to choose between staying in the apartment for a second month and paying the regular rent— much more than I could afford—in the hopes that I'd be luckier in the second month than I'd been in the first, or starting the apartment search all over again.

Happy ending: At the last minute, I ran into someone else in my building who was in the exact same situation I was in. He moved up one floor into my apartment and both of our problems were solved.

Unless you have enough money saved to comfortably cover your expenses for a few months, reduce the risk element wherever possible.

When to Call a Real Estate Agent

Going directly to a real estate agent instead of using the housing section of the newspaper may save you some time. You can describe your status to the agent (how many bedrooms you're looking for, how much rent you can afford, and so forth), tell her where you prefer to live, and she'll be able to check all of the suitable listings. You won't have to squint through newspaper ads that are of no use to you. Remember, though, to find out up front whether the agent is going to charge you for her services. And if so, how much.

You can find an agency by looking in the Yellow Pages or the Classifieds section of the newspaper. Set up a couple of meetings and find an agent who has listings in your desired neighborhood(s) and with whom you feel comfortable. It's best to work with one agent only; since agents have access to many of the same listings, they may take you less seriously if they know you're working with their competitors.

My friends and I moved to D.C. with the names of three or four real estate agencies and promptly contacted all of them. As it turns out, D.C. is a small town and the real estate community is a tight one. One of my friends has a distinctive last name, so it was not long before the agents became aware of our disloyalty. One agent actually called to reprimand us for working with other agents. She explained in no uncertain terms that using multiple agents was unethical and dishonorable. The other agents, though less passionate, were equally miffed. We were actually relieved when the only penalty was that we were moved down—way down—on their priority list.

Roommate Referral Agencies

Most, if not all, major cities have roommate referral agencies. These agencies relieve much of the uncertainty in the roommate search by letting you read profiles of roommate possibilities and then letting you choose with whom you think you might be compatible. Going through a referral agency also provides the opportunity to find housing and roommates simultaneously, since many people who use roommate referral agencies already have housing and are looking for someone to share it.

To find an agency, look in the Yellow Pages under "Roommate Referral Service" or in the Classifieds section of the newspaper. Call the agency to find out if an appointment is required. Ask what the fee is. Many agencies don't charge if you already have a house or an apartment and are looking for a roommate. If, on the other hand, you're looking to be matched with a person (or group) who already has housing, you'll have to pay a fee—usually, around fifty dollars.

Generally, the fee is well worth it. The odds are you'll find a roommate much sooner, and thereby save the cost of temporary housing. And the best agencies come with a guarantee: You can continue to use the agency's resources until you find your match.

When you go into the agency's office you'll be asked some basic questions. (For example, are you apartmentless or apartmented?) You'll then be given a series of written questions about yourself and, if you already have one, about your apartment. Questions range from

"Describe yourself" to "What are you fanatical about?" to "Do you have a religious preference?" You'll be asked to describe what you're looking for in a roommate and in an apartment. The questionnaire will most likely include a series of "yes" and "no" questions that range in subject matter from drugs to pets.

Filling out this questionnaire honestly is the key to finding a good match. Don't omit any habits or characteristics because you fear they would decrease your chances of finding a roommate. I have a chain-smoking friend who felt that if he were honest about his addiction, he would kill any chance of finding a roommate. He ended up living with someone who had a strong aversion to cigarettes, and every time he wanted to smoke, he had to go outside.

Your completed questionnaire will be placed in a binder. (There are separate binders for apartment-seekers and roommate-seekers.) You'll be able to look through the binders as often as you like. You can learn a great deal about the "potentials" before you meet them, much more than you could possibly learn from a four-line classified ad. You'll also have people seeking you out based on the way you filled out your questionnaire. You reduce the time it would normally take to find a roommate and you decrease the number of futile meetings you might otherwise have.

Back to School—Using College Listings

If there is a college or university in the area, take advantage of its resources. Call the housing office to find out its policy on nonstudent use. Most often, schools will allow the public access to their listings, both to look at listings and to post them. While students looking for roommates and student housing will be among the listings, you'll also see listings by other graduates who are looking for a new roommate or for housing in the neighborhood.

If you're planning to live alone, college housing offices are also the best place to find rooms for rent in private homes, by far the least expensive option you have. Professors and members of the community often advertise basement or attic apartments that are available in their homes. Living in a private home can, of course, be isolating; you're not surrounded by others as you are in an apartment building or a group house. But a home advertised in a college listing is likely to be in the vicinity of the campus; that can compensate for feelings of seclusion. And the benefits of living in a private home are that you generally get a very safe, clean room—and maybe even an apartment, perhaps even with character, and all for a reasonable price. Utilities are likely to be included in your monthly rent and there's a good chance you'll be allowed to use your landlord's laundry machine. A parking space in the driveway is also often included in the rent or is available for a small extra charge. If something breaks, your landlord is just a floor or two away and, since you're the only tenant and the landlord has a personal interest in the health of the house, s/he will probably attend to it sooner and more fastidiously than would a landlord in a big building.

Living with a family may also be comforting to you if you're far away from your own family. Remember, though, you'll have to be aware of the noise you make in your space, and in general, that you'll have to be respectful of the family's schedule and routine. If you like to blast your stereo, do aerobics late at night, or have loud parties, do not live in a private home. Chances are that the family will have an earlier bedtime than you and you won't last long in their home if they are kept awake by noise coming from your apartment. In many cases you'll even use their front door as your own, so you'll have to be doubly conscious of having late night guests.

A Radical Alternative—
Trading Your Services for Space

If the idea of living in a private home appeals to you, you may also want to consider trading baby-sitting or housecleaning duties for a room or small apartment. The hours you'll spend working in the household are usually minimal, and you'll be able to save a great deal of money on rent and utilities.

In this sort of situation you often become an extended part of the family, so it's much more important to find a family you feel comfortable with than it is if you're merely renting space in a stranger's home. Just as you'll want to find out as much as possible about the family, so, too, will the family want to know a great deal about you (especially if you're going to be caring for their children). Be prepared to supply them with several references and/or formal credentials.

You must also be prepared to give up much of your privacy. You may feel awkward bringing guests into someone else's home if your private domain consists only of your bedroom. You may never feel fully "at home" and probably won't be able to have parties. Unless you have an official contract, you may get stuck doing additional tasks if requested.

If this option sounds like a lot of trouble for a small payoff, keep in mind the major benefits: instant family, most likely a nice, safe home (typically, a family that has space for live-in help has a nice home), major savings on rent and, in many cases, on food as well. You may even get some serious perks: My friend Kim was taken along on two family vacations to Hawaii, a trip to Tahoe, and a weekend in Las Vegas, this in exchange for five hours a day of baby-sitting.

Bear in mind, though: It not only helps to like children, it helps to know something about child care.

"Mom Will Never Believe This"— Going to a Religious Institution

If you feel that going through the newspaper or an agency is simply too risky or too impersonal, you do have some other choices.

One option is to conduct your search through a religious institution. You need not be a regular servicegoer, and you must get rid of your gnawing feeling that anybody you'll meet through this avenue will be a proselytizing zealot. Many church-, synagogue-, or mosque-connected people make splendid roommates—thoughtful, responsible, all the positive elements of the common stereotype.

If you are yourself observant, this option is a natural: You'll have an important element of your background in common with your roommate, and you're likely to find that it's only one among many.

Call the local church or synagogue to see if it has roommate listings in its newsletter or posted somewhere in the building. You might consider putting in your own listing as well as taking advantage of the those that others have placed. Religious groups on college campuses almost always have housing bulletin boards. Since these organizations usually serve a postgraduate population as well as college students, you have a good chance of finding a roommate your age.

* * *

If, after thinking through all the options, you're still uncertain as to which kind of living situation would be best for you right now, don't worry. Try a couple of different avenues, see which one feels best, which works out. Check listings for single-occupant apartments and answer advertisements for shared housing. Keep all of your options open until you find a situation that feels comfortable. Keep in mind that you are not locked into anything. Even if you sign a lease and soon find that you're miserable, you can almost certainly find someone to sublet your space.

If you continue to be uncertain, consider limiting your exposure by finding housing with a short-term or month-to-month lease. If you've moved by yourself or on a whim, you might seriously consider this option: The transition can be easier psychologically if you don't feel trapped by a long-term lease.

What You Need to Know About Your New Home

By the time you've figured out with whom you're going to live and found a place that you like, you're probably going to be more than ready to move in. However, it's worth taking some extra time to make sure the housing is in sound condition and that you're satisfied with the terms of the lease. The landlord will assure you that the place is in tip-top condition; he's trying to rent it. As much as possible, you should rely on your own perceptions. Visit the apartment both during the day and at night so you can judge the noise level, how much light it gets, and how many people are out in the neighborhood. Take an inventory of the apartment, checking things like the number of electrical outlets and phone jacks.

- There are some questions, however, that you won't be able to answer for yourself. If at all possible, talk to another tenant in the building or, even better, the former tenant of your apartment. Other tenants will be able to give you an accurate idea of the quality of life in the building. You should find out about things like repairs and noise level. You should also get as much detail as you can from the landlord and write down his answers (he may feel more inclined to answer honestly if he knows his remarks are being recorded).

Apartment Checklist

Here's what you need to know before you sign a lease:

THINGS TO ASK AND THINGS TO CONSIDER

- When is the rent due? When is the rent considered late (usually three to five days after it's due) and is there a late fee? How much?
- How many months of rent do you pay up front? (Usually you pay first and last month when you move in.) How much is the security deposit?
- Is there a fee for having the apartment cleaned before you move in? (Make sure the carpets will be cleaned and the windows washed. Even if there's a charge, it's worth it. These are two tasks that you don't want to be stuck doing. They'll cause you a huge hassle; more likely, you'll find endless ways to postpone them.) Are you responsible for cleaning the apartment before you move out?
- What utilities are you responsible for and which ones are covered in your monthly rent? What's the typical monthly cost of the ones for which you'll be paying?
- How is the apartment heated: baseboard heat, blowers, or radiators? (Be careful of electric heat; it can be frightfully expensive. Radiators, which are old-fashioned, tend to generate a great deal of heat and it can be difficult to control the temperature—and often, the clanking.) Does each apartment in the building have its own temperature control? Which side of the building gets natural sunlight? (Obviously the cheapest form of heat.) Is the unit air-conditioned? (Even if it is, it's worthwhile to invest in some big fans; air conditioning will make your electricity bills soar.)
- Is the stove gas or electric? By and large, gas is preferable.
- How many electrical outlets are there in each room and where are they located? Is there enough electrical capacity to handle all your kitchen appliances, your stereo equipment, and your computer? Some older buildings might have a problem. Are there any three-prong outlets? (If not, and you have appliances with three-prong electrical cords, you can ask the landlord to switch some two-prong outlets to three-prong or you can

purchase converters. Converters are inexpensive and can be
purchased at any hardware store.)

- Where is the fuse box/circuit-breaker box? (If you have fuses
  rather than circuit breakers, make sure to keep a supply of the
  different sizes on hand and make sure when a fuse needs replacing that you use only the same size fuse.)
- How many phone jacks are there and where are they located?
  (This is largely a matter of preference. It becomes important if
  you own a fax machine or a modem.) Does the unit have more
  than one telephone line?
- How strong is the water pressure in the shower? (Check it out
  for yourself.)
- Who handles repairs? Is this person accessible twenty-four
  hours a day and how quickly does s/he respond to calls?
- What means of security does the building have? What kind of
  lock is on the front door and do visitors need to be buzzed in? Is
  there any lock mechanism on your apartment door that cannot
  be opened from the outside (e.g., door chain)? (Make sure to
  have your apartment locks changed when you move in.) Find
  out about garage security also. (The most secure buildings have
  a locked door between the garage and the apartment building so
  strangers can't get in through the car entrance.)
- How well lit are the halls, stairwell, and building entrance? Are
  the lights kept on throughout the night?
- Does the building have a parking lot or a garage? Is parking included in the rent or is there an additional charge? If there isn't
  parking, how close and how safe is the area in which you can expect to find parking? Do you need a neighborhood parking permit?
- Is there a second ready egress from your apartment? (Most
  cities require a second means of exiting the building, so check if
  there's a back staircase or fire escape.)
- What is the noise level like in the building? (You'll probably
  get the most accurate feel for the noise level by talking to some
  of the other tenants.)
- Will you be able to fit your furniture in the elevator or take it up
  the stairs, and will it fit through the doorway?
- How much closet space and cupboard space is there in the
  apartment? (If you don't think there's enough, see Chapter 4 for
  ideas on how to maximize space.)

- Does the building have extra storage space? Is there a fee for using it?
- Is there a garbage disposal? A dishwasher? (These conveniences will make it easier to keep your apartment clean; consider how important they are to you.)
- Where do you take your garbage? How often is it picked up and is pick-up included in your rent? Is there recycling pick-up?
- Are there laundry machines in the building? If so, are they coin operated or are they free? If there's no laundry in the building, where's the nearest laundromat?
- Are pets allowed in the building? (This is an obvious question if you have a pet, but if you don't, consider the added noise and mess potential of a building that allows them.)
- Can packages be left with the building manager/doorman or do you have to pick them up at the post office?

- It's very important to go over the condition of the apartment with the landlord and to document any existing damage. Your landlord may have a form that gives you room to record any pre-existing problems. If not, make your own list and have the landlord sign it. This document will be your insurance against extra charges when you move out. Without it, anything that is awry, be it nail holes in the wall or a stained carpet, can be blamed on you and subtracted from your security deposit.

After you have all of the answers you want, you're ready to sign the lease. You may be asked to have a guarantor (someone who will accept responsibility for fulfilling the terms of the lease if you don't) cosign. Most often, a guarantor is required when you don't have a rental history of your own and, especially, if you don't yet have a job. Your parents might be able to cosign, but some leases require the signature of a local guarantor. If you're not living where your parents are and if you don't know any responsible locals, this requirement could pose a problem. Ask the renter up front whose name s/he'll need on the lease, so you don't run into any problems when it comes time to sign.

Here's a sample lease, along with explanations of some of the more confusing and important parts. (Keep in mind that leases will differ from city to city, but you'll get something that resembles the following.)

SAMPLE

RHA
Rental Housing Association

STANDARD FORM APARTMENT LEASE
(FIXED TERM)
1995 EDITION

Date _____

_____
(Name)

_____
(Address)

Lessor, hereby leases to

_____
(Name)

_____
(Address)

_____
(Telephone No.)

_____
Lessee, who hereby hires

the following premises, viz: _____ _____ at _____
                             (Apartment)   (Suite)   (Street)

_____ Mass. (consisting of) _____
(City or Town)

for the term of _____, beginning _____

and terminating on _____. _The rent to be paid by the Lessee for the leases premises shall be as follows:_

RENT: **A:** The term rent shall be $ _____. payable, except as herein otherwise provided, in installments of $ _____
on the _____ day of every month, in advance, so long as this lease is in force and effect:

B: However, if in any tax year commencing with the fiscal year _____ the real estate taxes on the land and buildings, of
which the leased premises are a part, are in excess of the amount of the real estate taxes thereon for the fiscal year _____,
(herein called the "Base Year", and being the most recent year in which the Lessor has actually received a real estate tax bill for

If property taxes increase, the landlord can increase your rent by the percentage he writes into the lease (Section B). That's your safety net. →

TENANT:
This section governs Rent payments. In some cases, rent payments may increase during the lease term. Please be sure that you carefully read and understand this section. Please initial here when you are certain that you understand and agree with this section.
Lessee's initials:

This is where you find out who handles repairs. Note where this person is located and find out during which hours s/he is accessible. →

SAMPLE

> *If you want to paint, wallpaper, or change the apartment in any way, get written permission from the landlord first. Some landlords will even reimburse you for materials.* ⬆

3. **HEAT AND OTHER UTILITIES**

TENANT: This section governs utility payments. Be sure to discuss with the Lessor those payments which will be required of you for this apartment

The Lessee shall pay, as they become due, all bills for electricity and other utilities, whether they are used for furnishing heat or other purposes, that are furnished to the demised premises and presently separately metered. The Lessor agrees that the will furnish reasonably hot and cold water and reasonable heat (except to the extent that such water and heat are furnished through utilities metered to the demised premises as stated above) during the regular heating season, all in accordance with applicable laws, but the failure of the Lessor to provide any of the forgoing items to any specific degree, quantity, quality, or character due to any causes beyond the reasonable control of the Lessor, such as accident, restriction by City, State or Federal regulations, or during necessary repairs to the apparatus shall not (subject to applicable law) form a basis of any claim for damages against the Lessor.

4. **ATTACHED FORMS**

The forms, if any, attached hereto are incorporated herein by reference.

5. **CARE OF PREMISES**

The Lessee shall not paint, decorate or otherwise embellish and/or change and shall not make nor suffer any additions or alterations to be made in or to the leased premises without the prior written consent of the Lessor, nor make nor suffer any strip or waste, nor suffer the heat or water to be wasted, and at the termination of this lease shall deliver up the leased premises and all property belonging to the Lessor in good, clean and tenantable order and condition, reasonable wear and tear excepted. No washing machine, air-conditioning unit, space heater, clothes dryer, television or other aerials, or other like equipment shall be installed without the prior written consent of the Lessor. No waterbeds shall be permitted in the leased premises.

6. **CLEANLINESS**

The Lessee shall maintain the leased premises in a clean condition. He shall not sweep, throw, or dispose of, nor permit to be swept, thrown or disposed of, from said premises nor from any doors, windows, balconies, porches said building, any dirt, waste, rubbish or other substance or article into any other parts said building or the land adjacent thereon, except in proper receptacles and except in accordance with the rules of the Lessor.

7. **DEFINITIONS**

The words "Lessor" and "Lessee" as used herein shall include their respective heirs, executors, administrators, successors, representatives and assigns, agents and servants; and the words "he", "his" and "him" where applicable shall apply to the Lessor or Lessee regardless of sex, number, corporate entity, trust or other body. If more than one party signs as Lessee hereunder, the covenants, conditions and agreements herein of the Lessee shall be the joint and several obligations of each such party.

8. **DELIVERY OF PREMISES**

In the event the Lessor is not able through no fault of his own to deliver the leased premises to the Lessee at the time called for herein, the rent shall be abated on a pro rata basis until such time as occupancy can be obtained, which abatement shall constitute full settlement of all damages caused by such delay, or the Lessor, at his election, shall be allowed reasonable time to deliver possession of the leased premises, and if he cannot deliver such possession within 30 days from the beginning of said term, either the Lessor or Lessee may then terminate this lease by giving written notice to the other and any payment made under this lease shall be forthwith refunded. Lessee hereby authorizes and empowers Lessor to institute proceedings to recover possession of the premises on behalf of and in the name of Lessee.

9. EMINENT DOMAIN

If the lease premises, or any part thereof, or the whole or any part of the building of which they are a part, shall be taken for any purpose by exercise of the power of eminent domain or condemnation, or by action of the city or other authorities or shall receive any direct or consequential damage for which the Lessor or Lessee shall be entitled to compensation by reason of anything lawfully done in pursuance of any public authority after the execution hereof and during said term, or any extension of renewal thereof, then at the option of either the Lessor or the Lessee, this lease and said term shall terminate and such option may be exercised in the case of any such taking, notwithstanding the entire interest of the Lessor and the Lessee may have been divested by such taking. Said option to terminate shall be exercised by either the Lessor or the Lessee, by giving a written notice of exercise of such option to terminate in the manner described in Section 17 of this lease. Said option to terminate shall not be exercised by either party (a) earlier than the effective date of taking, nor (b) later than thirty (30) days after the effective date of taking. The mailing of the notice of exercise as set forth hereinabove shall be deemed to be the exercise of said option; and upon the giving of such notice, this lease shall be terminated as of the effective date of the taking. If this lease and said term are not so terminated, then in case of any such taking or destruction of or damage to the leased premises, rendering the same or any part thereof unfit for use and occupation, a just proportion of the rent hereinbefore reserved, according to the nature and extent of the damage to the leased premises, shall be suspended or abated until, in the case of such taking, what may remain of the leased premises, shall have been put in proper condition for use and occupation. The Lessee hereby assigns to the Lessor any and all claims and demands for damages on account of any such taking or for compensation for anything lawfully done in pursuance of any public authority, and covenants with the Lessor that the Lessee will from time to time execute and deliver to the Lessor such further instruments of assignment of any such claims and demands as the Lessor shall request, provided however that the Lessor does not assign to the Lessor any claim based upon Lessee's personal property or other improvements installed by Lessee with Lessor's written permission.

10. FIRE, OTHER CASUALTY

If the leased premises, or any part thereof, or the whole or a substantial part of the building of which they are a part, shall be destroyed or damaged by fire or other casualty after the execution hereof and during said term, or any extension or renewal thereof, then this lease and said term shall terminate at the option of the Lessor by notice to the Lessee. If this lease and said term are not so terminated, then in case of any such destruction of or damage to the leased premises, or to the common areas of the building customarily used by the Lessee for access to and egress from the leased premises, rendering the same or any part thereof unfit for use and occupation, a just proportion of the rent hereinbefore reserved, according to the nature and extent of the damage to the leased premises, shall be suspended or abated until the leased premises shall have been put in proper condition for use and occupation. If the leased premises or such common areas have not been restored by the Lessor to substantially their former condition for use and occupancy within thirty days after the damage occurred, the Lessee may terminate this lease by giving notice to the Lessor within thirty days following the termination of the thirty day period within which the Lessor failed to restore. If either party gives notice of intention to terminate under this section, this lease shall terminate on the last day of the then-current monthly rental period.

11. DISTURBANCE, ILLEGAL USE

Neither the Lessee nor his family, friends, relatives, invitees, visitors, agents or servants shall make or suffer any unlawful, noisy or otherwise offensive use of the leased premises, nor commit or permit any nuisance to exist thereon, nor cause damage to the leased premises, nor create any substantial interference with the rights, comfort, safety or enjoyment of the Lessor or other occupants of the same or any other apartment, nor make any use whatsoever thereof than as and for a private residence. No articles shall be hung or shaken from the windows, doors, porches, balconies, or placed upon the exterior windowsills.

12. GOVERNMENTAL REGULATIONS

The Lessor shall be obligated to fulfill all of the Lessor's obligations hereunder to the best of the Lessor's ability but the Lessee's obligations, covenants and agreements hereunder shall not (subject to applicable law) be affected, impaired or excused because the Lessor is unable to supply or is delayed in supplying any service or is unable to make or is delayed in making any repairs, additions, alterations or decorations, or is unable to supply or is delayed in supplying any equipment or fixtures, if Lessor is prevented or delayed from doing so because of any law or governmental action or any order, rule or regulation of any governmental agency, (other than those regulating rents) which is beyond the Lessor's reasonable control.

↑
If the state or any other public authority takes over or condemns the building (this very rarely happens), you can terminate the lease by giving written notice within thirty days of the takeover.

↑
If fire or any other casualty causes damage to part of the building, the lessor can terminate the lease.
If the lease isn't terminated, the lessor is responsible for restoring public areas (e.g., lobby) that were damaged, to former condition. If he doesn't, you can terminate the lease.

SAMPLE

↑

Note that unless otherwise specified, your landlord is not responsible for your personal property. For more on renter's insurance, see Chapter 4.

13. COMMON AREAS

No receptacles, vehicles, baby carriages or other articles or obstructions shall be placed in the halls or other common areas or passageways.

14. INSURANCE

Lessee understands and agrees that it shall be Lessee's own obligation to insure his personal property.

15. KEYS AND LOCKS

Upon expiration or termination of the lease, the Lessee shall deliver the keys of the premises to the landlord. Delivery of keys by the Lessee to the Lessor, or to anyone on his behalf, shall not constitute a surrender or acceptance of surrender of the leased premises unless so stipulated in writing by the Lessor. In the event that the exterior door lock or locks in the leased premises are not in normal working order at any time during the term thereof, and if the Lessee reports such condition to the Lessor, then and in that event, the Lessor shall, within a reasonable period of time following receipt of notice from the Lessee of such condition, repair or replace such lock or locks. Locks shall not be changed, altered, or replaced nor shall new locks be added by the Lessee without the written permission of the Lessor. Any locks so permitted to be installed shall become the property of the Lessor and shall not be removed by the Lessee. The Lessee shall promptly give a duplicated key to any such changed, altered, replaced or new lock to the Lessor.

16. LOSS OR DAMAGE

The Lessee agrees to indemnify and save the Lessor harmless from all liability, loss or damage arising from any nuisance made or suffered on the leased premises by the Lessee, his family, friends, relatives, invitees, visitors, agents, or servants or from any carelessness, neglect or improper conduct of any such persons. All personal property in any part of the building within the control of the Lessee shall be at the sole risk of the Lessee. Subject to provisions or applicable law the Lessor shall not be liable for damage to or loss of property of any kind which may be lost or stolen, damaged or destroyed by fire, water, steam, defective refrigeration, elevators, or otherwise, while on the leased premises or in any storage space in the building or for any personal injury unless caused by the negligence of the Lessor.

You may want to ask for permission for parking or owning a dog or a cat, even if you don't have a car or a pet at this time. You may acquire a car or a pet later, and it will be easier then if you already have permission.

↑

17. NOTICES

Written notice from the Lessor to the Lessee shall be deemed to have been properly given if mailed by registered or certified mail, postage prepaid, return receipt requested to the Lessee at the address of the leased premises, or if delivered or left in, or on any part thereof, provided that if so mailed, the receipt has been signed, or if so delivered or left, that such notice has been delivered to or left with, the Lessee or anyone expressly or impliedly authorized to receive messages for the Lessee, or by any adult who resides with the Lessee in the leased premises. Written notice from the Lessee to the Lessor shall be deemed to have been properly given if mailed by registered or certified mail, postage prepaid, return receipt requested to the Lessor at his address set forth in the first paragraph of this lease, unless the Lessor shall have notified the Lessee of a change of the Lessor's address, in which case such notice shall be so sent to such changed address of the Lessor, provided that the receipt has been signed by the Lessor or anyone expressly or impliedly authorized to receive messages for the Lessor. Notwithstanding the foregoing, notice by either party to the other shall be deemed adequate if given in any other manner authorized by law.

18. OTHER REGULATIONS

The Lessee agrees to conform to such lawful rules and regulations which are reasonably related to the purpose and provisions of this lease, as shall from time to time be established by the Lessor in the future for the safety, care, cleanliness, or orderly conduct of the leased premises and the building of which they are a part, and for the benefit, safety, comfort and convenience of all the occupants of said building.

19. PARKING

Parking on the premises of the Lessor is prohibited unless written consent is given by the Lessor.

20. PETS

No dogs or other animals, birds or pets shall be kept in or upon the leased premises without the Lessor's written consent; and consent so given may be revoked at any time.

21. PLUMBING

The water closets, disposals, and waste pipes shall not be used for any purposes other than those for which they were constructed, nor shall any sweepings, rubbish, rags, or any other improper articles be thrown into the same; and any damage to the building caused by the misuse of such equipment shall be borne by the Lessee by whom or upon whose premises it shall have been caused, unless caused by the negligence of the Lessor, or by the negligence of an independent contractor employed by the Lessor.

22. REPAIRS

The Lessee agrees with the Lessor that, during this lease and for such further time as the Lessee shall hold the leased premises or any part thereof, the Lessee will at all times keep and maintain the leased premises and all equipment and fixtures therein or used therewith repaired, whole and of the same kind, quality and description and in such good repair, order and condition as the same are at the beginning of, or may be put in during the term or any extension or renewal thereof, reasonable wear and tear and damage by unavoidable casualty only excepted. The Lessor and the Lessee agree to comply with any responsibility which any may have under applicable law to perform repairs upon the leased premises. If Lessee fails within a reasonable time, or improperly makes such repairs, then and in any such event or events, the Lessor may (but shall not be obligated to) make such repairs and the Lessee shall reimburse the Lessor for the reasonable cost of such repairs in full, upon demand.

23. RIGHT OF ENTRY

The Lessor may enter upon the leased premises to make repairs thereto, to inspect the premises, or to show the premises to prospective tenants, purchasers, or mortgagees. The Lessor may also enter upon the said premises if same appear to have been abandoned by the Lessee or as otherwise permitted by law.

24. NON-PERFORMANCE OR BREACH BY LESSEE

If the Lessee shall fail to comply with any lawful term, condition, covenant, obligation, or agreement expressed herein or implied hereunder, or if the Lessee shall be declared bankrupt, or insolvent according to law or if any assignment of the Lessee's property shall be made for the benefit of creditors, or if the premises appear to be abandoned the, and in any of the said cases and notwithstanding any license or waiver of any prior breach of any of the said terms, conditions, covenants, obligations, or agreements, the Lessor, without necessity or requirement of making any entry may (subject to the Lessee's rights under applicable law) terminate this lease by:

1. a seven (7) day written notice to the Lessee to vacate said leased premises in case of any breach except only for non-payment of rent, or
2. a fourteen (14) day written notice to the Lessee to vacate said leased premises upon the neglect or refusal of the Lessee to pay the rent as herein provided.

Any termination under this section shall be without prejudice to any remedies which might otherwise be used for arrears of rent or preceding breach of any of the said terms, conditions, covenants, obligations or agreements.

25. LESSEE'S COVENANTS IN EVENT OF TERMINATION

The Lessee covenants that in case of any termination of this lease, by reason of the default of the Lessee, then at the option of Lessor:
(A) the Lessee will forthwith pay to the Lessor as damages hereunder a sum equal to the amount by which the rent and other payments called for hereunder for the remainder of the term or any extension or renewal thereof exceed the fair rental value of said premises for the remainder of the term or any extension or renewal thereof; and
(B) the Lessee covenants that he will furthermore indemnify the Lessor from and against any loss and damage sustained by reason of any termination caused by the default of, or the breach by, the Lessee. Lessor's damages hereunder shall include, but shall not be limited to any loss of rents; reasonable broker's commissions for the re-letting of the leased premises; advertising costs; the reasonable cost incurred in cleaning and repainting the premises in order to re-let the same; and moving and storage charges incurred by Lessor in moving Lessee's belongings pursuant to eviction proceedings.

This is where you accept responsibility to return the space in the same condition it was in when you first rented it. Remember to make a list of any problems you find and have the landlord sign it.

(C) At the option of the Lessor, however, Lessor's cause of action under this article shall accrue when a new tenancy or lease term first commences subsequent to a termination under this lease, in which event Lessor's damages shall be limited to any and all damages sustained by him prior to said new tenancy or lease date. All rights and remedies are to be cumulative and not exclusive.

26. REMOVAL OF GOODS

Lessee further covenants and agrees that if Lessor shall remove Lessee's good or effects, pursuant to the terms hereof or of any Court order, Lessor shall not be liable or responsible for any loss of or damage to Lessee's goods or effects and the Lessor's act of so removing such goods or effects shall be deemed to be the act of and for the account of Lessee, provided, however, that if the Lessor removes the Lessee's goods or effects, he shall comply with all applicable laws, and shall exercise due care in the handling of such goods to the fullest practical extent under the circumstances.

27. NON-SURRENDER

Neither the vacating of the premises by the Lessee, nor the delivery of keys to the Lessor shall be deemed a surrender or an acceptance of surrender of the leased premises, unless so stipulated in writing by Lessor.

28. SUBLETTING, NUMBER OF OCCUPANTS

The Lessee shall not assign nor underlet any part or the whole of the leased premises, nor shall permit the leased premises for a period longer than a temporary visit by anyone *except the individuals specifically named in the first paragraph of this lease,* their spouses, and any children born to them during the term of this lease or any extension or renewal thereof without first obtaining on each occasion the assent in writing of the Lessor.

You need to get written permission to sublet your space. If you don't, you're technically in breach of the lease.

29. TRUSTEE

In the event that the Lessor is a trustee or a partnership, no such trustee nor any beneficiary nor any shareholder of said trust and no partner, General or Limited, of such partnership shall be personally liable to anyone under any term, condition, covenant, obligation, or agreement expressed herein or implied hereunder or for any claim of damage or cause at law or in equity arising out of the occupancy of said leased premises, the use or the maintenance of said building or its approaches or equipment.

30. WAIVER

The waiver of one breach of any term, condition, covenant, obligation, or agreement of this lease shall not be considered to be a waiver of that or any other term, condition, covenant, obligation, or agreement or of any subsequent breach thereof.

If any one part of the lease is waived, (e.g., you are given permission to have a pet), the rest of the lease is still legally binding.

31. SEPARABILITY CLAUSE

If any provision of this lease or portion of such provision or the application thereof to any person or circumstance is held invalid, the remainder of the lease (or the remainder of such provision) and the application thereof to other persons or circumstances shall not be affected thereby.

32. COPY OF LEASE

The Lessor shall deliver a copy of this lease, duly executed by Lessor or his authorized agent, to the Lessee within thirty (30) days after a copy hereof, duly executed by the Lessee, has been delivered to the Lessor.

33. REPRISALS PROHIBITED

The Lessor acknowledges that provisions of applicable law forbid a landlord from threatening to take or taking reprisals against any tenant for seeking to assert his legal rights.

IN WITNESS WHEREOF, the said parties hereunto and to another instrument of like tenor, have set their hands and seals on the day and year first above written; and Lessee as an individual states under the pains and penalties of perjury that said Lessee is over the age of 18 years.

_____   _____
Lessee   Lessor

                                                        _____
                                                        Trustee or Agent

TENANT: SUBJECT TO APPLICABLE LAW, THE LANDLORD WILL PROVIDE INSURANCE FOR UP TO $750 IN BENEFITS TO COVER THE ACTUAL COSTS OF RELOCATION OF THE TENANT IF DISPLACED BY FIRE OR DAMAGE RESULTING FROM FIRE.

The landlord agrees to give you up to $750 if you need to relocate because of a fire. ⬆

TENANT: MAKE SURE TO RECEIVE A SIGNED COPY OF THIS LEASE.   ⬆

In consideration of the execution of the within lease by the Lessor at the request of the undersigned and of one dollar paid to the undersigned by the Lessor, the undersigned hereby, jointly and severally, guarantee to the Lessor, and the heirs, successors, and assigns of the Lessor, the punctual performance by the Lessee and the legal representatives, successors and assigns of the Lessee of all the terms, conditions, covenants, obligations, and agreements in said lease on the Lessee's or their part to be performed or observed, demand and notice of default being hereby waived. The undersigned waive all surety-ship defenses and defenses in the nature thereof and assent to any and all extensions and postponements of the time of payment and all other indulgences and forbearances which may be granted from time to time to the Lessee.
WITNESS the execution hereof under seal by the undersigned the day and year first written in said lease.

Here's where the guarantor signs. ⬆

_____

_____

_____

ADOPTED BY THE **RENTAL HOUSING ASSOCIATION OF THE GREATER BOSTON REAL ESTATE BOARD**

Once you've decided on a place and moved in, you've passed a major hurdle. Regardless of how alienated and unsettled you still feel in your new city, at least you can return at night to a place that is your own. But an empty apartment or house can itself be pretty unsettling. It's going to take some work—and creativity—to make your new place feel like home. Don't know how to begin? Read on. The next chapter will tell you how to get started.

4. Furnishing Your Home: What Comes After Milk Crates?

If it's true that home is where the heart is, you're probably feeling pretty far away from home right now. Your heart may be back in Madison with your boyfriend or in Brooklyn with your family or in New Zealand where your four college roommates are. If, on the other hand, your loved ones are just minutes away, you may feel right at home in your city—even if you've just moved there. But you'll still probably feel more like a visitor than a resident in your new apartment until you fill it with your belongings and create a space that reflects your personality.

Setting up an environment in which you feel comfortable is critical to your transition. When you bomb two back-to-back job interviews and have yet to meet local friends with whom to commiserate, you want (at least) to return home to an apartment in which you feel comfortable, not to an impersonal space that's cramped and feels transitory. With all the other twists and turns you're going to encounter, a home base that feels like home can be a great source of comfort.

Creating that personal environment, though, won't happen overnight. Every time I move, I want to take care of setting up my home—start to finish—in one weekend. I can't stand the unsettled feeling of a new apartment. Living out of boxes, not having basic necessities, eating meals on the floor—the novelty lasts for about five minutes. But there's so much to be done when you move into a new apartment—buying furniture, household items, groceries, unpacking, setting up utilities—that it can't possibly be done in just a couple of days. It takes time to figure out how best to use your space and, therefore, what items you'll want to acquire. Why waste the time and money rushing out to buy a new desk, for example, only to find that you work and read sitting in the living room chair? If you force yourself to complete the furnishing process immediately, you'll end up making impulse purchases that are likely to end up being pricier, less useful, and less interesting than purchases that you take time to think about. (It's like going grocery shopping when you're hungry. Ding Dongs, anyone?) Start slowly, purchase only the most necessary items, and get things that you really love (or at least really like). The process will take a few extra weeks to complete but you'll end up with a more heartfelt attachment to your space. Indeed, your "space" will have a much, much better chance of becoming your home.

Where Are You and Do You Plan to Stay There?

The amount of money and time that you invest in setting up your apartment should reflect the length of time that you intend to spend living in the city you've chosen. If, for example, you're on a one-year program in a part of the country that you will probably leave when the program is through, it doesn't make a whole lot of sense—actually, it makes no sense at all, unless, of course, you have money to burn, in which case you can hire an interior decorator and skip the rest of this section—to spend money buying furnishings that are tailored for your current home and that you will be forced to ship or sell within several months. Likewise, if you're living somewhere new and aren't sure whether you'll end up staying for a significant period of time, think very carefully about the purchases you make. In the long run, you're better off saving the money and the hassle of figuring out what to do with your new belongings when you move. That's not to say that you should live out of a suitcase for the next year, but you can comfortably furnish an apartment temporarily. We'll talk about how to do that later on in this chapter.

If, on the other hand, the odds are that you'll be staying put for a while, you'll want to give serious consideration to ways to make your new home more homey and to investing in things that you think will withstand the test of time.

First Things Second: Painting

The very first thing you need to do, before you even get to the first thing on your "To Do/Buy" list, is to decide if your apartment needs to be painted. Many landlords will accept responsibility for painting the apartment before you move in. If you've reached an agreement with your landlord about painting, ask him/her to include it in the lease.

If you plan to paint the apartment yourself, take care of it a couple of days before you and your stuff move into the apartment. (If you want to paint the walls a color that's different from the current one, clear it with the landlord first. S/he may require that you repaint the walls the original color before you move out.)

In the lease for my Boston apartment, it was stipulated that the walls would be freshly painted before I moved in. When I showed up with the professional movers I had hired and a moving truck full of furniture and boxes, I saw that the apartment had not, in fact, been painted. Since I was not prepared to pay the movers for the extra time it would take for me to contact the landlord, locate painters, and have the walls painted, I moved in anyway. Two days later, at 6:30 in the morning, the painters showed up. They had to move all of my furniture to get to the walls and I had to suffer through a couple of days of noxious paint fumes. The hardwood floors (in the interest of which I had insisted the movers take extra-special care in moving my furniture) were completely and profoundly scratched by the painters, whose manner of extracting and later returning my furniture was, to put it delicately, indelicate.

A fresh coat of paint can have a big impact on an otherwise drab apartment, so even if your landlord doesn't take responsibility for it, it's worth doing it yourself. Creating a professional look—or, at any rate, a respectable amateur look—boils down to patience and organization. (For instructions on how to paint a room, see Appendix.)

Whether or not you choose to paint, you'll want to clean the apartment before unpacking. It may very well be included in your lease that the landlord will have the apartment professionally cleaned before you move in. If so, prior to unpacking see to it that the landlord meets his obligation. If it falls on you to clean the apartment, clean at least the kitchen and bathroom if it doesn't appear that the former tenant did so before moving out.

> The landlord for my Boston apartment must not have taken the lease too seriously because just as it stipulated that he would have the apartment painted before I moved in, it also stated that he was responsible for having the apartment cleaned. While different people have different standards for what qualifies as "clean," it seems to me that all people would agree that strands of dried spaghetti stuck to the top of walls and the kitchen ceiling do not a clean room make. It seemed that the previous tenants had gotten a little overzealous cooking al dente and my landlord had been a little underzealous in his cleaning efforts. Pasta's like hair in at least one way: If you're going to find it where it shouldn't be, you want it to be your own.

Sleep Tight

Your first priority for your new home ought to be a bed, because it is the single thing that can make you feel like you're *living* in your apartment and not just camping out there temporarily. Your bed doesn't necessarily have to be a real bed—it might be a futon or a pull-out sofa or a mattress on the floor—but you need to have somewhere to sleep, and a sleeping bag on the floor isn't going to cut it for more than a few nights.

If you have a bedroom, you'll probably want to purchase at least a mattress and box spring. Look for mattress factory outlets or discounters in the Yellow Pages under "Mattresses" and call around to find a place that delivers. You might also skip the Yellow Pages altogether and call (800) MATTRES [628-8737]. (Yes, that's just one

"S.") You can order your mattress over the phone and, if you live in a major city, your mattress will be delivered in a few hours. (It will take slightly longer if you live off the beaten path.)

Sarah borrowed a friend's pickup truck to transport her new mattress to her new apartment. Cruising down the highway, daydreaming about napping, she was jolted to attention by the frantic horn honking of the driver behind her. She pulled over to the breakdown lane to see what was wrong. The truck was fine—no smoke, no suspicious noise or odor—but no mattress either. The mattress had fallen off the truck somewhere along the way and by the time she was able to contact a highway patrolman to help, the mattress was gone.

If you don't purchase your mattress from a store that delivers, make sure the load is properly tied down. If you buy your mattress at a mattress store, a salesperson should be able to provide you with rope and help you secure your purchase.

Though a mattress and box spring work just fine on the floor, you might think about buying a bed frame that will give the bed a few inches of lift (as well as provide some storage space under the bed). Many discount mattress outlets will include a frame for free with the purchase of a mattress and box spring. Otherwise, the cost of a frame will be around twenty dollars. The standard and simplest frame is called a "Harvard frame."

It's critical to measure the space in which you plan to put the bed to determine what size you'll be able to fit into the room. Another important measurement, often overlooked, is the clearance of any door or stairway through and up which the box spring will need to be carried.

When I moved into my spacious bedroom in D.C., I immediately went out and purchased a full-size mattress and box spring. My roommates and I tied them to the roof of our car and carefully drove home. It took three of us to maneuver them up the stairs and through the front door of our apartment. We then faced the challenge of getting the box spring up and around the winding staircase that led to my bedroom. Though the three of us exhausted ourselves twisting and bending our bodies into unnatural positions, the fact was that the box spring itself could not be bent or twisted and could not, therefore, fit up the staircase. (Box springs, of course, lack the flexibility of mattresses.) In the end, we carried the box spring up the wider staircase of the adjacent apartment, out the sliding glass doors, across the roof, in the sliding glass doors of the floor above mine, and down the stairs that led to my bedroom. (I was lucky. When my friends Dana and Andy had their new couch, which was meant to double as kitchen chairs, delivered to their apartment, it didn't fit through the doorway even when they unhinged the door. The couch had to go back to the store and Dana and Andy had to spend another week eating dinner on the floor.)

Though a mattress is one thing you'll want to buy new, you can find great bargains on the rest of the bed at thrift stores. I purchased a a beautiful wooden headboard, footboard, and frame for twenty dollars at the Salvation Army store.

Know Thyself

Once you've purchased a bed, you have somewhere to sit to think about the following. What kind of look do you want to achieve in your home? How much time will you be spending at home and what will you be doing there? Are you a basically neat person who likes everything to have its place or do you thrive in a cluttered environment? Think about other people's homes that have appealed to you. Visit local furniture stores and flip through some design magazines to decide what style you're going to shoot for in the furnishings you obtain. Whether your taste gravitates towards country, modern, Victorian, ethnic, funky, contemporary, formal, informal, Southwestern, bohemian, comfortable, slick, minimalist, or cluttered, if you have a theme in mind before you go shopping, you'll end up with a more cohesive, deliberate design.

Design? That's probably the last thing on your mind. When your objectives are fundamentally basic (not having to eat dinner on the floor, for example) you don't give a hoot if your chairs are country or modern. (Cheap? That works for me.) But it is possible, even on a very tight budget, to create a distinctive style in your home. Inexpensive doesn't have to mean clashing, boring, or shoddy. Suppose you like the Southwestern look but an adobe hilltop house in Santa Fe is out of your price and/or geographic range. You can decorate your home in earth tones, buy some throw rugs with a Southwestern motif, get a few cacti and some bottles of colored sand. If the country look is more your thing, buy a few baskets, wreaths, patchwork quilts, wicker furniture, and loads of dried flowers. For a modern feel, decorate the apartment primarily in black and white and buy angular furniture. A bohemian look can be inexpensively achieved with a few tapestries, scarves over lamps (but be careful of fire), and extra-large throw pillows on the floor. Of course, you may go for the eclectic look: lots of things you love that have nothing at all in common with one another. There doesn't necessarily have to be a design behind your design.

The Basics

Since you are presumably on a limited budget, you have to figure out what furniture you need and can afford to purchase right away. Some things, like a bed, you absolutely need and—since we've already established that a sleeping bag will not suffice in the long term—a bed is the first thing you need to acquire. But as you put together your list of other things to buy, think about the function of the items you deem necessary and see if there isn't an alternative means to the ends that matter to you. It's best to have a list of things you require before you go shopping so you don't end up buying beautiful wooden porch furniture for the porch you don't have, or making other similarly impulsive and unnecessary purchases. Let your list serve as a reminder of the items that you truly need to have. The following is a list of some apartment basics—and some alternative items that would serve the same purpose. (Later in the chapter you'll read where to find these items.)

- *Dresser* (or somewhere to put your clothes). Some alternatives are shelves, a footlocker (works great for sweaters), baskets, and crates. If you have large closets you can probably forgo a dresser altogether. On the other hand, if your closets are too small, consider buying a clothing rack (perhaps with a folding screen to place in front of it). You might also give some thought to storing your off-season clothes in order to maximize closet space. Clothing storage bags, which can be purchased at houseware stores, fit under the bed.

- *Couch* (or something on which to sit). If you decide a couch is too large an investment, consider a futon, a mattress (which comes pretty close to a couch when you cover it with a cotton blanket, push it against a wall, and put some large pillows along the back), or large throw pillows.

- *Kitchen table* (or something upon which to eat) *and chairs*. Brawn over beauty on this one. The important thing is to get something sturdy; if it's ugly you can cover it with a tablecloth. A card table and folding chairs will work; porch furniture will also do the trick. If you have a high counter, you might purchase bar stools and leave it at that. (As you'll probably learn, if not in your apartment then in those of some of your less enlightened friends, the novelty of lap eating lasts only so long.)

- *Lamps* (or something by which to read). Unless you're prepared to purchase a megasupply of candles, there's no alternative to lamps. Of course, if your apartment is already well lighted you won't need to worry about this. Keep in mind that one halogen bulb will provide the same amount of light as several filament bulbs and will last much longer, so even though halogen lamps are more expensive, they're well worth the investment.

- *Window shades/curtains* (or something to block the nosy neighbor's view). Curtains are expensive; if you need a window covering, consider using sheets instead. All you need to do is buy an appropriate-sized curtain rod, slip it through the hem at the top of a flat sheet, and you've got custom curtains. You can put hooks on either side of the window and tie the curtains back with a scarf, fabric, or rope during the day.

- *Paintings* (or something to cover the holes and cracks in the walls). You probably won't be able to afford framed art painted by the masters—or even their apprentices—right now but, hey, art is a matter of personal taste, right? One tapestry can cover a huge amount of wall space. Shelves serve the dual purpose of providing an additional place to put your books or knickknacks/ tchatchkes while taking up wall space. Framed photographs will help personalize your space. Mirrors with interesting frames can be cheaply purchased at many thrift stores, and will make the space look bigger. Posters, too, will work, but make sure to frame them, even if just with a cheap plastic frame; your days of thumb-tacking posters to the wall should be over by now. Large floor plants or hanging plants can take up quite a bit of space—but purchase them only if you're prepared to care for them. (Dead floor plants or hanging plants do little to brighten a room, unless you go for the necropolis look.) Decorating the walls is a perfect way to liven up or personalize an otherwise uninteresting apartment. One friend of mine contacted a billboard manufacturing company to see if it had any old billboards to give away. Sure enough, he ended up with a wall advertising Miller Lite. Another friend had a painting party where each of his friends was responsible for a portion of the wall. (Later, when it was time to move, he failed utterly to convince the landlord that the wall was art and shouldn't be painted over.)

- *Coffee table* (or something upon which to put coffee, coffee-table books, or your feet). Just like the kitchen table—as long as it's not going to collapse, it doesn't matter what your coffee table looks like. Drape a tablecloth or some fabric over it, and even a footlocker works.
- *Dishes, pots and pans, silverware* (or something in which to cook pasta and on which and with which to eat it). You may come up with some creative alternatives, but it's really best to invest in at least a couple of dishes, a pot and a pan, and a few pieces of silverware. You can purchase them cheaply at houseware or Woolworth's-type stores. You can also begin to assemble an interesting collection by buying mismatched dishes at thrift stores.
- *Bookcase* (or somewhere to put your books). I have five bookcases in my apartment and I still use the floor for the spillover. A great alternative to bookcases and the floor is to make your own bookcase out of bricks (or cinder blocks) and boards. (You'll find both at a lumber yard.) You can decide how high and how wide you want the shelves to be; just make sure the

boards balance firmly on the bricks so your books don't end up
on the floor anyway.
- *Desk* (or somewhere to put your computer). A large board balanced on top of two file cabinets gives you both a work surface
  and storage space.

Once you have your list of the furniture you need, you're ready to
set about getting it. There are a number of different kinds of places
you can look for furnishings; think of your quest as a treasure hunt
(or scavenger hunt, as the case may be). Your treasure map will almost surely include some false leads and some dead ends, but if you
stick with it and venture down several different avenues, you'll more
than likely stumble across some great finds.

Used Furniture: Why Secondhand Doesn't Mean Second-rate

Chances are that at this point in your life you cannot afford high-
quality new furniture. Your choice, then, is between low-quality
new and high-quality used, and you may find yourself tempted to go
for the low-quality new. At first glance it looks spiffier. Forget it. It
will age very, very quickly if it doesn't fall apart first, and you'll
find that by the time of your next move (or your first upgrade) you'll
be ready for high-quality used. Save yourself the trouble and expense, and go used now. As designer Judith Bodie puts it, "If it's
made it this far, you know it has some value." If you don't like the
way a piece of used furniture looks, there are myriad ways to
change its appearance. You can refinish and/or recover old furniture
to give it an updated look if you like, but you're always better off
spending your money on quality merchandise even if it's been previously used.

You might want to bring your friend with the artistic eye shopping
with you to get a second opinion and some ideas for restoring old
furniture. Keep in mind that ugly designs can be covered; focus on
the sturdiness of the piece. Unless you're willing to undertake a major project, stay away from that which is wobbly, splitting, cracking, or in some other way deteriorating. (If you buy used appliances,
make sure to plug them in and see that they work, or, alternatively,

get a cash rebate or a guarantee including pick-up and delivery of re-placement by seller.)

"One Person's Trash Is Another Person's Treasure"

Finding good used furniture can be as simple as driving through a fancy neighborhood on garbage pick-up day. Many people don't know what to do with their old furniture or simply don't want to deal with it and leave it on their sidewalk for the city to pick up. (If you see furniture on the sidewalk and aren't certain that the owner has put it there to discard it, you can always ring the doorbell and ask.) My friend's mother, who has a home filled with beautiful antiques, found her most valuable piece of furniture in her neighbor's trash. (Sorry, I can't give you her neighbor's address.) When she discovered the chair, she couldn't believe he meant to throw it out. But there it was, on the sidewalk with the rest of his trash. Just to make sure, she asked her neighbor what his intentions were. He told her that he was thrilled she had found the chair; he hadn't known what to do with it and was hoping it would make its way into the home of someone who would appreciate it.

But you obviously can't rely on the chance of coming across valu-able antiques in other people's trash. You need to make a concerted effort to find the most affordable, most sturdy, most suited-to-your-taste used furniture.

Attics, Basements, and Garages. There is no furniture more af-fordable than free hand-me-downs from family and friends. Let your parents know that you would love anything they can spare (remem-ber, you can alter the furniture later to suit your tastes) and ask them to spread the word to their friends who live in your vicinity. People have all kinds of things crowded into their basements, attics, and garages, and might be relieved to have some of it cleaned out.

Thrift Shops. Thrift shops like the Salvation Army, Goodwill, and Hadassah sell merchandise that has been donated and use the profits to support their other activities. Though you usually have to sort through quite a bit of tacky merchandise, there are definitely treasures to be found. Antique sellers, designers, and other collectors often snatch the good stuff, so find out what day new goods are put on the floor and get there early.

Yard and Garage Sales. Whether the household sale takes place in the yard or in the garage, you can expect to find an array of household items, some old clothes, and maybe even some furniture. Anything worthwhile will definitely be purchased early on, so plan on getting there a few minutes before the sale is scheduled to begin. (When my mother had a yard sale that she advertised for 10:00 A.M., the professional collectors showed up at 8:30. We hadn't even finished setting up yet, and therefore resented their eagerness—so try not to get there too early—but they and the amateur early birds gobbled up everything of value by 9:30.) Yard and garage sales are generally advertised in the community newspaper and on signs posted around the neighborhood. Look for sales in the wealthier areas of town to find the best merchandise.

Estate Sales. When an entire estate is for sale (usually because of the owner's death, move, or bankruptcy), you can find anything from pots and pans to dining-room tables to bath towels. If the estate belonged to someone relatively wealthy, some of the merchandise will be valuable and, obviously, more expensive. Collectors know when a valuable estate is for sale and will arrive bright and early (or even dark and late, as it is not uncommon for serious shoppers to camp out the night before the sale). The number of people allowed into the house at the same time might be limited, so the early birds definitely have the advantage. Estate sales are advertised in newspapers.

Classified Advertisements. It's worth flipping through the newspaper's classified advertisements to see if anybody is selling something that you need. Major pieces of furniture are often advertised, but like anything else, you'll need to call early if you're interested. (When I advertised a box spring and mattress for sale, I received such a huge response that I had to change the outgoing message on my answering machine to say that they had already been sold.)

Many cities also have entire magazines filled with classified ads. In New England, for example, there's *The Want ADvertiser*. Check a newsstand to see what's available where you are.

Back to the Future—Transforming Used Furniture

When you buy a piece of used furniture that needs some aesthetic improvements, you can strip it back to its original state, cover it with fabric, paint over it, or merely touch it up. Stripping obviously works with certain kinds of furniture only. You can't, for example, strip a living-room couch or an easy chair. (Well, you can, but why would you want to?) The kind of furniture you want to strip is wood that has been treated with paint or varnish. You'll want to strip off layers of chipped paint or varnish even if you intend to repaint in order to avoid a paint job that looks bumpy and messy. A stripping solution can be purchased at a paint or hardware store and will have instructions printed on the can. Stripping is not a small job, so if the paint or varnish that's on the furniture isn't chipped and you're not going for the original look, don't bother. You can simply repaint.

Covering, on the other hand, works for any kind of furniture. If you don't want to paint them, you can cover tables with tablecloths, scarves, tapestries, or other fabric. Couches and chairs can also be covered with fabric—sheets are a good option. If sewing isn't your thing, you can use a staple gun to secure the fabric, but make sure that the messy part on the back will be against a wall. It's also important to make sure that the fabric doesn't cover the furniture too snugly; you don't want it to tear. The alternative to using a staple gun or sewing is to get fabric that is large enough to leave several inches dragging after the furniture is covered. The extra fabric can be tied into large knots or bows at the bottom of the furniture. (If you want to spend money rather than time, you can purchase slipcovers for couches and chairs.)

Remember, not all used furniture needs aesthetic improvements. You may find pieces that look perfect—or at least adequate—as they are.

First Time's a Charm: Buying New

If you prefer to buy new furniture, shop carefully and do your research to make sure that you're getting the best quality you can afford.

- Shop at factory outlets and save the retail mark-up costs.
- Shop at furniture discounters. Stores that discount prices usually say that they do in their Yellow Pages' advertisement.

- Comparison shop and look for sales.
- Inquire about buying display furniture; you should be able to get a discount.
- If you're going to buy more than one of an item, inquire about a volume discount. (I got twenty dollars off each of my desk chairs for buying two together.)
- Decide before you go shopping how much you're going to spend on each item and don't spend more than you budget.
- If you find flaws on a piece of furniture you want to buy, see if you can get a discount.
- Buy unfinished furniture and leave it as is or finish it yourself.

Renting Furniture

If you think it's a serious possibility that you'll leave the city to which you have moved within a relatively short time (say, a year or less), you might want to think about renting furniture. The advantage to renting is that you can get all kinds of furniture delivered right to you—and later picked up from you—and you don't have the hassle of selling, moving, or discarding it when you leave town. Renting is also a good temporary solution if you're not quite sure what you'll be able to afford once you've found a job, or if you have a few roommates and don't want to deal with divvying up the furniture when you part ways.

But whether or not renting saves you money is dependent upon the rental rate, of course, and the length of the lease.

When I moved to Seattle, I decided to rent a television rather than invest in a new one. I paid $30 a month to rent a small set for five months. I then went out and bought a used set for sixty dollars. For the two-ten I ended up spending, I could have bought a much nicer new set. (I also could have saved the $150 I paid to rent a set and bought a used one right away.)

You can usually rent month to month if you aren't certain for how long you'll need the furniture. Look in the Yellow Pages under "Furniture Rentals."

Transporting Your Treasures

If you have a car or, better yet, a truck, you already know how you're going to get your new furniture home. Just remember to secure the furniture tightly if you're putting it on top of your vehicle. Likewise, if you're shopping at stores that deliver, you don't have to worry about transporting your finds. But if you don't have a vehicle and you find furniture at a place that doesn't have delivery capabilities, you have to give some thought to how you will get your purchases home.

Presuming the furniture is too heavy to carry on public transportation and too large to fit in a taxi, find out if anyone you know has a van or truck, or knows anyone who has a van or truck. Your second option is to see if the store owner would be willing, for a few extra dollars, to deliver the merchandise even though that is not a service the store typically provides. Your final option is to rent a van for the day, which, depending on the number of places from which you make purchases and their locations, might end up costing less than a taxi anyway. If you have a roommate or friend who has also made purchases, split the cost of the rental and carpool.

These ideas might seem obvious, but when my roommates and I went shopping to furnish our first apartment, we took the Metro to the discount furniture store that had been recommended to us. We found several things we liked but we hadn't thought to call in advance to find out if the store delivered. Guess what? It didn't. We had to put all of the furniture on hold until we could rent a van and make a second trip to the store. (I hope my mistakes make your life at least a little bit easier. If not, I hope they at least give you a small—very small—chuckle.)

Designing Women . . . and Men

Some people think decorating is fun. These people can strut into an apartment, take a quick visual inventory, and immediately know what ingredients are required for a successful makeover. They whirl out to antique stores, yard sales, and thrift shops, where they quickly separate the junk from the treasures, bring home an array of furniture, trinkets, and baubles, and get to work. "We'll strip this, stencil here, recover that, a little paint over there," they explain, while those of us who are, shall we say, decoratingly challenged, respectfully watch them transform a dingy studio apartment into something straight out of a design magazine.

I was fortunate enough to live with a natural-born decorator for a few years in college and for one year after. Our limited budget didn't faze her in the least; she relied on her creativity and style to make the most out of what we could afford. She painted flowers on my father's old porch furniture (which we were using for dining-room chairs), covered our fading brown-and-orange-flowered tweed couch with bright cotton sheets, and strategically placed throw pillows and quilts to give the living room a cozy feel.

Though I will never be able to paint flowers on chairs adequate to make them presentable enough to go on my porch, never mind in the dining room, in the course of my three postcollege moves I've learned some design tricks that even someone as artistically inept as I can quickly master.

Some Advice

- Your apartment should reflect your personality. If you like to read, put bookcases in every room; if you're a sportsperson, hang your bike on the wall and keep your skis in the corner; if you're an artist, display some of your work. An apartment that feels like a generic hotel room is no fun. Surround yourself with the things that make you happy. (If you live with roommates, the apartment might develop a split personality. Later in the chapter we'll discuss issues for roommates to consider when designing the apartment.)
- If it's clear that you can't afford elegant furnishings, don't try to fake it by getting cheap imitations. Go funky instead.
- Consider the kitsch look, defined as anything pretentious and in poor taste. Just remember, it's essential to make it look as though you're in on the joke. When Lara bought a thirty-five-dollar oversize powder-blue velvet couch for her living room, she covered it with bright throw pillows and a quilt and placed it beside a hot-pink chair. She clearly didn't take the couch seriously; instead she celebrated its ugliness.

- If you have one or two of something quirky (in addition to your roommates), it or they will look random and uninteresting. If, on the other hand, you have an entire collection, you've suddenly got a conversation piece. For example, if you have two mismatched old-fashioned plates, they'll look as though they were left behind by the previous tenants or snagged from your grandmother's cupboard. But if you have a whole dinner party's worth of mismatched old dishes, the collection is clearly intentional and, therefore, interesting. Likewise, a room lit by an assortment of candles comes across very differently from a room with one candle glowing in the corner. A single colored glass bottle adds nothing to a room; three shelves of colored glass bottles, on the other hand . . .
- Take your sheets, pillows, and quilts out of the bedroom. Sheets make great curtains, as previously mentioned. They also provide a solution to tattered, torn, or ugly furniture. Throw pillows and quilts add color, comfort, and camouflage to couches and chairs. Interesting quilts can even be hung on the wall, which takes care of what to do with all that empty wall space.
- Flowers can significantly brighten up an otherwise dreary room. Consider interesting containers in which to display flowers; unusual bottles, jugs, or old canteens all work nicely. If the flowers are dried, they don't need water, so you can put them in almost anything: baskets, barrels, even boots.

Saving Space

If you're anything at all like I am, you have drawers full of clothes that you haven't worn in years but refuse to throw out in case the day comes when you need to wear those certain jeans. Or you're back to the weight you were when you bought them. You still have your third-grade book report for which you received an A++ and you have boxes full of magazines that you kept because they had articles you thought you'd want to refer back to. (What are the chances of that happening, when you have no system to remind you what the articles were about or in which magazines to find them?) Your mantra for cleaning house is "you never know," and since you never know when you'll want to wear a certain item or when you'll need a specific book or slip of paper, you keep everything, figuring that you're better off safe than sorry.

The apartment in which you now find yourself is probably not big enough to comfortably fit all of your belongings (and, in many cases, the belongings of your roommates as well). There are, however, ways to maximize the space that you do have and I've listed those below. If, after following some of the space-saving tips (and bending, folding, squeezing, squishing and/or mushing your things), you're still unable to find room for all your belongings, find out if the apartment management provides any storage space. If not, consider shipping some of your stuff to your parents' house (if they're generous enough to agree) or renting storage space. (See Chapter 1 for information on storage rentals.) If all else fails, enlist the help of an unsentimental friend to sort through your stuff and donate some of it to charity. Your problem can be someone else's solution.

Saving Space Everywhere
- Whenever possible, get things up and off the floor. You only have so much floor space and you'll probably be using most of it. But think about all the wall space and air space that could be used for storage. Shelves and hooks allow you to elevate things that would otherwise take up floor space. I have one friend who keeps chairs mounted on hooks on the wall. He uses them as shelves; each one holds a plant or a couple of books. When he has company, he takes the chairs down. (If he likes the company, he removes the plants and books.) You can save quite a bit of space by using your walls creatively.
- There are stores that specialize in space-savers. It's worth visiting one not only to shop, but also to get ideas of creative ways to save space.

Saving Space in the Bedroom
- If your bedroom doubles as the living room and/or dining room, consider using a futon as a bed. The advantage of a futon is that it can fold into a couch or chair during the day. You might also think about building a loft. One friend of mine added space to her tiny one-room apartment by elevating the mattress and designing a sitting area underneath. Another option is to sleep on a pull-out couch.

- If you have a mattress and box spring, buy a bed frame and lift your bed a few inches off the floor. The space under the bed is good for more than dust balls; it can serve as a perfect storage space for off-season clothes and shoes. (Make sure that any clothing you keep under the bed is stored in tightly sealed storage bags or you'll spend a fortune at the dry cleaners when the seasons change.)
- Put your bed against the window and use the window ledge as a nightstand.
- Get furniture that has drawers. Nightstands, desks, or tables with drawers are much more useful than those without.
- Hang your shoes on a shoe rack that fits over or on the back of the closet door and keep storage crates for clothes or files on the closet floor.

Saving Space in the Kitchen
- Buy a step stool and don't leave the top cupboard shelves empty.
- Buy lazy Susans (round shelves that spin) to add extra storage space in your cupboards.
- Hang your pots and pans on a pegboard near the stove.
- Stack your dishes wisely. If you put smaller dishes inside bigger ones, you'll save space and have more organized cupboards.

Saving Space in the Bathroom
- If you have one small medicine cabinet and three roommates, you'll quickly learn that it's not realistic to keep all of your various ointments, pastes, lotions, soaps, shampoos, razors, and creams—not to mention medicines—in the medicine cabinet. Consider getting individual buckets or baskets in which to keep your sundries and keeping them in your respective bedrooms. It's a little bit like dorm living but it works.
- Put extra towel/robe hooks on the back of the door. The best hooks are the ones that screw into the door, but if you're concerned about making holes, buy the kind that hook onto the top of the door. (Yes, the door will still close.) Stay away from the stick-on hooks; they fall off easily.
- Buy a shower shelf that fits over the shower head. You can find one at a housewares store or drugstore.

- Don't keep several half-empty bottles of the same product. Consolidate and create more space.

Saving Space in the Living Room
- Buy folding chairs that can be stored when not in use.
- Use a footlocker as a coffee table and store blankets or sweaters inside.

Settling In with Roommates

Setting up an apartment that reflects your personality and in which you feel comfortable and "at home" becomes more complicated when you have a roommate, and even more complex when you have two or three. Though you probably had a theoretical discussion about furnishing the apartment and setting up utilities when you were deciding whether or not to move in together, you might want to revisit some of these issues now that your theoretical home is a reality. (See Chapter 2 for additional discussion points for roommates.)

1. *Shared Space.* How do you envision using those areas that you share (e.g., kitchen, living room)? If one roommate thinks the living room is the room for partying, a second intends to use it as headquarters for his fledgling alternative music magazine, and you're planning on setting up your desk there to study for the Bar exam, work it out now. And how do you feel about keeping personal items in common areas? Do you want a charcoal sketch of your roommate's girlfriend hanging on the wall in your living room? It might take a few months of living in the apartment to get into a routine and figure out how you use a room, but discussing how you intend to use common areas will help iron out differences between you and your roommate(s) early on. Identifying the purpose(s) for which you intend to use the shared space will also help you determine the kinds of furniture that you'll want to acquire.
2. *Buying Together.* To avoid conflict when you and your roommate(s) split up, you might want to figure out now who is going to keep the items you've copurchased. It might make sense to have each person purchase specific pieces of furniture so that

ownership is clear cut. On the other hand, if you co-own major purchases, you're equally invested in maintaining them. If sharing ownership is the path you choose, make sure to record the price so you can settle up later when it comes time for the parting of the ways.

3. *Conflicting Taste.* If you already own some furniture that you want to put in the common area, show (or at least describe) it to your roommate first. You don't want to go through the trouble of transporting a piece of furniture that your roommate doesn't like. If it's something that you've owned for a while and aren't willing to recover or refinish or revise in any way, you may be resentful if your roommate doesn't want to put it in the common area. "It's good enough for me (or my family), why isn't it good enough for you?" Ditto for anything you want to hang on the wall. If you're respectful of your roommate's taste, the favor will probably be returned. On the other hand, you might agree that since you're starting from scratch, any furniture is good furniture and therefore no clearance procedures are necessary. Whatever you decide, decide together. That leaves less room for conflict, resentment, and hurt feelings.

Once in a while, a piece of furniture becomes intermingled with our sweetest memories. We think of that furniture not in terms of its finish or its pattern, but in terms of the emotions it evokes for us: safety, or comfort, for example—or even passion. For some people it's the cozy armchair where they spent hours nestled in their grandmother's lap listening to stories of the old country; for some it's the bunk bed that they and their brothers transformed into a tent on rainy Sundays; for some it's the kitchen table where they sat while their mother convinced them that their life was not in fact over because they didn't make the cheerleading team. For me, it was a hideous, electric-blue, S-shaped, legless chair.

To understand The Blue Chair, you need to understand its shape. Its curves met the body's curves perfectly; it was ergonomically correct before we knew what that meant. Reclining on the chair (its slopes made sitting impossible) was like getting a full body hug. My memories of the chair date back to my toddler years when my two older sisters would invite me to lie in it with them and watch the soaps. (It was the seventies then and the chair was totally groovy.) On the chair I wasn't the baby sister; I was included in their secrets and their giggling (except during the commercials, when they'd send me to the kitchen to fetch snacks). When I was seven my family moved and, sure enough, the chair was transported to its rightful place of importance in our new family room. As I grew older, the chair became the place where my family would veg out to watch *West Side Story* for the thirty-fifth time or to match wits in "Jeopardy." Later, it was the place to snuggle with various boyfriends. (The chair was always in high demand when I threw parties.)

So when I moved to D.C. and my mother said that I could take The Blue Chair with me, I was ecstatic. I was convinced that with The Blue Chair in our living room, there'd be nothing but good times and I'd be sure to develop a new world of wonderful memories. The one high-school friend with whom I planned to live was equally thrilled; she'd experienced the wonders of The Blue Chair and couldn't wait to make it a part of her life, too.

Our other four roommates, however, didn't see it quite the same way. What they saw was a hideous, electric-blue, S-shaped, legless chair. And they had no intention of having such a disgrace in their living room. They knew I would never abandon the chair to a bad home; leaving it on a stranger's doorstep wasn't a realistic option. Neither, in that regard and perhaps much to their dismay, was dumping it in the Potomac River. Forgoing pickets, protests, and petitions for more subtle means of opposition, my roommates set about finding a new home for the chair. When a friend of ours (who did not live in our apartment) said he liked the chair, they didn't waste any time in offering it to him. And since the chair was far too big to fit in my bedroom (I know; I tried), and since I was overruled by the majority, I was, in the end, forced to choose between my roommates and my chair. After hours of deliberation, I bade farewell to The Blue Chair, and with it to the symbol of my happy childhood memories.

To avoid similar scenarios, make sure you and your roommate(s) are in agreement about furniture that will be in the common area.

4. *Utilities.* Share the responsibility of your apartment and put different utilities in different roommates' names. If all of the

utilities are in your name, you will be the one in the awkward role of having to figure out how much each person owes and bugging the others to give you their prompt payment. You'll also be faced with the possibility that your roommates could conceivably take off unexpectedly without regard to outstanding debts. If one person uses the phone considerably more than anyone else in the apartment, make sure the phone service is in that person's name.

I have one friend who grew so tired of nagging her roommates for the phone payment that she eventually decided to teach them a lesson by letting the payments lapse so the phone service was shut off. Her roommates eventually paid up but the lesson cost her. She had to live without a phone for three weeks.

If you're all big talkers and you can afford it, consider getting more than one phone line. You won't have to worry about missing important calls and you won't have the hassle of splitting up the phone bill.

5. *Overnight Guests.* How do you feel about your roommate(s) inviting guests to spend the night? You might assume that overnight guests are part of the roommate bargain, but some kinds of behavior might be more than you bargained for. If there are specific issues about which you feel strongly, let your roommate know. If you need to be in the shower at 6:30 every morning, ask your roommate to let guests know that the bathroom is off limits at that time. If you and your roommate are sharing food, you might resent a semipermanent guest sharing that food as well. If your roommate develops a close relationship with someone, would you be comfortable if she gave him a key to the apartment? It's easier to talk about these issues when the boyfriend or girlfriend is hypothetical; that way your feelings aren't perceived as a reflection of the specific person.

Shop Till You Drop

No matter how many times you've moved, each time you settle into a new home you're faced with a major shopping trip to Woolworth's or Caldor's or some other "everything store." Though you buy every item on your three-page shopping list, you undoubtedly come home and realize that you completely forgot about extension cords or toilet paper. The following list should save you some time and energy. Cross off those things you don't need and add to it anything I've missed. (Those items that I've indicated in capital letters are absolute musts.)

1. Extension cords
2. Toilet paper
3. Broom and dustpan
4. Mop
5. Baking soda
6. Vinegar (for cleaning, explained in Chapter 9)
7. SPONGES
8. Dishwashing soap
9. Soap dish
10. Laundry detergent
11. Dish towels
12. Dish-drying rack
13. Contact or liner paper (for lining kitchen cabinets and drawers)
14. Silverware tray
15. Hooks
16. Can opener
17. Hammer and nails
18. Screwdrivers—both Phillips and flat head
19. Shower curtain
20. Shower curtain liner
21. Bath mat
22. More hooks
23. Hangers
24. Laundry basket
25. Fan
26. LIGHT BULBS
27. Tape

28. Scissors
29. Cutting board
30. Colander
31. Three-to-two-prong plug converter
32. Power strip/ surge protector
33. ADHESIVE STRIPS
34. Hanging shelf that slips over shower head
35. Toilet brush
36. Toothbrush holder
37. Magnets, bulletin board, or blackboard and chalk (for leaving messages to roommates)
38. Tissues
39. Paper towels
40. Baskets or crates (for socks, magazines, files, or anything else that doesn't fit anywhere else)
41. Rubbing alcohol
42. Disinfectant
43. Aspirin
44. Picture-hanging hooks
45. TOILET PLUNGER!
46. BATTERIES
47. FLASHLIGHT
48. CANDLES
49. Corkscrew
50. Bottle of champagne

Setting Up Utilities

If it's possible, you'll want to take care of setting up utilities a few days before moving in. You'll probably already know which utilities you're responsible for (at least the phone) and which ones are included in your rent (if not, check your lease or contact the landlord), but you may need to call to hook up even those services that are included in your rent. A quick call to the landlord will clear up which one of you is responsible for the various utilities and who will take care of setting up the service. If you're in a new city, ask your landlord for the names of the local utility companies. You should also be able to find the names and phone numbers of the utility companies in the front of your Yellow Pages in a section called something like "Getting Settled" or "Important Telephone Numbers."

You'll want to set up your telephone service first so that you have a local telephone number to provide to the other utility companies. The phone company will give you your new number when you make the arrangement, even before the phone is actually installed. You'll also need to provide your social security number, your landlord's name and phone number, your new address (of course), and maybe even an emergency phone number, so have that information ready when you make your calls. If you want to have more than one name on the bills, you'll need your roommate's information as well.

Telephone Service

As you've surely gathered by now, I am an enthusiastic advocate of getting more than one phone line if you have roommates who keep in touch via the telephone with long-distance friends and family. This has less to do with the fact that it can be extremely annoying when your phone is tied up, and more to do with the colossal pain it can be to itemize a lengthy phone bill. (Tucahoe? Who knows somebody in Tucahoe?) An added bonus to having individual lines is that you can each take advantage of long-distance service perks like frequent-flyer miles. If getting more than one phone line poses a financial or technical problem, consider signing up with a long-distance service that will give each household member a personal code to dial before making long-distance phone calls. The telephone bill for such a service will be divided by personal access codes so there will be no question regarding who called whom and who, therefore, owes what.

If you're going to share a phone line with roommates, you'll need to decide which added services you want. Do you want call waiting, three-way dialing, call forwarding, or instant redial? What about automatic message service? If you're living with roommates you don't already know or if you want to keep your phone messages private, consider signing up for a personalized message service. In your outgoing message, each roommate's name will be followed by a number for the caller to press in order to leave a private message for that person. (Ah, the wonders of technology.)

When you call the local phone company to sign up for service, you'll be asked to select a long-distance carrier. The local phone company will connect your phone to a long-distance service, but if you want any of the special long-distance calling plans (which you should definitely research because they can save you quite a bit of money), you'll have to call the long-distance company yourself. It's worth calling around to find out about the different long-distance services to find the one that provides the benefits that most suit your needs. You can reach the major long-distance phone companies at the following numbers: AT&T: (800) 222-0300; MCI: (800) 444-3333; Sprint: (800) 877-4646; Allnet: (800) 881-8860.

(While you're thinking about telephone service, jot a note to yourself to pick up some extra-long telephone wire—a twenty-five-foot cord is commonly available—so that if you don't have a phone in your bedroom, you can take the phone from the common room into a private place for personal calls.)

Safety

Your apartment may not be in the best neighborhood in town, but there are precautions you can take to make you feel safer—and be safer—at home. First, your apartment absolutely must have smoke detectors. If it doesn't, speak to the landlord or management company about installing them immediately. (In most places, they're required by law.) You should also have a fire extinguisher in your apartment; you can purchase one at a hardware store for twenty to forty dollars.

The front doorway of the building and the hallways should be well lit at night. You might want to speak to the management if the lighting is insufficient; you should also let them know when the light bulbs burn out.

Make sure that the locks on your apartment door are changed when you move in so the previous tenant doesn't have access to your apartment. If you're uncomfortable with the locks that are currently on the door, there are a number of locking devices that you can purchase at a hardware store. If you live alone or are especially concerned about the possibility of someone breaking into your apartment while you're home, consider purchasing a locking device that cannot be opened from the outside, such as a Jam Bar that wedges between the doorknob and the floor. Don't forget to leave a spare set of house keys at the home of a friend or neighbor whom you trust and who is often home.

The goal is for you to feel secure in your home. But despite locks and lighting and smoke detectors, apartment calamities do happen. Unfortunately, there's no foolproof way to prevent them. But there is a way to ensure that when they do happen, you're not financially devastated.

Renter's Insurance

Just as it is a requirement for all automobile owners to have automobile insurance, it ought to be a requirement for all renters to have renter's insurance. Renter's insurance is one of the most important investments you can make, and it is surprisingly inexpensive. It's difficult to justify spending even fifteen dollars a month "just in case" when you're living on a limited budget, but when "just in case" becomes "I never thought it would happen to me," you'll be glad you've taken financial precautions.

Returning from spring break in Florida to our chilly midwest apartment was difficult anyway, but when my roommates and I opened the front door and saw our apartment in utter disarray we were devastated. While we were gone, a bedroom window had blown open and let in sufficient cold air to freeze the pipes in the walls. The pipes burst on the second day of our vacation and flooded not only our ninth-floor apartment, but eighteen others as well. The apartment management had "dealt" with the situation by putting our drenched belongings in large plastic bags, so that by the time we got home, the mildew and the stench were unbearable. Most of our clothing and bedding could not be salvaged; our electrical equipment was destroyed. None of us had renter's insurance, and since it appeared that someone in our apartment had not closed the window securely, we had no recourse against the apartment management. We were, basically, out of luck.

One would think I would have known better since my sister

Nomi had survived an apartment fire and two robberies, and my sister Rachel's apartment and all of its contents were destroyed by fire. Which proves, alas, that apartment calamities are not that unusual and that it's therefore worth investing in renter's insurance to provide financial relief when they do happen. (One could argue that the evidence instead proves something about the luck of my family; a curse perhaps? But I also have several friends who have endured apartment fires and robberies.)

You might think you don't have many valuables in your apartment, nothing you'd be shattered to lose. But if all of your clothes were destroyed, you'd need to replace at least some of them. And what about your CDs and books? To get an idea of the value of your belongings, take an hour or so and write down everything you own. Estimate the value of each category of belongings. This exercise will help you realize what kind of financial investment you'd need to make if every item on the list were suddenly destroyed. It's also a useful document when you're trying to decide how much insurance to purchase. If you have a video camera, make a video of your apartment to have as a reference in case your belongings are destroyed. And yes, make sure to leave your video and/or inventory of belongings at someone else's home.

(Slightly relevant interruption: It's also useful to make a list of the contents of your wallet in case it's ever lost or stolen.)

There are two kinds of insurance you can purchase. Actual Cash Value takes into account the depreciation of the item. If you purchased a stereo several years ago for two hundred dollars that is now worth only one hundred dollars, you will get one hundred dollars from the insurance agency. (Minus the deductible, of course.) Replacement Cost, on the other hand, pays you the amount it would cost to replace the item, so you'd get two hundred dollars for your old stereo. Replacement Cost insurance is more expensive than Actual Cash Value, but for the added value, it's probably worth it. An insurance agent will be able to explain the differences in greater detail and to help you put together the plan that makes the most sense for you.

Renter's insurance doesn't only cover possessions that are in your home. It covers specified damages to your possessions while you're traveling, and it also protects you against liability for some accidents that occur in your apartment.

Note that with renter's insurance, as with virtually all similar insurance, the deductible is a key element in the price. Essentially, the amount of the deductible is the amount for which you're insuring yourself; if there's a loss, you eat that amount. The higher it is, the lower the cost of the insurance. Opt for the largest deductible you can reasonably handle; unless you're accident prone (and therefore file claims frequently), you'll save money that way.

The Independent Insurance Agents of America publishes a free pamphlet for college graduates: *The Graduate's Independent Guide to Insurance*. The pamphlet includes answers to basic questions about various kinds of insurance and contains a listing of state contacts who can provide you with additional information and with the name of a reputable agent in your city. To obtain a copy of the pamphlet, call (800) 991-7722.

All this may seem like a lot, but it's worth expending the time and energy to shape a place that you look forward to returning to in the evening and to which you want to invite your friends.

But what if you don't have any friends to invite?

That's what Chapter 5 is all about.

5. Mixing and Mingling: Is There Social Life After College?

Making friends in college is as easy—and as natural—as skipping class on a sunny day. On campus, after all, there's an essentially endless supply of preselected people, a decisively nonrandom universe of people your age who are all doing roughly the same things you're doing. Even the ones least like you straggle to the beat of the same drummer. Strangers, strange as they may be, are not really strangers, since you will almost invariably share a class, an acquaintance, a dorm, what have you. The social dynamic of a college campus urges students towards camaraderie, and the making of friends is aided and abetted by the fact that most students care at least as much about their social life as they do about their classes.

Once you've left school, however, meeting new people is no longer built into the scheme of things. It takes effort. In unfortunate fact, it's never again going to be as easy to meet good friends and maintain relationships as it has been up to this point in your life. Consider:

1. You're no longer living among thousands of people your age; not only is it harder to come into contact with new friends, but it's much less convenient to see your old ones.
2. You're no longer doing the same thing as all of your friends. Though your friends at school had different majors, professors,

and classes, you could relate to what they were doing. They were students and so were you—sociology or biology, just a three-letter difference. Most important, the school calendar was the same for everybody: finals, vacations, summer break, and so forth. Now, though you and your friends may all be working, you'll likely be in different fields with distinctive pressures and challenges. You won't be able to identify in the same way with how your friends spend their days, hence with your friends.

3. When you were in school, you and your friends were all at the same stage of life. For the most part, you all finished one semester and went on to the next at the same time. Now, you and your friends are going to be moving at different paces. If you're on the fast track in a high-pressure business career and your friend is serving lattes at a coffee bar, you may begin to feel some distance develop between you. Likewise, if you're living in the city and playing the dating game, you'll notice a change in how you relate to your friend who gets married and moves to the suburbs. Which isn't to say that seemingly mismatched friendships can't flourish; friends are friends, not clones. But as you continue to make major decisions and enter new stages, old relationships are going to be put to new tests and you may well feel the need for new friends with whom you have, at least for the time being, more in common.

4. Friendships that develop in college are uniquely intense. Except for the few hours a day of classes, you're able to spend the majority of your waking hours with your peers. You live together, eat together, study and party together. Now, you will spend (I know this seems—and often more than merely "seems"—depressing) the majority of your waking hours at work. It's going to take a much greater effort to find time to see your friends, and when you do, it will be for a shorter period of time (a cup of coffee, say, instead of the whole pot). This is going to mean both a major adjustment in the friendships that you've brought with you to your new life as well as a need to make a greater investment in forging new friendships.

All of the preceding probably seems discouraging, so keep in mind that there's a major up-side to postcollege friendships. Though the number of friends and acquaintances that you have will almost surely decrease, the quality of your friendships may well be richer. College friendships have something of the quality of shipboard romances: Thrust together by common situation, you spend a great deal of time with people you wouldn't necessarily choose as friends, and your time together can be wonderfully intense. But when the situation changes—when you reach port, as it were—you have little to say to each other beyond trading reminiscences. As to your new friendships, based as they almost necessarily are on intention rather than coincidence, they come not only with a more durable foundation but also with some useful advantages: You'll probably find that because you have less time to spend with your friends, you'll value the time you do spend together much more than you did in the past; as the peripheral friendships that you had in college dissipate, you'll develop a greater sense of which friendships were really provisional and which ones you care to maintain. The college friendships that sustain the transition take on a whole new meaning, and will likely prove lifelong.

You'll also find that you spend more time alone and invest more energy in developing your personal skills and interests than you did in college. You will have a greater sense of self and have, therefore, more to offer in a friendship. Since you'll be meeting people through a variety of situations now that you're out of school, you can also expect to have a much more diverse group of friends. They will no longer all be of the same age and socioeconomic status, following the same path as you. In short, you're likely to find that your postcollege friendships are far richer than those that developed circumstantially in school, and that their intensity and depth will greatly enhance your life.

To pull it off, you'll need the Three I's: Inspiration, Initiative, and (a little bit of) Ingenuity.

The Inspiration part is simple. Though your social life may now take a backseat to other concerns (at least until your job situation stabilizes), you don't want and don't need to become a hermit. In fact, a support network is at least as important now as it was in college. Whether you're having trouble with a co-worker, a roommate, or a lover, nine times out of ten it's your friends who will help you get through this crisis, and the one just around the corner, too. Plus, friends aren't only for the hard times; the good times wouldn't be nearly as good without them.

If you've moved by yourself, the need to start building a social life will be immediately obvious. But even if you've moved with old friends, or somehow have an already established social network in your new city, you're still going to want to meet new people.

The question then becomes how to go about meeting these new friends, and that's where Initiative enters. While it's true that you'll meet many people purely through serendipity (more about that later in the chapter), serendipity works on its own schedule, not on yours. Unless passivity's your thing, your job is to seek out the settings and the connections that expand your prospects. As my friend's mother said to her three months after graduation (interrupting yet another home video rental), "New friends are not going to come walking into the living room and find you." (Six months later, by the way, that friend was engaged. And not to the pizza delivery man.)

Networking

If there were a better word I would use it. When we hear the word "networking," most of us think of slickly shmoozing one's way up the corporate ladder. I use the word simply to mean meeting people through other people. And networking, in that sense, is the easiest and best way to meet new friends.

To get started, begin spreading the word to as many people as possible that you're planning to move (or have just moved). Find out if your family or friends know anyone who lives in your new city. Collect as many names as you can. Your Aunt Ida's neighbor's daughter may not turn out to be your new best friend but she might know of a job opening or a great apartment. You never know—that is until you actually call the people whose names you've gathered. You'll probably feel a bit awkward calling perfect strangers, so ask the person who gives you the name to call ahead and explain who you are. That way, your call will be expected.

You should also be prepared to accept all invitations extended to you once you've moved.

A friend who had just moved to Seattle, upon his parents' urging called their close friends just to say hello. They promptly invited him to dinner and although he didn't have a sincere interest in accepting, he did so to please his parents. It turned out that the parents' friends had two kids his age: The daughter soon became his girlfriend and the son his roommate.

On the other hand, before I moved to Seattle, I was given the name of a friend of a friend who had moved there the previous year. From the description it sounded as if we'd hit it off beautifully. She was told I was moving, and she couldn't wait to meet me. I called her just after I arrived and we met for lunch. That's how we got started. That's also, as it turned out, how we ended. Our one lunch comprised the entirety of our "friendship." For whatever reason, we just didn't connect.

The important thing is to follow up on every contact, no matter how tenuous it may seem. Some will be dead-ends; others will end up costing you a couple of wasted hours. Big deal. But now and then you'll meet someone who will have a positive impact on your life, perhaps become a new friend. And even if a friendship doesn't result, the meeting may still be valuable. You can come away with the name of a dentist or the name of the funkiest restaurant in town. And the more people you meet and the sooner you meet them, the faster your new city will become home.

Networking doesn't only mean calling complete strangers. As you begin to meet people in your new city, through a temporary job or your new neighbor or the children of your parents' friends, you'll begin to meet the people they know, and your circle will slowly expand.

Another good way to meet people is to become involved in activities, associations, or clubs that interest you. Whether you choose to work on a political campaign or join a skeet-shooting club, you will be taking part in something that you care about and you won't be able to avoid meeting people with whom you have something in common. It's important to remember, though, to commit only to those activities in which you have a genuine interest or curiosity and not simply use them as an avenue to meet people. The idea is to meet people with whom you share a common interest, conviction, skill, etc. So think about the ways in which you'd most like to spend your spare time and consider the following:

Volunteer Work

With all the transitions you're currently experiencing, you are certainly absorbed if not completely obsessed with the details of your own life. Volunteer work forces you to restore a healthier balance to that life. There is no shortage of causes and organizations that would benefit from your time and energy, and the people you'll encounter there are very often well worth knowing. Few of them regard their work on behalf of others as a sacrifice; most feel enriched by it.

Some kinds of volunteer work lend themselves more easily than others to meeting friends, so keep that in mind when choosing your project. For example, Habitat for Humanity, a nonprofit organization that responds to the problem of inadequate shelter by forming partnerships between people in need and those willing to help, is a great way to meet people, because you will work together with a team of volunteers building housing for families in need. (You can contact Habitat for Humanity at 121 Habitat Street, Americus, GA 31709; (912) 924-6935.) On the other hand, if you will be working in a situation where you are the sole volunteer (e.g, tutoring), your contact with others will be limited to those you tutor and to general volunteer meetings.

There are a number of ways to find out about volunteer opportunities in your city.

- *The Encyclopedia of Associations: The Regional Volume* is an encyclopedia of state and regional associations. The book is divided into sections, including several that list associations for causes that may provide interesting volunteer opportunities (e.g., social-welfare organizations, public-affairs organizations, and health and medical organizations). You should be able to find the book in the reference area of your local library. If you have a cause in mind you'd like to work for, look for an association that relates to that cause and ask to be referred to appropriate local organizations with volunteer opportunities.
- City Cares of America, a national umbrella organization that operates in twenty-six cities around the country, promotes community service among young professionals, and strives to make volunteering more accessible by coordinating volunteers and placing them in appropriate settings. Group meetings touch on

central themes of volunteer work, making your service more effective while giving you the opportunity to meet other volunteers. To find out if there's a City Cares organization in your city, call City Cares at (202) 887-0500.

- *Stand Up and Be Counted: The Volunteer Resource Book* by Judy Knipe (Simon & Schuster, 1992) is a directory of nonprofit organizations and publications divided into general category of service (e.g., environment, community service, children). Listed within the general categories is information about specific organizations, including the name, address, phone number, and a description.

- *Community Jobs: The Employment Newspaper for the Nonprofit Sector* is a monthly national newspaper focusing on job and volunteer opportunities in the nonprofit sector. A one-year subscription costs $69, but you might be able to find all the information you need by subscribing for just six months. Three-month trial subscriptions are also available. You can subscribe by calling ACCESS at (202) 785-4233 or by writing to: ACCESS, 1001 Connecticut Avenue, NW, Suite 838, Washington, DC 20036.

- Many newspapers regularly list volunteer opportunities. If the listing isn't evident, call the local newspaper to find out if they do in fact run such listings and on what day of the week they are printed.

- If you know the cause you want to work for but don't know of an appropriate organization to contact, try looking in your phone book. Look under the subject in which you are interested; you'll probably find at least one listing of an organization associated with your cause. Even if the organization listed doesn't use volunteers, it will likely be able to refer you to an organization that does. You can also look under "Charitable Organizations."

Professional Associations

There's a national association of professionals for most careers. Local chapters of the association sponsor events such as lectures, workshops, and meetings related to the career. You may not yet be employed, but if you're interested in finding a job in a particular field, joining a professional association will put you in contact with others working in the field. This can be a good way to meet friends and a great way to make professional contacts.

Two books that will direct you to professional associations are:

- *The Encyclopedia of Associations: The Regional Volume*
- *State and Regional Associations of the United States*

You should be able to find both in the reference area of your local library. Find out if there is an association listed for your area of interest. Contact the association and ask to be put on their mailing list. Find out if there are any upcoming events that interest you. You might also consider volunteering for the association, particularly if you are not yet employed. You'll meet more people in the field and you can add the experience to your resume.

Book Clubs

If you like to read, think about joining a book club (a.k.a. reading group). Local libraries usually sponsor at least one book club, so they're a good place to start. Major bookstores sometimes sponsor clubs as well. (If your neighborhood store doesn't already have a club, you might want to speak to the manager about starting one.) You can also contact the community adult-education program—most communities have one—to find out if it has a reading group. If you know a couple of people in the area, think about starting your own club. (For a guide to starting a book club, check out either *The Reading Group Handbook*, Rachel Jacobsohn (Hyperion, 1994) or *The New York Public Library Guide to Reading Groups*, Rollene Saal (Crown, 1995). You might also look into author readings and book-signing events at your local bookstore.

Athletics

The benefits of joining a sports team are many: increased energy, keeping in shape, and the myriad other values of working out. Sports teams are also one of the best ways to meet other people. Regardless of your athletic powers, you should consider this option. Most leagues have different levels, so even if the last time you kicked a soccer ball was in sixth-grade gym class, there's still probably a division for you. To find out about the sports leagues and teams in your area:

- Contact the local Department of Parks and Recreation.
- Look in the phone book under Recreation Centers and call for information.
- Call the local YMCA or community center to see what sports teams they have.

Outdoor Activities

If you're more interested in individual recreation (such as hiking, mountain climbing, biking, skiing, etc.), a good way to find out about groups in your area is to talk to people who work at stores that sell the equipment needed for the activity. A clerk at a store that sells back-country ski equipment will likely know a great deal about the merchandise, probably know quite a bit about the sport, and is likely to be a back-country skier. Specialty stores or major recreation stores often have fliers or even bulletin boards listing regional events.

Adult Education

If you've just graduated from college, signing up for another class may be low on your list of priorities. But community adult-education courses are often nonacademic in nature, with courses ranging from wine tasting to meditation to jewelry making. Courses usually meet once a week for a few months and are an excellent way to meet people. To find out about the program in your area, look in the phone book under "[Your Community] Adult Education" and call to request a course catalogue.

If you have an unusual skill or are knowledgeable in a specific area and want to try your hand at teaching, you might consider teaching an adult-education class as well. Contact the program staff

and ask about the procedure for submitting a proposal. The pay
won't be great (you'll have to keep your day job) but you'll expand
your professional experience and meet the other teachers as well as
your students.

Politics and Public Interest

If you're interested in politics, think about volunteering for a campaign. You can locate party offices in the phone book. Call and find
out what campaigns, local or national, are currently taking place. See
if there's a candidate or proposal that you strongly support and
would like to work for. Volunteers are always needed and your
involvement can range from voter registration drives to grassroots
organizing to rallies to fundraising.

You might also think about joining a local chapter of an organization focusing on a cause you feel strongly about. If you're concerned
about human rights, think about joining Amnesty International.
Amnesty's basic goal is to protect the basic human rights of people
throughout the world by 1. seeking the release of prisoners of con-
science; 2. working for fair and prompt trials for all political prisoners; 3. opposing the death penalty and other cruel punishment of
prisoners. There are more than one million members of Amnesty
International and thousands of local groups around the world. Involvement usually consists of writing letters to the government,
publicizing obstruction of human rights around the world, and participating in human rights campaigns. To find out more about the organization and to locate the chapter nearest you contact Amnesty
International U.S.A., 322 Eighth Avenue, New York, NY 10001;
(212) 807-8400.

If you're interested in nature and concerned about conservation,
think about joining the Sierra Club, North America's largest grassroots environmental organization. The goals of the Sierra Club are to
protect the global environment against acid rain, global warming,
ozone depletion, pollution, and similar threats. Members promote
conservation by influencing public policy through grassroots ac-
tivism, lobbying, and public education. The Club also sponsors national and local activities and excursions. There are sixty-three local
chapters of the Sierra Club. To find out more about the organization

and to locate the chapter nearest you, contact Sierra Club, 730 Polk Street, San Francisco, CA 94109; (415) 776-2211.

These are just a couple of examples of ways to become involved politically. Whatever cause you believe in, there is almost certainly an organization for you to join. Your involvement can be as great or as minimal as you choose; you'll feel the positive effects of working to further the goals of a cause in which you believe; and you'll meet others who share your convictions.

The Arts

If you're a performer, you already know that working on an artistic production is one of the best ways to meet people. The cast and crew spend a great deal of concentrated time together and develop intense relationships. If you aren't a performer, you can still be part of a production by working on sets, props, makeup, costumes, lighting, or sound.

- Look in the Yellow Pages under "Theater." Some of the listings you'll see there are professional companies, and the distinction between those and community theater groups won't necessarily be clear from the listing. Professionals should be able to refer you to the nonprofessional groups in your city.
- Contact performing schools in the area, if there are any.
- Call the theater department of any nearby college.
- Subscribe to local entertainment publications. (This is also a good way to find out about performances you may want to attend.) People whom you contact through the avenues listed above should be able to tell you the names of the best publications.

Even if you are merely a lover of the arts and have neither the talent nor the inclination to be part of a production, there are still many ways to become involved. Because most arts organizations are, unfortunately, underfunded, they rely on the help of volunteers for a variety of tasks. Theater, ballet, symphonies, and other performing companies depend upon volunteers to usher and sell tickets. In exchange, volunteers get to attend the performance free of charge.

Museums use volunteers to lead tours, work in the children's room, and sell tickets. You can find out about volunteer opportunities by contacting the local arts organization, theater group, museum, or community center.

Religious Groups

Even if your involvement in organized religion consists of attending services just once or twice a year, you might want to think about locating a local church, synagogue, or other religious institution. Religious groups usually offer an array of activities from fundraising events to performances to discussion groups and lectures. Religious communities are likely to be supportive and welcoming of new members. If you live near a college campus, try contacting the campus branch of your faith. Campus groups often have postgrad groups that meet for nonreligious activities as well as devotional ones.

Philanthropic Organizations

Philanthropic organizations can also be a productive way to meet people: Do good, make friends—hard to beat that. Philanthropic organizations sponsor fundraising events for a variety of causes. The events themselves can range from gala balls to dances to lectures and workshops. By working on a committee that plans special events, you will work closely with a group of people that are committed to the charity or cause and, as a bonus, you'll be able to attend the events for free (tickets to the events are often costly). And growing numbers of philanthropic organizations have young people's divisions, with well-developed programming and as much committee work as you can handle.

Alumni Associations

Many people feel a strong connection with the college from which they graduated and feel a continuing bond with other graduates. Odds are there are other people who went to your school who are now living in your city. Alumni associations offer a range of activities, from social activities similar to those that take place on campus (watching sports games, happy hours), to talking to high-school seniors about the college, to conducting alumni interviews for college applicants.

Call your college alumni office to see if there's a local chapter in your area; even if you don't live in a major city, there may well be one. (Special note if you're a graduate of the University of Michigan: There is a very embryonic chapter of the University of Michigan alumni club on the moon. When two astronauts who were graduates of the university landed on the moon, they left behind a University of Michigan flag.)

Workplace

Your workplace may be among the very best places to meet people. After all, you spend more of your waking hours at work than anywhere else, and if nothing else, you at least have your work in common with your co-workers.

Some work environments are more social than others. If you work for a large company with a number of people your age or for a company with a training program, you'll find it's easy to meet friends at work. If you regularly work as part of a team, or simply work in a sociable, easygoing atmosphere, you'll find you have no trouble establishing friendships with your co-workers. Sometimes it's the most stressful jobs that lend themselves most easily to the development of friendships; shared pressure can create strong bonds.

If, on the other hand, you work in an atmosphere in which people tend to keep to themselves, it's still possible to make friends—it will just require a greater effort. Don't feel strange about asking a co-worker to lunch, even if it's someone you hardly know. Most people are grateful to have an opportunity to break up the monotony of their routine day and will appreciate the invitation. (When you do socialize with your co-workers out of the office, whether it's during lunch or over a post-work drink, try to avoid discussing two taboo subjects: co-workers and salary.) Once you have one or two friends in the office, your workday will become more enjoyable and Monday mornings may even seem less depressing. And even if you find it a bit much to hang out with your co-workers after hours, they may be a good starting point for meeting other people.

Establishing a Routine

Unfortunately, not all workplaces provide the opportunity to meet other people. My first postcollege job was in a two-person office and my co-worker (who was, in any case, my boss) was on the road for weeks at a time. On the other hand, two-person offices can sometimes provide the best opportunity to develop a relationship with your co-worker. One friend of mine in D.C., who worked with just one other person, chose to consolidate work life and social life and married her officemate.

Even if there's no hope of becoming friends with your co-workers (much less marrying one of them), there are still many ways to meet friends during the workday. When I worked in the two-person office I became good friends with someone who worked in an office down the hall. (His situation was even less socially promising than mine; he worked in an office by himself.)

By establishing a routine to your workday, you'll see the same people every day and can, if you choose, meet some of them. If you catch the 8:10 bus daily, you'll start to recognize the regulars. If you eat lunch at a restaurant near your office three days a week, or bring your lunch to the nearby park, you'll probably meet others who work nearby. And remember that there are ways to greatly increase the number of people with whom you interact on a daily basis, so keep this in mind when planning daily routines. Consider the following examples of typical days in the lives of Ralph and Rachel, apartment-mates living in Boston.

1. Ralph awakes on a given weekday a bit later than perhaps he should; he's overslept and has just enough time to hop in the shower, dress, and fill his travel mug with coffee for the commute downtown. He drives into the city, parks, and manages to make it to the office with a few minutes to spare. He settles into a busy day of paper-shuffling, and decides shortly after noon that in order to get some extra work done he should order a sandwich from the downstairs deli to eat at his desk. He fin-

ishes an exhausting day at six, drives home, and collapses on the couch. Too tired even to go out to eat, he puts together a simple dinner in the kitchen and spends the rest of the evening watching a movie, television, or perhaps reading. He retires at around midnight.

2. Rachel wakes early in order to get in some exercise before work, and takes a run or walk around the local reservoir. On her way home, she stops in a local coffee shop and picks up a coffee, returning to the apartment in time to shower and dress before she leaves to catch her trolley. She rides the trolley downtown, and settles down at her desk for a long day of work. At lunchtime, she chooses to eat at the downstairs deli rather than order in, but takes just a short break and returns to work. At five she leaves the office, stopping off at the local pub for a beer. She takes the trolley home, changes out of her work clothes, and decides to go out. She has dinner at a local restaurant, and walks to the movie theater to catch a new release. After the movie, she returns home and goes to bed.

Obviously these are extreme examples, but the point is clear. On an average day of his pod-existence, Ralph actually interacts with (not including co-workers) a total of about two or three people: the parking-lot attendant, the deli delivery person, and perhaps Rachel. Rachel, on the other hand, has maximized her potential to meet friends, not only because she is in contact with people exercising, at the coffee shop, on the trolley, at lunch, at the pub, at the restaurant, and at the movie theater, but because some of these are daily rituals. Seeing the same people every morning on her run, at the coffee shop, or on the trolley will inevitably lead to nodding acquaintants, which in some instances logically lead to companionship, even if only for the morning run.

The Unexpected

Whether through networking, community involvement, work, or daily ritual, you *will* start to meet people and develop a new circle of friends. You'll find that friends crop up in the places you expect them to as well as, in some cases, surprising places. Chance encounters can occur anywhere, any time, and you never know what kind of relationship might develop.

I asked some of my friends in what unexpected places they had met friends or boyfriends/girlfriends:

Julie went to college in Bronxville, New York. On weekend nights she would regularly go out in New York City and then catch the last train back home. One night, she and a friend were riding the train home when two young men sat down beside them and struck up a conversation. Though wary of the obvious attempt at a pick-up (which probably would have turned her off even if she hadn't already had a boyfriend), Julie was interested by the fact that the men played in a band. She gave one of them her phone number and asked him to call her the next time they were playing. He coyly waited twenty-four hours, then called to ask her out. Since she had been interested in the music, not the musician, she declined. He was determined, though, and continued calling. Finally, he gave up. End of story? Not quite. One year later, she and her friend were riding the last train out of New York City, when, lo and behold, there he was. (And no, he hadn't been catching the very last train every night for a whole year in hope of seeing her.) His technique was less obvious this time (and much more successful), and when he called two weeks later to ask her out, she accepted. Their relationship lasted for three years.

After spending an unplanned evening in a New York City emergency room, Becky and her boyfriend stopped at a local restaurant for a late dinner. The boyfriend left briefly to make a phone call and cancel plans he had for the night, and while he was gone, the waitress struck up a conversation about Becky's new arm cast. By the time her boyfriend returned, Becky and the waitress had exchanged phone numbers. They've been close friends for several years.

Liz moved from Boston to San Francisco a year after she was graduated from college. Jobless and virtually friendless, she went to the neighborhood coffee shop each morning to eat breakfast, read the paper, and get out of her apartment. In time, she became friendly with a woman who worked at the coffee shop and they made plans to go hear her friend's band. "When you move to a new city you have to be up for anything," says Liz. "There's no sense in moving if you're going to act as sheltered as you would at home." The invitation to see a band not only was the start of a friendship between the two women, but resulted in Liz finding a job. It turned out that the bass player in the band had a friend whose father needed a receptionist. Liz was hired one week later.

Sandy spent the better part of her twenties as a very eligible bachelorette—a quick-witted doctor and avid outdoorswoman, she found she had trouble meeting men who were not intimidated by her busy schedule. Flipping through the personal ads, she saw an enticing advertisement and gave the guy a call. As it turned out, he lived in a different city. That didn't deter Sandy. She got his E-mail address and started what turned into a three-month computer correspondence. By the time they finally met, they had become good friends. Now, they're married.

Shortly after moving to Minneapolis, Jim interviewed for a job assisting the director of a music festival. During the course of the interview it became clear that he was not well suited for the position—nor it for him. On the way out, the receptionist asked him how the meeting had turned out. He explained that his job search was not over. The receptionist told him that her position was temporary and she was looking for permanent employment as well. They decided to get together for lunch to talk about their respective job searches, and ended up becoming close friends.

Interviewing potential roommates to fill a vacancy in my apartment, I met a woman who seemed like a perfect candidate—until she asked me how I felt about cats. I explained that even thinking about cats made me start sneezing. We were both disappointed since we had gotten along so well. Though I didn't get a new roommate, I did gain a new friend.

Meeting people will take time; meeting people who come to be friends will take even more time. But before too long, you'll find you're no longer worried about how you're going to meet new people; you'll be much more concerned about how you're going to find time to see all of your friends, or how you're going to fit private time into your busy social schedule. Remember, new friends are not going to walk into your living room and find you. So get up, get out, and find them.

SECTION TWO

YOUR JOB SEARCH

6. What to Do? Getting Started in the World of Work

"**Y**ou can be anything you want to be," we're told from an early age. The implicit assumption is that we know or soon will know *what* it is we want to be. Talk about pressure. In the first place, most of us haven't even heard of one fiftieth of the jobs that exist. What, for example, is an ombudsman? A yeoman? A zymurgist? And what does a controller control? For that matter, what does a comptroller do? Comptroll? Why isn't an occupational therapist a career counselor? And what exactly does a joiner join? Finally, what if, in keeping with current earth-friendly trends, you have your heart set on becoming an ecowriter, which, as it turns out, is nothing more than a pencil made from recycled material? How can we know what we want to be if we don't even know what there is to be? Further, how do we know whether the jobs with which we are already familiar are right for us? Apprenticeships are outdated; going into the family business is no longer (in most cases) the assumption. And just because we choose one college major over another doesn't necessarily mean we intend or are qualified to pursue a career in that field. I, for example, majored in political science and Judaic studies. I chose those majors, not for the professional doors they might later open, but because I enjoyed courses in those majors more than most others. And upon graduation, I was no closer to figuring out what I wanted to be than I had been when I first arrived on campus four years earlier, or, for that matter, than I was on my fifth birthday when my mother first told me I could be anything I wanted to be. It's great to know we can be anything we want to be, but how in the world do we figure out what that is?

When my friend, Kara, was graduated from college she was, as were most of my friends, thoroughly confused about her future. She found it immensely helpful to talk to people whom she admired, who had been out of school for five to ten years, about the paths that led them to their careers. "I was worried that I'd make a bad choice and set off on the wrong track. But when I talked with people who were in these great careers, I found out that they hadn't always known what they wanted to do." She learned, in short, that switching fields and changing jobs within fields is the norm, not the exception. "I was reassured about my own confusion and felt less pressure about making the 'right choice' for my first job." Consider the twisted paths that led the following people to their current careers:

A series of random decisions and incidental conversations led Kirk to his current job as a program developer for an educational-software consulting company. When he was graduated from Tulane University, Kirk had absolutely no idea what kind of career he wanted to pursue. Although he had lived in several different parts of the country, he had never lived on the West Coast and decided to give Seattle a try. "Since I had zero direction," Kirk says, "I was free to move to Seattle where I didn't know a soul. I figured there was no sense in being around all of my great connections if I didn't know what to do with them." He started temping as soon as he got to Seattle and continued temping on and off for several months. About the time he'd had enough of the temping lifestyle, one of his housemates told him that there were some available positions at the day-care center where she worked. Although he had no child-care experience, he decided to give it a try; he ended up working there for seven months and learning, to his surprise, that he enjoyed the work and had a knack with children. Then, just as he was coming to the decision to move on, a friend of his in D.C. offered to help him get a job at the elementary school where she was teaching. She raved to the principal about Kirk, and after just one phone conversation he was hired as an "after-school" teacher. And then, even before he moved to D.C., he got his first promotion; the principal called and offered him a much higher-paying job teaching in the computer center. Kirk thought it the better part of wisdom to refrain from informing the principal that he had neither real teaching experience nor any computer experience whatsoever. "I was lucky," Kirk says now, "because I was able to learn the basics from the teacher who previously held the position. The rest I picked up from my sixth graders." Two years passed, and Kirk decided that neither D.C. nor teaching was for him any longer. He decided to try living in Roanoke, Virginia, where he had some close friends. In a chance encounter with one of the other teachers he mentioned his intention to move. Twists and turns: that teacher had a sister in Roanoke who owned a computer consulting company and, of all things, was looking to hire a teacher who could bring the viewpoint of the students to the company. A couple of phone calls back and forth to Roanoke and Kirk had himself a job, and, given how much he loves it, most likely a career. Try charting the course that brought him to where he is now: five years, three cities, several false starts (well, not really "false," but less than "true") several rest stops along the road (and some off-road), and a few accidental conversations that turned out to be turning points.

Does that mean that in the end it's a matter of luck? Perhaps. But if there's such a thing as "dumb luck," Kirk's is an example of "smart luck," of keeping yourself alive to possibility, of being the kind of person others want to help and feel comfortable recommending, of what can happen if you come to the search as a thoughtful adventure.

When she finished college, Jen was hired for a six-week freelance project at the documentary film company at which she had interned her senior year. She found the project completely boring and began looking for a full-time job almost immediately. Her strategy boiled down to looking at listings in her college career newsletter. She followed up on any listing that sounded mildly interesting. Having worked on a presidential campaign while in college, she had enough experience to be hired by a nonprofit political lobbying group. Jen stayed there for a year and a half, but realized that the only part of the job she enjoyed were those tasks that involved communications. She decided to look for a job in publishing.

Jen quickly learned how competitive the publishing world is. She went on a series of informational interviews but wasn't getting any closer to finding a job. Then she got a call from a contact she had met through the informational process. "I know of a job," the contact told Jen, "but I'm sure you won't be interested. *Esquire* magazine needs someone to come in for two weeks and clean out the fashion closet." "I took it because I wanted to get in the door," Jen says. And if the door only led to a closet? "I was willing to take the risk." Jen used the vacation time she had accumulated to take the assignment. She had difficulty making contacts since she was in the closet all day, but she stayed late every evening and asked to take on additional tasks. Soon she was hired on a part-time basis and continued her job at the nonprofit as well. Before long, though, she was hired as an editorial assistant. And now? Jen's the associate features editor at *Elle* magazine.

Cheryl always knew she wanted to pursue a career in which she could use her writing skills. After college she worked for a couple of publishing and public-relations firms in the Boston area. "I learned a lot from those jobs and made some great friends, but the nine-to-five-plus world was never really for me," she says. "I always felt like I was going to hyperventilate. So about five years ago, I started my own business, writing newsletters, articles, brochures, and so forth for corporate and nonprofit clients." A few years in the working world gave Cheryl the perspective to figure out that she wanted to work for herself, on her own terms (as well as giving her the experience and connections to make that dream a reality). "I often work seven days a week. I don't get paid holidays, vacations, or medical insurance. I feel isolated at times, so I talk to the cat more than a healthy person should. And I have to make sure that the work and the checks keep coming in. But the pros outweigh the cons. I can work the hours I want as long as the job gets done. I can take time off during the day to ride my bike or run errands. I don't have to wear pantyhose or heels, ride the trolley during rush hour, deal with office politics, or tell someone I have a doctor's appointment."

You shouldn't feel that your first postcollege job is going to determine the company or even the industry in which you'll work for the rest of your professional life. Most people change jobs and fields many times throughout their lives. For now you should be concerned about getting a job that you think might make you happy (or at least not unhappy) *now*. Your objective is to take your first step on what will presumably be a long and illustrious career path. (The bumps, sharp turns, and potholes are all par for the course.) That piece of comfort offered, you can't switch fields or change jobs until you've got a field and a job to switch from. Where, and how, do you get started?

Two facts about looking for a job: 1. Most people would avoid doing it if they could; 2. most people will do it several times in their lifetime. As with most activities in which the majority of people participate, there are countless strategies, theories, and formulas about the easiest and most effective way to do it. There are career and employment centers that exist solely as resources for job seekers, libraries full of books wholly focusing on the job hunt, and people whose careers are built exclusively around helping other people in the search for a career of their own.

This may very well be your first time looking for a full-time permanent job; this may even be your first time looking for any kind of job. So: With all of the resources out there, where should you begin? How do you sort through all the information that's available to you and determine how most effectively to invest your time and money? That's what this chapter's about.

Let's start with the basics. If you don't know what it is you are looking for, it will be difficult to find it. (On the other hand, if you don't know where you're going, you can't get lost.) That's not to say it will be impossible. If you start off by pursuing a variety of jobs, you may stumble across a field that suits you perfectly. And even if you don't find an impeccable match, you'll certainly weed out those jobs that seem horrific and thereby begin to narrow your search. Still, finding the "right" career through a process of elimination can easily take several lifetimes. Job-seeker resources exist for a reason. They're there to help you narrow your options by figuring out what you *do* want in a job.

What Are You Searching For? or Self-Assessment (or The Job as a Four-Legged Chair)

Happiness and fulfillment at work are dependent upon four factors: *what* you are doing, *where* you are doing it, *who* you are doing it for/with, and *why* you're doing it (i.e., what you get out of it). If you're discontent with any one of those four elements, you will not be thoroughly satisfied with your job. (Your chair, as it were, won't support you comfortably if one of the legs is missing. If two are missing, it may be time to look for a new chair.) Lest you develop unrealistic hopes, please realize that many, many people spend their entire lives looking for a job with a what, where, who, and why that satisfies them. Your first job, therefore, is unlikely to do so. However, the more precisely you're able to define the ingredients that would satisfy you, the shorter your journey to the ideal job is likely to be. And the job-seeker resources can help you develop your definition.

You can use job-seeker resources to figure out *what* you want to do at work. They'll help illuminate the possible relationship between the choices you've made in the past (e.g., how you've chosen to spend your free time, what you chose as a major) to your career choices for the future. Think about it. Have you chosen mostly group activities or independent ones? Have you been a camp counselor? Are you a performer? Have you participated in student government? Have you spent your free time volunteering in a soup kitchen? What books do you like to read? Do you prefer hectic activities or relaxed ones? The activities that you've chosen say a great deal about your skills, values, and interests. Suppose you participated in student government. From that you can learn the following: You enjoy working with a team, you're a problem solver, you're a leader and a people person, you're interested in policy and decision-making, you work well in a structured environment, and so forth.

The resources may also help you work through the nature of the environment that suits you. Where you work is critical to your happiness at work. You may already know that you'd rather spend forty hours a week sitting in a toll booth than stuck in an office. The thought of putting on a business suit may make you just crazy enough to warrant a straitjacket. But there is more to the work environment than office or no office, formal or casual. There are endless other variables that help define the work environment and that may be central to you: big, small, fast-paced, relaxed, bureaucratic, creative, high tech, nonprofit, for-profit, academic, corporate, financial, medical, environmental, community based, international in scope, and/or team-oriented, to name a few.

Figuring out *who* you'd like to do your job for and who you'd like to do it with, is largely a gamble; you're not going to know much about your boss and co-workers until you've been at the job for at least a day. (Job-seeker resources, therefore, won't provide much help on this one.) Your instincts may flash a warning sign when you meet your prospective boss at the interview or, alternatively, you may develop an instant affection (watch out if it's *that* kind of affection) for him/her. More likely, though, you'll be too nervous to develop an accurate impression. As for your co-workers, a general idea of the sort of people who choose to pursue your selected career path is really all you have to go on, unless you are given the opportunity to meet with them during the interview process.

The resources may also help you determine *why* you want to do your job. Are you looking for monetary rewards or security? Is rapid advancement the most important criterion for you, or are you looking for a job that will provide the best opportunity for skills development? Do you want a job with status or glamour or do you want a job in which you help others? Do you want your first postcollege job to be the first step on your career path or do you want, simply, to land your first postcollege job? (Keep in mind that the preceding are not necessarily mutually exclusive.)

Determining what you want to do, where you want to do it, whom you want to do it for/with, and why you want to do it—all that's an evolving process. As your interests and values develop and change, you'll probably find you want different things from your job—and from and for yourself. So remember: You're not making lifelong decisions here, you're simply getting started.

Career Counselors/Centers

If you can afford it, make an appointment with a career counselor. The cost of a session varies but you can expect to pay thirty to seventy-five dollars for a one-hour session. Career counselors have distinct styles, but with any good counselor you can expect help with: (1) self-assessment, (2) selecting appropriate career choices, and (3) preparing a job-search strategy. Many career counselors help you self-evaluate by administering inventories (tests) that measure personality or interests in order to help guide career choices. (For more on the use of tests as self-assessment instruments, see the next page.) Career counselors also use written exercises and discussion that help you define your skills, values, and interests, and zero in on potentially fulfilling careers. Working one on one with a professional career counselor is among the best ways to clarify your job search. But, as with any kind of counseling, success depends largely on how well the counselor gets a sense of who you are, and it might take more than one session to reach your goal. If you can afford the investment, it will probably be worth it.

Career counselors are often affiliated with career centers/libraries that are full of resources (e.g., books, magazine/newspaper clippings, handouts, job listings) to help you in the job search. But you don't necessarily have to see a counselor in order to use the center's resources. Many libraries will charge you a nominal fee (around ten dollars) to purchase a membership card that allows you to use its resources as often as you like.

To find a career counselor/center in your area:

- Call the career center of any university or college in your area and ask about its policy for nonstudent use. Those that restrict privileges to students may be able to refer you to other centers in the area that do not.
- Look in the Yellow Pages under "Career and Vocational Counseling."
- Net-Research publishes a series of books by Donald D. Walker and Valerie A. Shipe that lists career centers, employment agencies, and executive search firms in specific regions. The book is called *[Your Region] Job Seeker's Sourcebook* (e.g., *Boston and New England Job Seeker's Sourcebook*). You can find the book in your library or bookstore, or call (800) 455-5340 to find out if there's one for your region.

Self-Assessment Inventories (Tests)

Self-Assessment Inventories are tests you can take that help guide your choice of occupation by evaluating your interests or personality type. Note that though these are called self-assessment inventories, they are not self-administered. Nor, for that matter, will you be able to interpret the results on your own. Call a local career center (see pages 125–26) to inquire about test administration.

The two most popular tests are the Myers-Briggs Type Indicator and the Strong Interest Inventory.

The Myers-Briggs Type Indicator (MBTI) has been widely used since 1943. It recognizes sixteen different personality types that are various combinations of four personality and preference scales (i.e., extroversion–introversion, sensing–intuition, thinking–feeling, and judgment–perception). The test is used as a tool to clarify one's natural strengths and weaknesses, which are then used as an indicator of one's ideal work style and environment.

The Strong Interest Inventory has been used since 1972 to measure interest in various occupations and suggest which fields might prove to be most fulfilling. The test-taker is asked to complete a range of questions dealing with many jobs, activities, academic subjects, and so forth. The answers are matched with those of people already working in a variety of fields and similarities are measured to determine which careers are worthy of further exploration.

Books

There are hundreds and hundreds of books to help you with your job search. Most of the ones I recommend, like most of the good ones in circulation, help the reader identify a job goal through self-assessment discussion or exercises, and serve as guides for the entire job hunt. I've chosen the following because of their careful attention to self-evaluation, their readability, and their accessibility to readers who are looking for a job for the very first time.

- *What Color Is Your Parachute?* by Richard Nelson Bolles (Ten Speed Press, yearly editions). This book is an easy-to-read manual with self-assessment exercises to help you determine what skills you most enjoy using and where you want to use them. Every aspect of the job-hunt is covered, from finding a job to interview success to salary negotiation. An extra bonus is the "pink page" section at the back of the book which provides listings of additional resources, including further reading suggestions and state-by-state listings of vocational resources.

- *How to Create a Picture of Your Ideal Job or Next Career* by Richard Nelson Bolles (Ten Speed Press, 1991). This is the self-assessment portion of *What Color Is Your Parachute?* If you don't want to invest in the book, you might consider picking up this workbook of exercises that help you develop an idea of your perfect job.
- *Career Success Workbook: Five Essential Steps to Career and Job Satisfaction* by Urban G. Whitaker (Learning Center, 1992). This is another workbook of exercises that help the reader 1. assess values, 2. assess skills, 3. match values and skills to appropriate careers, 4. develop a learning plan to develop additional skills needed for an identified career, and 5. improve job-seeking tools, such as resumes and skills such as interviewing.
- *Career Starter* by Jack O'Brien (Kiplinger Books, 1993). This is a planner to help the reader design a game plan for the job search. It's one of my favorites because it's graphically inviting and very easy to use. Exercises help the reader identify values, interests, skills, and then match them to an appropriate career. Information is provided about where to find work, how to plan and organize a job campaign, how to market yourself, interview, and make a decision once the offers start pouring in.
- *Landing Your First Job Out of College: The Ultimate Job-Hunting Handbook* by Matt Gordon (St. Martin's, 1993). This book is written, as the title indicates, for the new college graduate. It covers the same issues as the others—establishing criteria for a first job, building a resume, generating interviews, and dealing with job offers—with the understanding that the reader is going through the process for the first time. A small handbook, it's a good basic introduction to the job search.
- *Jobsmarts for Twentysomethings* by Bradley G. Richardson (Vintage, 1995). Yet another book that leads you through all aspects of the job search, from preparing for the job hunt all the

way to succeeding on the job. Richardson's book is written from the viewpoint of someone in his twenties and is loaded with examples of new job-seekers' experiences. An added bonus is an index to select industry profiles that includes information on where to start, what skills you need, the typical career path, and where the jobs are. The second half of the book focuses on issues you confront once you have a job, so this is a book you'll want to keep after you've been hired.

- *Nine Lives, from Stripper to Schoolteacher: My Yearlong Odyssey in the Workplace* by Lynn Snowden (W. W. Norton, 1994). Snowden's thesis is that what you do from nine to five determines who you are during the rest of the day. Your work defines you in the sense that it plays a part in whom you socialize with, where you live, your status in the community, how others view you, and, ultimately, how you view yourself. To test her theory, Snowden spent a year in nine different jobs, ranging from (hence the title) a stripper to a schoolteacher. I recommend this book not only as a fun read but also because it illustrates, through actual experience, the importance that the selection of a career can have in every aspect of your life.

Memoirs

To get direct insight into a specific employment field you might consider taking a leisurely drive down the memoir avenue. The style is a growth industry these days, and it is now hard to avoid memoirs by investment bankers, movie producers, weight-lifters, and virtually everyone in between, as also their chauffeurs, cooks, and stepmothers, along with the indicted, the lawyers of the indicted, the members of the juries of the indicted. While it is important to keep in mind while reading this type of book that you're getting only a single person's perceptions, thoughts, and opinions, note as well that it is in just such reflections that pros and cons you may not have considered will be spelled out. I have a close friend who once gave serious consideration to running for Congress, but changed his mind in a flash as soon as he read then Congressman Don Riegle's memoirs, *Ah, Congress*, which described in truly painful detail the lot of a freshman congressman (at least in the pre-Gingrich era). Most memoirs can be found cross-referenced in libraries and bookstores both in the biography section as well as in the section pertaining directly to the field.

Workshops

Workshops can help you in every phase of the job search, from networking to resume writing to interviewing. For information about relevant workshops taking place in your area:

- Call all local career centers and ask them what, if any, workshops they are sponsoring.
- Read the *National Business Employment Weekly*. In the "Calendar of Events" you'll find listings of career workshops and panels by region and state. You can purchase this newspaper for $3.95 at many bookstores and newsstands, or call (800) JOB HUNT [562-4867]. (Also, check out the College Edition of the *National Business Employment Weekly*.)
- Check out the "Calendar of Events" section in your major and community newspapers.

Software Programs

There are a number of interactive computer programs designed to help with the self-assessment/career evaluation process. The benefits of these programs are that they take a relatively short time to complete (approximately two hours—much less time than it takes to get the results of a written self-assessment inventory), and since the computer responds to information that you, the user, plug in, the information you get is much more personalized than what you read in a book. The programs described below are administered primarily through colleges and universities and are usually free to use.

- SIGI Plus® System (System of Interactive Guidance and Information Plus More). SIGI Plus is divided into eight sections that relate to distinct stages of making a career decision. SIGI Plus is primarily distributed to colleges and universities, so the first place to look for it is at the career center of any college or university in your area. Schools that restrict use to students may be able to refer you to other SIGI locations in the area. If you have trouble locating SIGI, contact: Educational Testing Systems, Rosedale and Carter Roads, Princeton, NJ 08540; (800) 257-7444, and ask for the most convenient location.

- Discover. Put out by American College Testing (ACT), Discover is an interactive program designed to assess the user's interests, abilities, experiences, and values, match these characteristics to appropriate careers, and provide information about occupations. Two special features of Discover are (1) when the user plugs in a college major, the program produces a list of logical career choices and (2) for each career, names and addresses of organizations to contact for more information are provided.

Discover is used primarily in college career and placement centers, although some public libraries and private career centers carry the program as well.

Informational Interviewing

One of the best ways to learn about different kinds of careers is to talk to people already in them. When you learn exactly what people do while they're at work, the path that led them to their position, what their work environment is like, and what the field in general is like, you can get a sense of whether their career appeals to you and thereby continue to narrow down and hone in on what it is you are searching for.

The first thing to do is to think about the jobs of people whom you know and make a list of anyone you know whose job you'd like to learn about. Next, find out if people you know (friends, relatives, professors, neighbors, dentists, etc.) know anyone in the field that you're considering. (The nice thing about informational interviews is that whether or not they know you, most people will be happy to meet with you to talk about themselves for a half hour.) If your list of prospects still seems flimsy, consider calling your college alumni office and inquiring whether any graduates who live in your area work in your field of interest. You can also look in the *Encyclopedia of Associations* (located in the reference area of the library) to find an association for the occupation in question. The association might be able to put you in touch with local professionals.

You only need a few names to begin the informational interviewing process. Each person you meet should be able to refer you to other people in the field, so that once you have even one meeting, your list of potential interviewees will multiply.

You might feel queasy about calling a stranger and asking to schedule a meeting. Don't. Informational interviewing is a standard part of the world of work. Most people have done it at some point and will be more than happy—flattered even—to oblige. Moreover, since you've recently graduated, you're not expected to know anything about the field you're considering; people will understand that you're engaged in a process of exploration.

On the other hand, you should respect that the people you contact are probably busy; that means you should be prepared both when you make the initial contact and at the meeting itself, so that you don't waste their time. (In fact, you don't want to waste their time even if they're not busy.) If it makes you more comfortable, write out a script for the initial phone call. You should begin by explaining who you are and how you got the person's name. Tell him/her you'd love the opportunity to learn about what s/he does and ask if you could have fifteen or twenty minutes of his/her time. Schedule the interview, thank the person, and hang up. Phew.

To prepare for the interview, think about the information you want to obtain during the meeting. If you prepare some questions in advance you'll feel more confident during the conversation, you'll be more likely to leave with the knowledge you need, and you won't waste the person's time. Remember, you requested the meeting; be prepared to manage it. Make a list of questions as you prepare in order to help organize your thoughts. If you think it will make you more confident, bring the list of questions with you to the interview. This is a learning opportunity, not a test, and crib sheets are perfectly acceptable. You should also bring your resume with you. (See Chapter 7.) The person will probably want to know about you as well, why you're interested in the field, so be ready to talk about yourself. (And yes, the fantasy that just five minutes before you arrived the interviewer learned of an opening for which, by the end of your meeting, s/he thinks you're ideal, is not only permitted, it's virtually irresistible. Just don't let your hopes get in the way of the point of the meeting.)

The following list of questions, courtesy of Radcliffe Career Services in Cambridge, Massachusetts, provides some examples of questions to ask.

Informational Interview Questions

1. What is your job title, and what are the responsibilities of your job?
2. What do you like most about your work?
3. What do you like least about your job?
4. What does your typical work day, week, and year consist of?
5. How is your time divided between working with people, data, things?
6. How many hours do you work each week?
7. How closely do you work with others?
8. How much variety is there in the work you do?
9. How severe is deadline pressure in your field?
10. Are your hours flexible?
11. Do you ever bring your work home with you?
12. Whom do you supervise and to whom do you report?
13. How much contact do you have with people outside of your company? Who are they and what is your relationship to them?
14. How much, if at all, do you travel for work?
15. What career path led you to your current position?
16. What is the typical job path in your career? What are the opportunities for advancement?
17. How good are the future career opportunities in your field? What is the job market outlook in the field and where are some of the best opportunities?
18. What kind of educational preparation is necessary and/or desirable for advancement in your career?
19. What are the entry-level jobs in your field?
20. What are the minimum qualifications a person would need for an entry-level job?
21. Are there any on-the-job training programs in this field?
22. What kinds of job hunting strategies would you suggest to get into your field/organizations?

23. What kinds of advice can you give me on my resume and the way it presents my experience for this type of work? What additional experience would I need to be considered for an entry-level position?
24. What books or journals would you recommend that I read?
25. Could you suggest any additional people or organizations I might contact for more information? (Be sure to get enough information so that you can locate the correct phone number or address.)

Follow-up

As soon as possible after the interview, write out a personal record of the meeting, including the person's name, your impressions (both positive and negative) of this area of work, and any suggestions you were given for further action. You should also send a thank-you letter (see Chapter 7) within two days of the meeting. If you have any interest in the field, you should keep in touch with the people who've been helpful to you during your job search. For example, if you have a meeting with someone they recommended, drop them a note afterward to let them know. If you read a book they suggested, write a letter letting them know what you thought of it. You'll remain in their thoughts and if they do hear of an appropriate job opening, you'll come to mind.

On-the-Job Experience

If you want to learn about a particular career and figure out if it's right for you, there is no substitute for real-life experience. Internships and temporary work are ways to explore potential fields. And, while you're busy investigating different career paths, you're also gaining valuable skills to put on your resume, meeting job contacts, and acquiring local experience.

Internships. An internship is a short-term work experience designed to give an overview of a particular field. The benefits of internships are that you:

- Spend time in a work environment that interests you and have a foundation upon which to develop a sense of whether the field is right for you
- Acquire relevant work experience to put on your resume
- Acquire local experience to put on your resume
- Obtain free job-training
- Get in the door of a company that interests you
- Meet a wide range of job contacts

The downside to interning is:

- Most internships are not paid. If they do pay, it's not likely to be much.
- Some employers view interns as low-level laborers. Your internship may involve more copy-making, phone-answering, and coffee-fetching than valuable experience.
- Full-time internships cost you time, time you might be out there looking for a "real" job. You won't have the flexibility to continue your job search while you're working.

You want to make sure you're making a good investment with your internship, so do your homework first. Make sure that the job will offer valuable experience. Some grunt work is fine, but you want to get a feel for the meaningful aspects of the job. Find out how much personal attention you will receive. Is there an established internship program? If so, supervisors will be more likely to understand the needs of interns and to offer you the guidance you want.

To find an internship:

- Look at Peterson's Guides' annual Internship Guide *(Internships 1996)*. Indexed by field, state, and employer, the information provided includes general company information, internship program information, benefits, requirements, and contact's name, phone number, and address.
- Look for postings at local career-resource libraries.

Temporary Employment

In the search for your ideal working environment, temporary work is one of the most valuable self-assessment tools. You get to try out different work environments, see how they suit you, and (though it won't make you rich) you get paid for it.

Getting a paycheck isn't the only benefit of temporary work. You'll also:

- Acquire local work experience for your resume.
- Be able to explore different work environments—no strings attached.
- Make job contacts.
- Have the potential to be in the right place at the right time should a permanent position become available. (This happens more often than you might think, even if less often than you would like. Temps are often called upon to fill a vacancy while the employer is in the hiring process. A temp who is able to get the job done becomes an obvious candidate. That's how I got my first postcollege job.)
- Experience variety with each job placement.
- Be able to make your own work schedule (if you request short-term assignments, you can decide which days you want to work), and continue your job search at the same time.

The disadvantages to temporary employment are:

- The pay tends to be on the low side. The entire paycheck goes directly to the employment agency and, in turn, the agency gives you a percentage of the earnings. (The agency makes its profit by charging the employer more than it pays you.)
- Many temporary assignments are boring. Temps are often hired to do necessary tasks that can be learned quickly, like answering phones or coordinating mass mailings.
- It takes time to become comfortable in a new work environment. If you choose to accept short-term assignments (which can be as short as a couple of hours), you will constantly have to learn new office procedures and equipment. You may also feel like, and be treated as, an outsider in the organization.

If you're uncertain as to whether temporary work makes sense for you, consider trying a couple of assignments and seeing if you like it. Here's how it works:

1. Call a temporary employment office and schedule an appointment. To find a temporary service, look in the Yellow Pages under "Employment Contractors—Temporary Help." You might want to register with more than one agency to increase your chances of getting assignments when you want them. Also, call to schedule your interview as far in advance as possible, especially if it's during the summer (when you're competing with students for jobs). You may have to wait several days, even weeks, to get an appointment.

2. Bring two pieces of identification with you to the meeting. Make sure one is a birth certificate or passport, necessary for your W-4 form. (A W-4 is an IRS form that helps you figure out the number of withholding allowances you should claim. You need to fill one out whenever you start a new job.) During your interview, you'll meet with a personnel manager to discuss the kind of work that interests you. You will be given a couple of basic tests (e.g., computer, math, spelling) to assess your skills. Many agencies offer computer clinics if you need a refresher.

3. After you officially register with the temporary agency, it's to your advantage to call regularly to check if there are assignments for you. Sure, the agency is supposed to call you if an appropriate position becomes available, but one personnel manager handles many temporary workers and it's the squeaky wheel that . . .

If you're interested in learning more about temporary work, check out *Temp: How to Survive & Thrive in the World of Temporary Employment* by Deborahann Smith (Shambhala, 1994), which is a thorough guide to the world of temping.

You get the picture. Internships and temporary assignments can provide you with practical information to further your self-evaluation process. True, you may wind up in some environments that have absolutely nothing to offer other than a great "my day was worse than yours" story at happy hour. But they also have the potential to provide valuable work experience, contacts, and skills development.

If your objective is to get a feel for whether the field is appealing to you, you'll have to do more than just sit at the front desk answering phones for eight hours. Try to get to know those employees for/with whom you're working. Learn as much as you can about the organization and the industry. And if you decide that you might indeed be interested in pursuing a job in the field, let your supervisor know. When you've completed your regular duties, ask if there's anything else for you to do. You're not only going to get in the front door, but you are actually going to be given the opportunity to prove yourself as an employee, so make the experience count. There may not be a position for you where you're working, but if you make a positive impression, people might think of you when they hear of a job opening in the field.

The tools in this chapter are meant to help you define what kind of job you are looking for. If you've identified more than one field of interest, you're in good shape. Many people have difficulty identifying even one career that sounds appealing. You can pursue a couple of different paths simultaneously and see which one produces the best results. But if, after trying different self-assessment tools, you're still completely confused and cannot think of any job that seems right for you, you'll have to rely more heavily on the process of elimination. That might require surviving your first or second nightmare job before you are able to characterize what it is you *don't* want in a job—and, therefore, the beginning of a definition of what you *do* want. On the other hand, any new job is a gamble. Maybe you'll draw a winning hand on the very first deal.

7. Your Head in the Clouds, Your Feet on the Pavement: Pounding Forward

In an ideal world, prior to graduation you'd receive a job catalogue of available positions listed alphabetically by industry. You'd be able to register either by mail or in person for the position you wanted. If the position had already been filled, you could choose another, or try to convince the boss to squeeze you in anyway. Alas, in the Real World, there's no catalogue of job listings. (The closest is the "Help Wanted" section of the newspaper but it, as you'll read below, includes only a small fraction of job openings.) Most positions are never publicized.

So how do you find out what's out there? And once you do, why can't you just sign up? After all, if you know you're the right person for the job, wouldn't it be much more efficient to just call the boss and let him/her know when you're reporting for work? But try doing that, and you'll hear a dial tone before you even finish informing your new boss of your salary and vacation schedule.

In short and obviously: In order to make a prospective employer realize that you're The One for the job, you need to succeed at a multi-step process that includes cover letters, resumes, and interviews.

One could argue, and many do, that looking for a job is in itself a full-time job. But unless someone is paying you to conduct your job search (in which unlikely case, take your time, and then some), you're not going to have forty hours a week to devote to your search. What to do? Designate a reasonable and realistic amount of time each day to your campaign, keeping in mind that the more time you devote, the more contacts you'll be able to make, the quicker, therefore, your search is likely to be successfully concluded. During that block of time you'll generate leads, respond to advertisements, conduct follow-up to the letters you've sent and to the meetings you have. This chapter discusses how to do all that, plus how to develop your strategy, how to find out about unadvertised positions, and how to write successful job correspondence.

The first two hours, or four (or however long it takes because it's critical to your success), should be devoted to *organization*. Here, in a nutshell, is how to organize:

- *Go Shopping.* Remember shopping every autumn for school supplies? This is the same idea (except your parents probably aren't paying). Get all your job-search supplies together, so you won't need to postpone mailing a resume because you don't have a stamp. You should get: stamps, copies of your resume (more on that later) and matching stationery, envelopes, a calendar, and an appointment book.
- *Set up a record-keeping system.* You need to devise a method, whether it's a three-ring binder or an index-card organizer or a computer file, to keep track of your search activity. You're going to be making contacts through a variety of avenues, and the last thing you want is to get a call to schedule an interview based on your response to a newspaper ad—and find that you haven't the foggiest idea what opening the person on the phone is talking about. Keep your records in alphabetical order by organization name and include the following information:
  - A copy of the ad (if there was one)
  - Referral source (if there was one)
  - Contact name and phone number
  - A copy of your letter to the organization
  - Summary of any phone conversations
  - Summary notes of the interview
  - Copies of any follow-up correspondence
  - Records of the dates on which all communications occur

- *Change the message on your answering machine.* Your message helps frame the first impression a potential employer develops of you, so keep it short, straightforward, and professional. This isn't the time to test new stand-up comedy material, share your favorite new Pearl Jam song, or get your roommates together for a campy group message.

Let the Search Begin

By now you have some idea, vague though it may be, of what you're looking for in a job. You've got your job search headquarters set up; you're raring (I know, I know, but let's pretend) to go. You buy the local Sunday newspaper, browse through the help-wanted ads, clip an ad or two, and respond with a cover letter and resume. So much for Sunday.

Come Monday, you're wondering how it's possible to devote time to your job search *every* day. You've responded to the week's help-wanted advertisements; what else is there to do?

Network, Network, Network

A couple of chapters back I defined networking as "meeting people through other people." Now that you're looking for a job, the definition needs to be slightly expanded: Networking for a job is "meeting people *who might be in a position to offer you a job or help you in some way in your search for a job* through other people." And networking is your best bet for finding a job.

Think about it from the employers' point of view: They can place an advertisement in the newspaper (this costs money). They'll then receive some hundreds of resumes that will need to be weeded through (this costs time). They will then have to contact the promising applicants and conduct a series of interviews (more time). If employers are lucky enough to find one or two candidates who seem right for the job, they can rely on their intuition and hire one. But even if the candidate's references are checked (let's face it, most people are not going to provide a reference that isn't positive), the employer is still taking a chance, working with very sketchy information—the more so, of course, if the person s/he's hiring doesn't have much, or any, work history. The result? Potential disappointment. More time, more money wasted. So it's clearly to the employers' advantage to call a couple of friends or colleagues—people they trust—and ask if they can recommend anyone for the job opening.

It's your objective, therefore, to make as many people as possible aware of the fact that you are looking for a job. Talk to your friends, your friends' friends, your friends' parents, your parent's friends, your parents' parents—whomever. Use your imagination.

My friend changed his answering machine message when his brother was looking for a job to say something like: "Hi, this is Gerry Gold, brother of David Gold, who is currently unemployed. He's superbly qualified in a variety of things. If you know of any job openings, please let me know." Another example: Returning home from a job interview, I met a man at the bus stop. In the course of our conversation—small talk, really—I mentioned that I was coming from a job interview. He gave me the phone number of a friend of his who had recently started his own business. I called, had an interview the very next day—and wasn't interested in the job. But the point is that I got the interview. And yet another: Liz was looking for a way to develop her photography skills over the summer. Pulling into the parking lot of a bank to use the ATM, her mother noticed a car with a "news photographer" license plate. Seeing only one person at the ATM, she asked if the car belonged to him. It did, and in response to her next question he assured her that he was in fact a working photographer, employed by a major newspaper. That was all she needed to hear. She told him that her daughter was looking for a job in photography and asked if Liz could call him. That was all it took: Liz followed up, had an interview, and sure enough was hired as an apprentice for the summer.

Networking is about more than just spreading the word that you're looking for a job and then sitting back and waiting for employers to call you or, alternatively, combing the streets hoping to run into someone who can get you a job interview. That wouldn't be an effective use of the daily time you've designated for this process. You need to be assertive and take initiative. Ask people if they know anybody who works in your field of interest, and, if they do, whether you can use their name when you call. In the best of circumstances, they'll offer to call the contacts for you and let them know to expect your call. (You can also contact people without a referral, but that's a different exercise, and will be covered in the next section.) The object is to get an interview with people who work in your field, *even if they don't know of any current job opening*. The fact is that most people you contact won't have a job opening when you contact them—but they will be able to give you advice, put you in touch with other people in the field, and keep you in mind should they hear of an appropriate position.

In the last chapter, you read about informational interviewing as a means of exploring different careers. Now that you've zeroed in on your field(s) of interest, informational interviewing is one way to learn of job openings. The drill is the same, except that you'll tailor your questions to reflect your interest in the field. You've already done your research, so you don't need to ask as many general questions. You can be more specific and ask about organizations in your area. (For a list of informational interview questions, see pages 133–34.)

The vast majority of jobs are filled through networking, so take the process seriously. Keep in touch with the contacts that you make; always, always send a thank-you letter after your meeting, and follow up every few months with a short note letting the person know how your search is going. Make sure to notify all your contacts when you are hired. Your newly established network will remain useful to you as long as you remain in the field.

Cold-Call, Broadcast, or Bullet Letters

If, after asking every single person you've ever met in your entire life, you still can't come up with any contact names in your profession, it's time to start sending letters and resumes to people you don't know. Such correspondence is also know as cold-call, broadcast, or bullet letters. And if the number of possible jobs in your field of choice is limited (say, for example, a high-school teacher), you can send a letter to every single potential employer.

When Andy graduated from college, he knew that he wanted to work as a high-school teacher in a private school. He bought a directory of secondary private schools and counted eighty-plus schools that were within reasonable proximity to his home. After sending a cover letter and resume to each and every one, he sat back and waited for the offers to pour in. To his dismay, they didn't even trickle. He received ninety-plus rejections (rejections even from specific departments within schools, so in the end the number of rejections was greater than the number of resumes he had sent out) and just two calls for interviews, neither of which paid off. Came the end of August, his prospects looked bleak. Upon his father's urging, he began calling each of the schools he'd contacted to see if perhaps a position had become available in the interim. Contacting the schools in alphabetical order, it took only until the C's for him to get a positive response. (Which shows that persistence does sometimes pay off.) He went in for an interview the very next day and learned that there was just one other candidate being considered for the position. The other candidate, Andy was told, had quite a bit of teaching experience and, understandably, wanted a salary commensurate with that experience. In response, Andy said "I'll take half of what you'd pay her." Voila! He started teaching one week later. (Persistence, especially if you're prepared to live in penury.)

The odds on getting a positive response to a cold-call letter are slim; unless your experience is outstanding (a college major and a summer internship do not qualify as outstanding), it boils down to timing. If an employer receives a letter from you on the day that an employee quits or funding comes through to create a new position, you can bet s/he'll call you to see if s/he can perhaps avoid the hassle of publicizing the opening. That's what happened to my sister. On her first round of letters. During her first job search. What's important is to make sure your cover letter and resume are top-notch (see pages 149–61) so that maybe, just maybe, they'll elicit a positive response.

Your odds may improve if you contact key people and ask for an informational interview as opposed to an actual job interview. The people you contact won't feel as if you're trying to get something from them (i.e., a job) and will likely oblige. During the course of your "informational" conversation, you might learn that there are in fact job openings in the organization. If not, you've made a new and potentially valuable contact who can refer you to others within the field.

Help-Wanted Ads

Responding to help-wanted ads is usually much less effective than networking; still, it's an important part of your job campaign and should not be ignored. Even if just for the sake of feeling that you've covered all the bases, it's worth responding to help-wanted ads. And obviously, it's not purely symbolic behavior; there are people who've found their jobs through an ad in the "Help Wanted" section. It's just that most jobs are never advertised, and those that are receive a huge response, so your chances of being hired via the "Help Wanteds" are significantly reduced.

Still, it's worth a try, and since it's worth doing, you might as well do it in a way that enhances your prospects.

The first place to look for ads is the obvious place, your city's major newspaper. Sunday's paper will have the most extensive listings, although most papers have ads listed daily as well. You should also check the ads in community papers and any city magazines. Look for ads in trade and professional journals, which also give you an idea of the kinds of jobs available in the profession you're pursuing. Finally, seek out career centers or libraries that carry job listings. (You may be charged a nominal fee to use the center's resources.) To find a career center or library, see page 126.

Placement Firms/Headhunters

There are two kinds of job placement firms—those that charge you when they find you a job and those that charge your employer. A headhunter, on the other hand, is always paid by the employer. At this stage in your career, neither placement firms nor headhunters are going to be helpful. Here's why: Agencies or individuals that require you to pay them if they find you a job are inherently suspect. Since the way they make their money is by finding you a job, they are going to aim to do that as quickly as possible. They are not likely to give much consideration to what kind of job they find for you; they merely want to find you a job so that they can earn a paycheck. These agencies are often sleazy; stay away from them.

Why aren't employer-paid firms or headhunters equally suspect? They just want to find the employer a warm body as quickly as possible so they can get paid, right? Wrong. Firms that are paid by the employer want to do as much business as possible with the employer. If they recommend one or two or twenty mismatched candidates, the employer isn't likely to trust their matchmaking skills and won't use them in the future.

A headhunter or placement firm, therefore, that is paid by the employer when you are hired, can be a very valuable tool in the job search—but only after you've gained work experience and are worth the added cost to the employer. (Typically, the employer pays as much as 30 percent of the annual salary of the new hire.) Employers very rarely contract with intermediaries to find the entry-level employees they need. As one placement specialist put it, "Nobody will pay extra to hire somebody with no experience."

Campus Recruiters

Campus recruiters, on the other hand, are looking for people straight out of college who, though probably lacking in experience, exhibit great potential. They come right to your campus, you don't pay them a penny, and you might get hired without writing even one cover letter. But: They're most interested, often only interested, in graduating college seniors. They also usually represent corporate industries such as investment banking or sales, or industries that look for students with very particular skills-oriented majors, such as hotel management. And even if you are a graduating senior pursuing a career in finance, you can expect to be compared to every other graduating senior with a business major—the competition is stiff.

Temporary Jobs and Internships

In the last chapter, you read that practical experience is one of the best ways to figure out what kind of job you want. In this later phase of your job search, practical experience can help you actually find a job. There's simply no equivalent to getting your foot in the door and having the opportunity to prove yourself as an employee. You spend your entire day in an office full of contacts, and you acquire relevant work experience for your resume. If you're not yet convinced, see pages 134–38 for additional benefits (and how to find a temporary job or internship).

> On my second temp assignment in Seattle, I was given a two-day placement answering phones for a national nonprofit agency. On my second day, I read the organization's newsletter. Having a bit—not really more than that—of experience with newsletter publishing, I immediately noticed that the publication was atrocious. (It was so atrocious, in fact, that my experience was irrelevant; anybody would have been appalled by it.) It looked horrible, was filled with typos and grammatical errors, and was boring as could be. When I asked my supervisor, I learned that the organization was paying a freelancer an enormous amount of money to produce the newsletter. I gave her my resume and explained that for a great deal less money, I could produce the newsletter in-house. Within a month, I was hired as the organization's director of communications.

Recap. You are going to find a job through one of the following methods:

1. *Networking.*
   a. Alert all the people you know and whom you have ever known, as well as all the people all of them know, that you are looking for a job.
   b. Ask them if they know anybody who works in your chosen field. In the best of worlds, they'll break the ice by contacting that person on your behalf and telling him/her to expect your call. Failing that, it's still a big step forward if you can use their name when you call. The vast majority of jobs are found this way; approach this part of the search in an especially serious and organized manner.

2. *Cold Approaches.* Identify organizations within your chosen field and contact someone in the organization for an informational interview. You have a good chance of finding a job through this method. Although you might have to deal with quite a bit of rejection (e.g., letters or phone calls that don't get returned, assistants that won't put you through to the boss, people who refuse to meet with you—yes, it's worse than trying to find a date for the prom), every positive response you receive will open new doors.

3. *Want Ads.* Although answering ads is the first thing most people think of when they contemplate looking for a job, it's one of the least effective methods of finding one. On the other hand, it does work sometimes and should, therefore, be included in any comprehensive search.

4. *Placement Firms, Headhunters, Campus Recruiters.* You are probably too young (read: inexperienced) and too old (read: nonstudent) to benefit from these methods. If, however, you have unusual or valuable experience, by all means contact an employer-paid placement firm or a headhunter. And if you are reading this while you're still in college, get over to the Career and Placement Center immediately.

5. *Temp Jobs/Internships.* Practical experience offers a host of benefits. One of the most valuable is that you are given the opportunity to prove your worth to an employer through your work (and may even be able to avoid the challenge of trying to stand out from a crowd on the basis of a twenty-minute interview).

The more paths you pursue, the more leads you will generate, and the quicker you are likely to find a job. You may want to set a goal for yourself—for instance, try to generate three new leads every day. It's true, as you've most likely heard, that your success will in the end largely depend on luck and timing. But the more people who know you are looking for a job and the greater the number of desks that have your resume on them, the greater your chances of "lucking out" and being in the right place at the right time.

Correspondence

At every stage of the job-search process there are written documents—resumes, cover letters, cold-call letters, and thank-you letters—that you'll need to prepare. Each is an important element in your quest. It's one or another of these that will convince a potential employer to interview you (or not to), to develop a positive first impression of you (or not to), and to hire you (or not to). Your correspondence will give its reader an idea of who you are (what you've done, what your skills and interests are, and so forth) and whether or not you're a good match for the position. Though different employers will certainly be looking for different things when they read your correspondence, you can bet on the fact that no employer will take seriously a candidate whose letter or resume is messy (smudged, wrinkled, or otherwise unreadable), contains typos, grammatical errors, or misspellings, or is confusing or difficult to read. Always keep in mind the profession you're trying to break into and tailor your correspondence accordingly. If you're applying for a job in a conservative field, stick to the standard formats. If, however, you're applying for a job in a creative field, don't be afraid to display your creativity in your correspondence.

Dawn wanted to work for a funky magazine when she finished college. Although she was a journalism major, had worked on the campus magazine, and had some freelance writing experience, she knew the competitive nature of the industry and wanted her correspondence to stand out from the rest. She took a risk and printed her resume and cover letter on hot-pink paper. Her cover letter was bold, beginning with "Let me tell you why you should hire me." The response? Overwhelmingly positive, including a personal phone call from one magazine's editor-in-chief. Dawn took a risk and it got her noticed.

Colin was applying for a position as a graphic designer and wanted his talent to be evident from his correspondence. He printed his resume on red paper, and rather than laying out his information from top to bottom in the standard format, he designed a quirky layout. The result was a resume that showed his design skills and was difficult to ignore.

You might want to balance your off-beat letters with some that are more conventional, but don't be afraid to take chances and let your personality shine (or at least leak) through.

Your Resume

What's the Point? The most common and important use of a resume is to pique an employer's interest and win you an interview. Resumes are also used to:

- Give your contacts a summary of your skills and experience so they can refer you to appropriate people.
- Serve as a basis for discussion during both informational and standard job interviews.
- Remind people of your qualifications after an interview.

The Basics. There are shelves and shelves of books devoted entirely to writing a winning resume. But if you think that you're going to learn to write the perfect, unrejectable resume from the lessons you learn in a book, you'll quickly find that (1) there is no such thing as an unrejectable resume and (2) the books can leave you much more confused than you are now. Different resume books prescribe conflicting advice: Never ever put an objective at the top of your resume, don't even think about sending out a resume without an objective; don't include references, always include references; don't include your photograph, do include your photograph (if you think it will be an asset). On the other hand, most of the books on resumes provide samples and are a useful source of ideas for design and for ways in which to present your experience. Make sure to look at the publication date of any resume sources you use. Resume styles and standards have changed over the years, and you'll want to make sure that the samples you look at are current.

The fact is that your potential employer will probably look at your resume for one minute, if you're lucky. Minor details (such as whether you "acted" as a waiter, "served" as a waiter, "worked" as a waiter, or simply "waited") are not likely to make a significant difference, so don't obsess over them. What's important is that your resume is organized, neat, and complies with the following basic principles:

1. Your name, address, phone number (and, if you have them at home, fax number and E-mail address) should be at the top of the page, in bold, and in a bigger point size than the rest of the resume. If you are living somewhere other than at your permanent address, include both your temporary and permanent addresses. Your resume should inspire the reader to contact you; it's no help for you to succeed at the inspiring part and then fail at making it easy for the employer to act on the inspiration.

2. Organize your experience as it relates to the field you are pursuing. Include all of the following that pertain to you:
   a. Education: schools attended and degrees awarded (include GPA if 3.5 or over), study-abroad programs
   b. Related coursework
   c. Work experience: paid, part-time, internships, volunteer work, community service
   d. Research experience
   e. Extracurricular activities
   f. Honors and awards
   g. Computer skills
   h. Special skills: including foreign-language ability
   i. Interest and/or hobbies

3. Every listing under "experience" should include the company name and location (city and state), your job title, dates of employment, and your job responsibilities.

4. Begin every description with a verb. (e.g., "Led hiking trip in Colorado," rather than "I led a hiking trip in Colorado." Whoever reads your resume will understand that it's not Vladimir who led the hiking trip.)

5. Your resume should be consistent. It doesn't matter if you boldface company names and italicize job titles or vice versa as long as it's the same throughout.

6. Limit your resume to one page. Years from now, maybe, you can expand it to two pages—but only if you have two pages worth of experience.

7. Don't lie. There is a tendency to exaggerate on resumes, in order to make your experience, however mundane it might be, dazzle. There is also a tendency, among those who lack even mundane experience, to lie on a resume. These tendencies are

risky—you may be found out before your interview (if, for example, the reader of your resume has friends at a company where you claim to have been employed and asks about you); during your interview (if you cannot comfortably talk about your experience); or even after you've been hired (in which case you will probably be fired immediately). Stick to the truth and let it be your personality that dazzles. One day your experience will as well.

8. Your resume *must* be typed. It should be printed on a heavy paper stock, at least 24 pound, 8½ × 11. (Laid and linen both look nice.) Consider mailing your resume in a 9 × 12 envelope. It will stand out from most of the regular mail and it will remain crisp and unwrinkled. Be aware that extra postage is required for a 9 × 12 envelope even if it is under one ounce.

My sister once sent out a mass resume mailing in 9 × 12 envelopes with 32 cents postage on each envelope. She was slightly dismayed that she had received no response after a week, but she figured it was still early. Then, one day, her mailbox was overflowing. Requests for job interviews? Rejection letters? Neither. Every one of her letters was returned marked, "insufficient postage." She had to slice the envelopes open, put the letters into new envelopes, address the new envelopes, and apply the correct postage. It was a huge waste of time and money.

9. You might consider showing a draft to a couple of people who have already written resumes and asking for critical feedback. And when it's complete, have at least one other person proofread your resume.

If you don't have a computer or typewriter, if you feel unprepared, or if you just don't want to deal with putting your resume together, there are services that will do it for you. Look in the Yellow Pages under "Resume Services." Prices vary from company to company (usually between fifty and two hundred dollars) and will depend on how much, if any, of the actual writing, as distinguished from the design and production, the service does for you. Call a few companies to check the rates and be sure to ask to see some samples.

If you do have a computer, you might consider purchasing a resume software program to help you create a resume. There are several different resume programs; check out a software store in your neighborhood to see what's available.

What Works . . . What Doesn't. The first three samples that follow (A, B, and C) are all examples of effective, professional-looking resumes. There are hundreds of ways you can design your resume; which one you choose is a matter of personal taste. Resumes A, B, and C all convey the same information. Resume A is a standard resume format. It's clear, the key information (i.e., dates, positions, companies) is easy to spot, and Noah Bailey comes across as a well-rounded person with focused experience. Sample B is a more specialized resume. Highlighting skills at the top of the resume distinguishes Noah's experience and interest in written communications. This focus carries through the rest of the resume; note that writing/editing and public relations are separate subheads. A glance at this resume lets the reader know what skills characterize Noah. Sample C shows another way to highlight specific experience: By putting a profile at the top of his resume, Noah immediately conveys his significant skills and experience. The headings, format, and wording of the three resumes vary, but they all succeed in providing a sketch of Noah.

Sample D, on the other hand, is pathetic. It is obviously (I hope) an exaggeration of a bad resume. It breaks all the fundamental rules of resume preparation and it is doubtful that any employer would look at it for more than two seconds before throwing it in the trash. (That's a full fifty-eight seconds less than you're counting on.) If it's not immediately clear to you why this resume fails, go back to The Basics and memorize them.

Noah P. Bailey
12 Humner St.
Brookline, MA 02146
(617) 555-5555

EDUCATION: 1996 1994	***University of Michigan,*** Ann Arbor, MI BA in communications; GPA: 3.8/4.0 ***University of Madrid,*** Madrid, Spain **Honors:** National Dean's List (three semesters) National Communications Honors Fraternity

RELATED COURSEWORK:

Marketing Communications	Advanced Public Relations
Promotions	The Art of Newsletter
Introduction to Public	Publishing
Relations	History of Mass Media

WORK EXPERIENCE:

1995–1996

Associate Editor
Campus Talk Magazine, Ann Arbor, MI
● Wrote an average of three articles a month
● Edited two sections of magazine
● Assigned articles to staff writers

1995 (summer)

Intern
Short Story Magazine, New York, NY
● Evaluated unsolicited fiction submissions
● Researched and assisted in production of semi-annual book review

1994 (summer)

Intern
Museum of History, Los Angeles, CA
● Led tours of museum exhibits
● Provided administrative support in office of public relations

1992, 1993 (summers)

Field Guide
Hiking Association, Bozeman, MT
● Led two-week hiking trips throughout Montana
● Taught daily workshops on environmental issues

ACTIVITIES:
● Intramural soccer team
● Member, Documentary Film Club
● Volunteer, Linda's Soup Kitchen

SKILLS & INTERESTS:

Microsoft Access	Hiking
Microsoft Word	Film Buff
PageMaker	Proficient in Spanish

SAMPLE B

Noah P. Bailey   12 Humner St. ◆ Brookline ◆ MA 02146 ◆ (617) 555-5555

SKILLS

Writing ◆ Editing ◆ Desktop Publishing
◆ Public Relations ◆ Fluent in Spanish

EDUCATION

University of Michigan, Ann Arbor, MI, 1992–1996
University of Madrid, Madrid, Spain, 1994

degree

Bachelor of Arts, Communications, 1996

distinctions

Grade Point Average: 3.8/4.0
National Dean's List, seven semesters
National Communications Honors Fraternity

communications
coursework

◆ Marketing Communications
◆ Advanced Public Relations
◆ Promotions
◆ The Art of Newsletter Publishing
◆ Introduction to Public Relations
◆ History of Mass Media

EXPERIENCE

writing
and editing

Campus Talk Magazine, Ann Arbor, MI
Associate Editor, 1995–1996

Wrote an average of three articles a month for bimonthly student interest magazine, edited two sections of magazine, developed story ideas and assigned articles to staff writers.

Short Story Magazine, New York, NY
Intern, Summer 1995
Produced written evaluations of unsolicited fiction submissions for review by senior editor, researched authors and wrote draft biographies for semi-annual book review.

public relations

Museum of History, Los Angeles, CA
Intern, Summer 1994
Led tours of museum exhibits for groups of 25–30 museum guests, provided administrative support in office of public relations, assisting in preparation of press releases and museum newsletter.

Hiking Association, Bozeman, MT
Field Guide, Summers 1992, 1993
Led two-week hiking trips throughout Montana for groups of teens, taught daily workshops on environmental issues, assisted in recruitment of participants throughout the year.

ADDITIONAL

◆ Volunteer, Linda's Soup Kitchen
◆ Member, Documentary Film Club
◆ Intramural soccer team

SAMPLE C

Noah P. Bailey

12 Humner St.
Brookline, MA 02146

Telephone
(617) 555-5555

Profile
- Two years experience as associate editor of free campus magazine, circulation 40,000
- Computer skilled: proficient in Microsoft Access, Microsoft Word, and PageMaker
- Bachelor of Arts in communications, graduated with honors
- Strong administrative and organizational skills; detail-oriented; fast learner

Education

B.A., Communications
University of Michigan, Ann Arbor, Michigan   1996
- Deans list, seven semesters
- National Communications Honors Society

Semester Abroad
University of Madrid, Madrid, Spain   1994
- Fluent in Spanish
- Traveled extensively throughout Europe

Professional Experience

Campus Talk Magazine, Ann Arbor, MI   1995–1996
Associate Editor
- Wrote articles for campus magazine on issues affecting students
- Created and edited two sections of magazine
- Worked with staff writers on story development and execution

Short Story Magazine, New York, NY   1995 *summer*
Intern
- Read and summarized fiction submissions
- Researched and wrote biographies for semi-annual book review

Museum of History, Los Angeles, CA   1994 *summer*
Intern
- Served as tour guide for museum exhibits
- Assisted with museum public relations, including press releases and newsletter

Hiking Association, Bozeman, MT   1992, 1993 *summers*
Field Guide
- Worked as field guide for teens on hiking trips throughout Montana
- Developed curriculum and taught daily workshops on environmental issues

Extracurricular
- Intramural soccer team
- Member, Documentary Film Club
- Volunteer, Linda's Soup Kitchen

SAMPLE D

Noah P. Bailey 12 Humner St. Brookline, MA 02146 (617) 555-5555

Education: Graduate of the University of Michigan, Bachelor of Arts in Communications; Semester Abroad in Madrid Spain at University of Madrid. Graduated in 1996.

Experience: For two years I was the associate editor of the school magazine, <u>Campus Talk</u>. I wrote numerous articles, edited a major portion of the magazine, and served in a supervisory capacity. During the summers, I had two internships, one at <u>Short Story</u> magazine in New York City and one at the Museum of History in Los Angeles. My experience in these positions was mostly as a gofer but when given the opportunity, I read fiction submissions and led museum tours. I also spent a couple of summers leading hiking trips in Montana.

Activities: I was in a documentary film club. I played on an intramural soccer team. I volunteered at a soup kitchen.

P.S. I am computer proficient and fluent in Spanish.

Your Cover Letter

What's the Point? A cover letter accompanies your resume when you respond to a job advertisement and is used to:

- Tell the reader why you are writing (e.g., you're responding to an ad that you saw in the *Daily Chronicle*).
- Provide a basic introduction, let the reader know how your skills match the needs of the job, pique the reader's interest so that s/he reads your resume.
- Expand on one or two items from your resume that illustrate why you're a good match for the position.

The Basics

1. In the first sentence of the cover letter, state why you are writing.
2. Keep your cover letter short and simple. A basic cover letter contains three paragraphs. In paragraph one, explain why you're writing. In paragraph two, provide a general overview of your experience and what you have to offer an employer. Let the reader know how your skills match the job needs. In paragraph three, state your intention to contact the employer within a few days.
3. Don't start every sentence with "I." It's a challenge to write a letter outlining your experience and qualifications without starting most sentences with the word "I," but you don't want your letter to sound tedious—or egomaniacal.
4. Let the employer know what you have to offer the company. It's easy to explain why you want the position, but the employer is more concerned with what you have to offer than what you stand to gain.
5. Don't be afraid to display confidence.

What Works . . . What Doesn't. Sample A is a great cover letter that ought to win Noah an interview. The very first sentence lets the reader know why Noah is writing. He clearly states his relevant experience and highlights his special skills, explaining why he thinks he'd be right for the position. In the opening paragraph, he explains why he's interested in the position. He closes by giving a specific date on which he will follow up. He comes across as a poised, competent, and assertive candidate.

Sample B is horrible. The entire letter focuses on why the job would be right for Noah; there is no mention of why Noah is right for the job. He doesn't mention specifically where he saw the advertisement. Every single sentence starts with the word "I." He communicates no intent to follow up. After wasting a few seconds reading this letter, there is no reason why an employer would want to spend time reading Noah's resume.

SAMPLE A

Noah P. Bailey
12 Humner Street
Brookline, MA 02146

June 16, 1996

Ms. Petra Peterson
Director of Public Relations and Marketing
The Art Museum
300 A Street
Boston, MA 02210

Dear Ms. Peterson:

I am extremely interested in the position of Marketing Associate which was advertised in the Boston Globe, Sunday, June 10. One of the benefits of growing up in Boston, as I did, is the presence there of the Art Museum, a benefit of which I often and with great pleasure took advantage. You may imagine, then, how excited I feel at the prospect of working there. I am enclosing my resume and a few samples of my writing to give you an idea of my background, talents, and qualifications.

I was recently graduated from the University of Michigan in Ann Arbor. As a communications major, my coursework included classes in marketing communications, public relations, and promotions. In these courses I learned to write press releases, newsletters, and other promotional materials. During my junior and senior years, I was an associate editor of *Campus Talk*, a student magazine. In that capacity, I wrote an average of three articles a month, edited numerous articles, and assigned stories to staff writers. I have also held administrative positions which have honed my organizational skills and my ability to set priorities and meet deadlines. My additional qualifications include:

◆ Internships at the *Museum of History* and *Short Short Story* magazine.
◆ Excellent communication skills, both oral and written.
◆ Proficiency with PageMaker, Microsoft Word, and databases.

I would enjoy the opportunity to meet with you and discuss the role of Marketing Associate. I will call you on June 21 to see if we can schedule an appointment. Thank you for your time and consideration.

Sincerely,

Noah Bailey

SAMPLE B

June 16, 1996

Ms. Petra Peterson
Director of Public Relations and Marketing
The Art Museum
300 A Street
Boston, MA 02210

Dear Ms. Peterson:

I am writing because I saw your advertisement. I am very interested in the position because I have been looking for a communications position in Boston.

I am a graduate of the University of Michigan and have always wanted to work for the Art Museum. I think it would give me some really great experience that would help me achieve my long-term career goals. I am enclosing my resume so you can see why my experience makes me the perfect candidate.

I hope to hear from you soon.

Sincerely,

Noah Bailey

Your Cold-Call, Bullet, or Broadcast Letter

What's the Point? A cold-call letter accompanies your resume when you contact someone without knowing if a job is available. This kind of letter is used to:

- Develop job leads.
- Expand your network.
- Impress the reader enough that s/he will want to meet with you.

The Basics
1. The structure of your cold-call letter will be similar to that of your cover letter. The major differences will be in the introduc-

tory paragraph. Since you don't know if there are any openings at the company, you'll need to explain how you got the person's name (e.g., "I'm writing at the suggestion of Mr. X" or "I came across your name in my research" or "I read the latest article on your company").

2. You don't want to put the reader off by stating that you are looking for a job at his/her company; if there are no openings, s/he may throw your letter out. Instead, write that you would love the opportunity to meet with the person to discuss the field, to get some advice, and/or to critique your resume.

3. There will be a slight difference in the second paragraph as well. Instead of talking about how your skills meet the job needs, you'll just talk about your skills.

4. In the closing paragraph, state that you will follow up with a phone call and give a date when you will call.

5. A cold-call letter needs to have more oomph than a cover letter. Your letter is coming out of the blue, so you need to give the reader reason to take the time to read it.

What Works ... What Doesn't. Sample A starts off with a bang. The first sentence entices Ms. Peterson to continue reading. The letter continues with a thorough portrayal of Noah's qualifications. Noah's request for a meeting doesn't sound as though he's looking for Ms. Peterson to hire him, so she's unlikely to feel threatened. He also makes it clear that he respects her busy schedule.

If it isn't immediately clear to you why Sample B fails, forget about memorizing the basics. Go back to school.

SAMPLE A

Noah P. Bailey
12 Humner Street
Brookline, MA 02146

June 16, 1996

Ms. Petra Peterson
Director of Public Relations and Marketing
The Art Museum
300 A Street
Boston, MA 02210

Dear Ms. Peterson:

Professor Ed Rathbone may just be your biggest fan. For my public-relations course at the University of Michigan, Professor Rathbone had us read several of your articles. He also referred to you frequently as a "museum marketing maven." I've just moved to the Boston area and Professor Rathbone suggested that I contact you as I commence my search for a job in the museum industry.

Last month, I was graduated from the University of Michigan in Ann Arbor. As a communications major, my coursework included classes in marketing communications, public relations, and promotions. In these courses I learned to write press releases, newsletters, and other promotional materials. During my junior and senior years, I was an associate editor of *Campus Talk*, a student magazine. In that capacity, I wrote an average of three articles a month, edited numerous articles, and assigned stories to staff writers. I have also held administrative positions which have honed my organizational skills and my ability to set priorities and meet deadlines. My additional qualifications include:

◆ Internships at the *Museum of History* and *Short Story* magazine.
◆ Excellent communication skills, both oral and written.
◆ Proficiency with PageMaker, Microsoft Word, and databases.

I would very much appreciate the opportunity to speak with you briefly and would sincerely welcome your insights concerning the industry and my job search. I will call you on June 21 to see when it might be convenient for us to have a conversation. Thank you in advance for your time.

Sincerely,

Noah Bailey

SAMPLE B

June 16, 1996

Ms. Petra Peterson
Director of Public Relations and Marketing
The Art Museum
300 A Street
Boston, MA 02210

Dear Ms. Peterson:

I am writing because I'm looking for a job in a museum in Boston and I was hoping you'd be able to help me.

I'd love it if we could get together for an hour or two so you could tell me all about the Art Museum and introduce me around. I know the Museum would be a great place for me to work so I'm really hoping you can help me.

I'll drop by next week sometime.

See you then,

Noah Bailey

Your Thank-You Letter

What's the Point? It's always important to follow up after an interview with a thank-you letter because:

- It's expected. If you don't send one and your competition does, it will reflect poorly on you.
- It's a good way to remind the interviewer of you and of your interest in the position.
- It's one more chance to sell yourself.
- It's courteous.

The Basics

1. Send your thank-you letter as soon as possible after the interview, while your impressions of the employer and the position are fresh in your mind.
2. Your letter can be short: Thank the employer for meeting with you and reiterate your enthusiasm about the position, explain why you are a good match for the position, let the reader know you look forward to further discussion.
3. Send a thank-you letter whether the interview is informational or for a specific job.
4. If possible, comment on something that was discussed during the interview, thereby demonstrating that you've not just tossed a form letter into the mail.

What Works . . . What Doesn't. The following is a sample of an effective thank-you letter. It conveys Noah's enthusiasm for the position, reminds the interviewer of Noah's relevant experience, and mentions something that was discussed during the interview (i.e., the interviewer's pending trip to Seattle).

There is no sample of a bad thank-you letter because as long as it's well written, there's no such thing as a bad thank-you letter. The most important thing to remember about a thank-you letter is to write it.

Noah P. Bailey
12 Humner Street
Brookline, MA 02146

June 29, 1996

Ms. Petra Peterson
Director of Public Relations and Marketing
The Art Museum
300 A Street
Boston, MA 02210

Dear Ms. Peterson:

Thank you for meeting with me to discuss the marketing associate position. I am very excited about the possibility of joining your team.

As I said when we met, I believe that the skills that I developed as a communications major at the University of Michigan would be easily transferable to the opening at the Art Museum. You mentioned that good writers are hard to find; I hope my writing samples prove that you've found one in me. I think that my communications experience, coupled with my creativity and energy, would make a good match with the position. After looking through the museum publications that you gave me, I am confident that I can succeed in the capacity of Marketing Associate and be an asset to the Art Museum.

Thank you again for your time. I look forward to talking with you again in the very near future.

Sincerely,

Noah Bailey
(617) 555-5555

P.S. I hope you had a successful conference in Seattle!

Letters of Reference

Though *you* don't write them, letters of reference are a major part of the correspondence involved in getting a job. The tricky thing about letters of reference is asking for them. Genuinely enthusiastic letters (and especially telephone calls) can go a long way in convincing an employer to hire you. But a letter of reference that wins you a job has to be from somebody who believes in you. When you ask that kind of person to write a letter on your behalf, you need to allow him/her to get off the hook without damaging your relationship. You should say something like, "Would you be comfortable writing a letter of recommendation to Mr. X for me?" Do not take it personally if s/he says no. S/he may not feel that his/her name would do you any good with Mr. X. If, however, the person you ask says no a few times, you should probably take it as an indication that s/he doesn't feel comfortable recommending you. Ask somebody else.

8. Who's Asking the Questions? The Art of Intelligent Interviewing

Ask me no questions and I'll tell you no fibs.
—Oliver Goldsmith

Once you've finally lined up the elusive job interview, the first half of the battle is over. But the second half—surviving and maybe even succeeding at the job interview—can be an even greater challenge (and the cause of much anxiety and stress). There's no way to make the interview entirely worry-free; after all, the structure of an interview is inherently such that the interviewee is required to demonstrate grace under pressure. But there are many ways for you to feel more confident and ensure that you not only survive the interview, but that you actually succeed at it. That's what this chapter is about.

Which One of Us Is Being Interviewed, Anyway?

An interview is, in a sense, like a blind date. It boils down to two people checking each other out. And that's the thing you have to remind yourself on the way to the interview and all the while it's under way: Two people are interviewing/being interviewed, not one. Just as the interviewer is trying to get an impression of who you are, you need to learn as much as possible about the company and position—and, if the person interviewing you is also going to be your supervisor, about that person—*so that you can figure out if the job is right for you.*

The tendency is for you, the interviewee, to get so worked up about your appearance, responses, and the overall impression you make that you overlook the opportunity to get the information you need. Again and again: The interview is mutual, reciprocal, a two-way street; you're both evaluating at the same time. And if you can keep that in mind, you'll make a very different and much better impression than the interviewee who is sweating the impression s/he's making. Think of it this way: You're going *for an interview*, not *to be interviewed*. (Better yet: You're going on a blind date. You're excited. You want your date to like you—and you want to like your date. And if it works, you'll . . . Okay, so the analogy has its limits.)

The Art of Preparation

If you walk into the interview prepared to talk intelligently about both yourself and the company to which you are applying for a position, prepared to answer most of the questions you're likely to be asked, and prepared with questions of your own, you reduce the potential for surprises, you create an impression of confidence, and you ensure that both you and the interviewer leave with the information you both need to make any further decision.

I'm not easily dumbfounded. As nearly as I can recall—and instances of being dumbfounded are, alas, readily recalled—only once in my life have I been totally dumbfounded. That was during a job interview for which I didn't prepare. Temping for a major athletic-shoe manufacturer, I got a telephone call from a woman in the human resources department alerting me that a new position had opened up and an interview had been scheduled for me on the following day. I inquired about the nature of the position and was told, simply, "It has something to do with P.R., I'll try to get back to you with more information." Didn't happen. So the next day, I walked into the interview with exactly no concept of the position. We started talking, general chit-chat—who I am, what I've done, etc.—and then it happened: The interviewer told me that Mr. X (very famous athlete of whom I'd never heard) was going to climb K-2 (very big mountain of which I'd never heard) wearing this company's sneakers. "So," he said, "how ya gonna package it?" It was as though all power of speech had left me. I had absolutely nothing to say and couldn't even think clearly enough to fake a semi-intelligent answer (or, for that matter, any answer). I think I've repressed what I actually did say and how I managed to make it through the polite good-byes and then out of the room. What I do remember is how much laughter and guffawing the story elicited when I told it to my friends. That, and my pledge never again to walk into an interview with zero preparation.

Phase I. Prior to an interview, try to learn as much as possible about the company to which you're applying. Your first stop should be the library. The research librarian should be able to help you locate relevant information. Directories such as the *Corporate Yellow Book* (with industry-specific volumes) will give you basic information, including a description of the company. You can also call the local chamber of commerce and inquire whether they have any information about the company.

Your research will depend on the kind of company at which you're interviewing. If you are trying to get hired at *Newsweek*, of course you're going to be familiar with the last several issues. For a publishing company, know the specific works they publish; at any kind of manufacturing company, learn about the product. For a job at a nonprofit you'll want to familiarize yourself with the kind of work the organization does, the major issues involved, and the other organizations that do similar work. If you're looking for a job at an advertising agency, find out about some of its major accounts (and you'd better be reading *AdWeek*).

You should also be reading the newspaper every day during your job search. If any company in the industry you're trying to break into has a newsworthy development and you aren't aware of it, you'll be regarded as a less serious candidate. Reading the newspaper is also critical simply as a conversation starter. If, while being escorted from the lobby to the interviewer's office, the interviewer says "How do you like what happened in China?" and you don't know whether to say "Isn't it wonderful?" or "What a tragedy!" you're in trouble.

Phase II. The second part of preparing for the interview is to familiarize yourself with the kinds of questions that are likely to be asked and to shape answers for them. Study your resume and be prepared to discuss, in depth, anything that it includes. That way, when the interviewer says, "Tell me about yourself," you can reply, "As you can see from my resume, I'm a graduate of X. While there I . . ." Also be ready to answer the question, "Where do you see yourself in five years?" The interviewer knows that recent graduates, as a rule, don't have much past work experience to discuss, so questions about future goals are a natural—and popular—substitute. Another common set of questions deals with your achievements in college. And the almost certain bet is that you'll also be asked what you consider your greatest weaknesses. When asked about your weaknesses, try to make something negative look positive. For example "I get too invested in my work," or "I'm a perfectionist." The following is a list of questions commonly asked during an interview. (I have been asked every question on the list—never, thankfully, all in the same interview.) You might want to ask a friend to do some role-playing with you; that will give you the opportunity to run through the answers you draft.

Commonly Asked Job Interview Questions

1. Tell me about yourself.
2. Why do you want a career in X?
3. Where do you see yourself in five years?
4. What is your greatest achievement?
5. Why did you major in X?
6. Why did you select your college?
7. What courses did you like best? Least? Why?
8. What is your greatest strength? Tell me about a situation in which you used it.
9. Tell me about a problem you've encountered and how you dealt with it.
10. How do you define success?
11. What qualities do you look for in a supervisor?
12. What things are important to you in a job?
13. How would your friends describe you?

14. If you were having a dinner party and could invite any five people, living or dead, whom would you invite and why?

Questions that inquire about your age, race, religion, and any disability are illegal, unless they are legitimate job qualifications.

Phase III. Just in case you've forgotten: The interview process is a two-way street. Accordingly, not only should you be prepared with answers to commonly asked questions, you should also have questions of your own to ask. Some of the questions you prepare will undoubtedly be answered over the course of the interview, so it's a good idea to have at least five questions in mind beforehand. After the interviewer has exhausted his/her list of questions, you will almost certainly be asked if you have any questions. Unless you do, you come across as unintelligent, desperate for a job, not interested, or just plain dull.

Some Questions to Ask During the Interview

1. What would an average day in this position be like?
2. Can you describe the company culture?
3. How many people work in the company? In the department?
4. How do you see the company developing in the future?
5. What is the growth opportunity within the company?
6. What kind of position would this job train me for?
7. What are the training opportunities within the company?
8. What are some of the current projects being worked on and what would my role be?
9. What are the major challenges of the position?
10. How do you measure the success of somebody in this position?
11. What is your timetable for filling the position?

This is probably not the time to ask the following questions:

1. When do I start?
2. How big will my office be?
3. What does my secretary look like?

Phase IV. Under no circumstances should you arrive late for an interview. In fact, you should try to arrive a few minutes early. So, make sure you know the exact address of the meeting place and exactly how to get there. If the directions are confusing, practice the route the day before the interview. You're going to be stressed enough as it is; you don't want to be worried about getting lost.

Judging a Book by Its Cover

At a job interview, the fact is—despite what we've been taught—the book is judged by its cover. The interviewer will develop an impression of you within the first couple of minutes of the meeting that may determine whether or not you're hired. The other stuff that happens during the interview—how well you answer the questions, how prepared you seem, how you conduct yourself under pressure—is important, of course. But the initial impression that you make is critical to how the interviewer listens to what you say throughout the interview. It's just like the blind date: If, when he greets you at the door, you're turned off at first sight, you're not going to care much that he's been to the moon, developed a cure for a rare disease, and plays professional baseball.

I've read many books that instruct the job-seeker to dress conservatively for a job interview. Men should wear a dark suit and women a knee-length navy suit, these books insist. If you're looking for a job in a conservative industry such as finance or insurance, by all means get your dark suit to the dry cleaner. (And make sure it gets back in time.) But there are many industries in which conservative dress is not only unnecessary, but discouraged. If you're applying for a job at a fashion magazine, for example, your knee-length navy suit isn't going to exhibit your flair for fashion. (I have a friend who went to her very first interview at a fashion magazine. She wore a classic Ann Taylor suit that she had purchased specifically for the occasion. The interview was short, and at its conclusion the interviewer said, "Why don't you come back in a couple of years when you've developed some style?") You don't need to wear a pinstriped suit to be hired as a chef. The idea is to determine the style of the industry, and dress accordingly.

Obviously you should make sure that your clothes are clean and pressed; avoid the rumpled, I-slept-in-my-clothes look. Pillow creases on your face aren't a good idea. Whatever you wear should be tasteful and inoffensive, and project an image of professionalism.

Sheila had a high-powered career in Boston when she decided to move to New York City. She contacted a headhunter who promptly arranged an interview for her there. Sheila drove to New York, handled the interview beautifully (she thought), and returned home. The next day she called the headhunter to inquire whether there had been any feedback from the interviewer. She was completely stunned by the response: "I have to be honest with you," she was told. "I've heard that you didn't wear a suit to the interview and that you had a run in your stocking." After an interview that had lasted an hour, the only comments the interviewer had regarding Sheila were about her clothes. Clearly in Sheila's industry, in New York City, a power business suit is required. Needless to say, she was not called in for a second interview. And needless to say, she was neither surprised nor disappointed.

Pete was thrilled when he received a call to interview for a job at a holistic medicine magazine. He arrived at the interview bright-eyed and enthusiastic, decked out in a crisp suit he had borrowed specifically for the occasion. Waiting beforehand in the lobby, he noticed that all the employees were dressed casually. He didn't think much about it; his attire, he thought, was appropriate for an interview. The next day he received a call from the school counselor who had helped him arrange the interview. "The editor thought it was cute that you were wearing a suit," she said. Not exactly the kind of impression Pete had hoped to make.

Most often, you will not hear feedback—during the interview or after—on the image you project. If you don't get called back you usually don't know why. But the examples of Sheila and Pete show that, superficial though it might be, your appearance does matter. Take the time to figure out what people in the company wear, and invest in or borrow a couple of appropriate outfits.

Talking About Money

Until you've been offered a position, try to avoid talking about specific salary figures. Here's why: Suppose you're asked what kind of salary you are hoping for and you say twenty-four thousand dollars. If the interviewer has a budget for the position of twenty thousand dollars, s/he may automatically rule you out. If, on the other hand, the interviewer has a thirty-thousand-dollar budget, you probably just lost six thousand dollars. So unless you're explicitly asked, don't raise the issue yourself. And if you are asked, try to be as vague as possible. You might say something like, "What's the salary range for employees in comparable positions?" or "Did you have a salary in mind for this position?"

You should, however, have an ideal—albeit realistic—salary range in mind (see Chapter 9) in case you are pressed.

When interviewing for a job at a publishing company, the interviewer (later my boss) asked me how much I wanted to earn. I tried to get away with a vague response but he insisted I give him a specific figure, stating that he needed an exact number to present to the publisher.

Sometimes you don't have a choice, so be prepared with an answer just in case. And remember that your salary package consists of more than just your paycheck. Also included are benefits like insurance, investment plans, and bonuses. These "extras" can add quite a bit to your salary (around twenty percent), so make sure to get all the details when the conversation ultimately turns to compensation.

Keeping Your Spirits Up

The process of looking for a job can be extremely stressful. In normal life, it's considered rude for people not to return phone calls; a relationship consists of give and take; and people are, for the most part, straightforward. For some reason, these rules of courteous behavior mysteriously vanish during a job search. It's tiring to spend so much time trying to get people to give you so little of theirs. You constantly have to swallow your pride. You're also going to confront so many ups and downs that you'll get motion sickness. You find a job you really want, are led to believe it's in the bag, and then get a form letter of rejection. What's worse, a normal job search lasts six to eight months. How can you take your job search in stride and not let the feelings of stress and frustration take over the rest of your life?

- Just as you set aside time every day to focus solely on your job search, set aside time during which you don't think about it at all. It's easy to let the job search consume you; give yourself a couple of hours a day to put it totally out of your mind.
- Stay active. You've heard the statistics—regular exercise helps alleviate stress, keeps you energized, and boosts your self-confidence. Exercise, then, is an antidote for the side effects of a job search.
- Enlist a partner in your job search. If possible, find someone you know who is also looking for a job; if no one fits that bill, coerce a good friend or family member. You're going to need somebody to help you strategize, proofread your correspondence, prep you for interviews, and lend an ear or a shoulder on a regular basis.
- If you aren't working while you're looking for a job, make sure you're taking part in some kind of activity. Whether it's a personal project, social activity (see Chapter 5), or volunteer work, having something other than your job search on which to focus will help keep things in perspective. You might also think about setting personal goals for yourself that are unrelated to your search. The frustration of not finding a job right away can be alleviated by the satisfaction of realizing other goals in your life.

Dealing with Rejection

During my first full-time job search, I had an epiphany: Although your job search is the most important thing to you, it is not the most important thing to the people who are interviewing you. If somebody says, "I'll get back to you," the getting back may take two weeks, a month, or, worse, may never happen. During my first job search, I thought that as long as I didn't get a rejection letter or phone call, I could assume that I was still a live candidate. A month or two would go by, and when I finally called to inquire about the status of the position, I'd learn that it had been filled six weeks earlier. Getting a job is your number-one priority. Your getting a job may not even make last on your prospective employer's priority list. And courteous follow-up when s/he hires someone else is a coin toss. So don't sit around waiting for the phone to ring, don't be upset when you receive a standard rejection letter instead of a thoughtful personalized letter, and please don't take it personally when you don't get the job. (If you haven't heard after a few weeks, it's perfectly acceptable to call and inquire about the status of the position.)

Why shouldn't you take it personally if you don't get the job? Because most often, you don't know who *did* get the job. Maybe the owner's cousin applied for the same position. Maybe the interviewer's neighbor's son applied for the position. Maybe there was a qualified internal candidate who took precedence over outsiders. Maybe someone who went to the same college or was in the same fraternity or grew up in the same home town as the interviewer applied for the position. Maybe the interviewer is trying to learn Spanish and someone from Spain applied for the position. Maybe someone who had seen the same Star Trek movie the interviewer had seen the previous night applied for the position. Or maybe, just maybe, you completely botched the interview, wore the wrong clothes, fumbled your answers, and had sweaty palms. But you don't know, and the odds are you will never know. So why get worked up over it? There will, I assure you, be other jobs.

If you have several unsuccessful interviews—say, twenty or more—it may become somewhat difficult for you to refrain from taking the rejections personally. And maybe it's time for you to check out whether you're routinely doing something wrong. While I hate to blame the victim, and after twenty rejections you are for sure feeling like a victim, this is when you might want to consider contacting a career counselor for some interview coaching. Tell him or her that while you haven't had any trouble getting in the door, once inside the door something strange is happening. Apparently, you're not coming across well. Can s/he shed any light on the matter?

8½ Addendum: What to Do When the Job of Your Dreams Isn't So Dreamy After All

How to Survive a Boring Job

After all the time and energy you invested in your job search, after surviving all the ups and downs of your job search, after the expense of your job search, it would be nice to think that you'll end up with a stimulating, rewarding, be-all and end-all job. A job so great that you not only look forward to work in the morning, but you groan when the day is done—you want to work overtime and weekends, too. A job so fulfilling you want to stay in it for the rest of your life and never ever have to go through a job search again.

That's probably not going to happen.

Most entry-level jobs are boring. (That doesn't necessarily apply to those positions that require specialized training—e.g., engineer, computer technician, school teacher—and in which therefore you do substantive work, even at the lowest level.) Have you heard of the corporate ladder? You're on the lowest rung. That means that you're a whole lot closer to the bottom than you are to the top. You've gone to college, maybe graduate school, too; you have a wide breadth of knowledge; you want to make an impression; and you're stuck in a job where your knowledge is irrelevant and your motivation is very nearly beside the point. You're interchangeable with the twenty-five applicants who didn't get the job or, for that matter, with half a random selection from the roster of the unemployed. You may well find yourself doing nothing. (And it's little consolation that the people at the top of the ladder may also be doing nothing. Their nothing is considerably more lucrative than yours.)

Entry-level jobs are often defined as "administrative," and that is what they often are, in fact. You may spend your entire day administering the telephones, administering the copy machine, and/or administering a mailing. You may even administer the cleaning of the coffee cups. For this you went to college? Back there, in the sheltered groves of academe, your brain was thought to be (at least potentially) a thing of value. Now and then, even your opinions were taken seriously. At commencement, the speaker indicated that commencement is a beginning, not an ending, and that there were worlds to be conquered.

And now? Now, you're a pair of hands connected to a brain that's being asked to function at far less than capacity. You have an opinion? Save it for happy hour, this is how we do things here, don't rock the boat, opinions are things you get to have after you've put in your time in the mines.

So here you are, a specialist in boredom. How can you deal practically with being bored for much of your day, your week, your month? And, aside from the practical, how do you deal with it conceptually, how do you adjust to the realization that your work is neither stimulating nor, in any compelling sense, significant?

My first year out of college, I lived with five other recent graduates. Although we were all in different fields, all of us were in entry-level jobs and all of us were, no matter our titles, essentially receptionists. I would talk on the phone with one friend or another—always prepared to make it sound like an important business call should the boss walk by—at, say, 9:18. "I can't believe we have seven hours and forty-two minutes left," one of us would say. We'd speak again at 10:32 and comment on the remaining six hours and twenty-eight minutes. (If nothing else, we were at least honing our math skills.) These conversations would continue throughout the day. Twice a day there'd be a new topic—where to meet for lunch and, later, where to meet for happy hour. None of us stayed in our jobs for more than a year; a couple of us went back to school, some were promoted, and one or two switched fields. When we look back at that first year out of school, the jobs we had seem blurry; what we remember is the lunches and the happy hours.

What to do?

1. Take initiative at work. If your job is to answer phones or transcribe notes or send out weekly mailings, do those tasks as well as possible, but make it clear that you're interested in taking on additional responsibilities as well. If you drag into work, halfheartedly do your job, and rush out, you won't make a name for yourself, you'll perpetuate your boredom, and it will take a lot longer to get promoted and move out of a boring job. Whether you want to move ahead within the company or in a different organization, the more varied kinds of experience you have and the greater your responsibilities, the quicker you're likely to advance—and the more glowing the letter of reference your current employer is likely to write on your behalf.

2. When you're bored for the better part of the day, the tendency is to become demoralized, sluggish, and depressed. Happy hour at workday's end may give you a lift, but the lift will be only temporary. With the hour's end, you'll become painfully aware that you don't have much to look forward to except getting up in the morning and going back to being bored, bored out of your mind. The remedy? Take a deep breath, muster what little energy you have left, and find something to do in your off-hours that gives you a lift, and a life. Something, for example, that helps remind you. Remind you of what? No, I mean "remind" as in "re-mind," something that restores your mind to its natural status as a useful organ. Work may be a large part of life, but you don't have to let it become life itself.

   Participating in some kind of intellectual endeavor outside of work, whether it's an established activity such as a reading club (see Chapter 5), or reading the classics on your own, or writing in a journal, or whatever, will help you exercise your mind. If you're frustrated because your work is meaningless, take part in a political campaign, volunteer, or do something else that you care about a couple of nights a week. If you take part in other kinds of stimulating activities or are excited about your social life, your work won't seem like such a heavy burden. When the rest of your life is going well, work becomes a mere eight-hour interlude rather than the focus of the day. In other words:

Do not spend *every* night vegging out in front of the TV, the empty pizza boxes slowly accumulating off in the corner. In the long run, that will only make you more depressed. And do not try to drink your way into oblivion; oblivion is, after all, what you're trying to escape, not extend. (See Chapter 10 for further discussion on achieving a balanced lifestyle.)

3. Try to make personal connections at work. If you have a friend or two at work, the day becomes much more bearable. Whether it's somebody to go to lunch with, compare notes with on the weekend, or gripe about the fact that it's eighty degrees outside and you're stuck inside, you'll feel much less alienated and depressed knowing that you're not alone. Misery loves company.

4. Make the most of your lunch hour. If you can schedule something fun to do during lunch, you'll break up the day and the time will go much faster.

5. Don't compare yourself to your friend who has landed a great, cool job. You might have a friend who is working as a production assistant on a film or doing some other job that seems glamorous and exciting to you. (When, on the same day, my friend who works as an assistant to a producer called from LA to tell me she'd spent the entire day in wardrobe with Keanu Reeves and my friend who works at *Elle* called to tell me John F. Kennedy, Jr., had dropped into her office, I was plunged into despair. I'd spent the entire day crammed into a cubicle a few inches larger than my desk, working on spreadsheets. It may not be healthy but there are times, it turns out, when comparison is unavoidable.) But it's not going to do you any good to focus on the seductions of your friend's job. Try instead to believe that one day your prince(ss) will come, too.

6. Think of your first job as a rite of initiation into the world of work. It's something you have to survive to move ahead into an interesting position. Most people start at the bottom and

have, at some point in their career, answered phones, made copies, and collated mailings. Don't take it personally when you are asked to do menial tasks. It's not a reflection on your intellect or ability. The fact is that there are phones to be answered, copies to be made, and mailings to be collated. Somebody has to do it, and as an entry-level person, you're the obvious candidate. The good news is that if you do these things well (you'd be amazed at how many people botch up these seemingly simple tasks) and have a good attitude about doing them, you'll find you're asked to do more complicated and interesting tasks as well.

7. Remind yourself that your job is temporary. Unless it is totally, irretrievably, unmitigatedly intolerable, you should stay in your first job for at least a year. If your job doesn't improve at all after that, you can justifiably pursue either a promotion or a new job. If you have a personal time frame, it's easier to deal with the situation. You will not be in this job for the rest of your life. (What to do if your job *is* totally, irretrievably, unmitigatedly intolerable? See below.)

Take This Job and Shove It

Your first or second job probably won't be all you've always dreamt of. Chances are you aren't going to be jetting off to important meetings and "doing" lunch at glamorous restaurants. Again: First and second jobs are often highly administrative in nature, so try not to have unrealistic expectations of how you'll spend your workday.

That does not mean, however, that any disgrace, disillusionment, or despair you feel at work should be chalked up to first-job doldrums. It is entirely possible that despite all of the self-evaluation, preinterview research, and careful consideration you devoted to your job search, you'll wind up in a job that clearly isn't for you. If you've given your job a fair try (generally at least three months) and are still completely miserable, you shouldn't feel obliged to stick it out for an entire year. If you have a good reason for leaving and are prepared to explain your actions to your next interviewer, leaving shouldn't have any negative implications. In fact, it might even work in your favor. It looks much better to take a positive step toward finding the right career than it does to stay in a bad situation. (Chances are that the interviewer will have made some sharp turns in his/her career path also.) Just be prepared to discuss why you think the company at which you are interviewing will be a better match for you than the one you've left. If the job makes you sufficiently miserable, get out of the situation even if you don't have another job waiting in the wings. You can support yourself while you look for a new job by temping or by trying some of the money-making ideas in Chapter 9.

Kristen had earned her masters degree in psychology when she was hired to be the manager of benefits and employee relations at a major department store. When she showed up for the first day of work, a month after she was hired, she learned that the woman who had hired her had since been transferred to another department; Kristen would, therefore, be working for a new supervisor. Kristen's new boss had brought her own team to work with her and had already given the responsibilities that Kristen had been promised to one of her own. Kristen was put in a back room filing records from 8:30 in the morning to 5:00 in the evening. When questioned, the supervisor denied that the position had been changed. Kristen felt that the supervisor was hoping she would quit—and after nine days that's exactly what she did.

Jon had been working at a newspaper for three months when his supervisor was fired. The position was left vacant, and Jon ended up ignored, his workload eradicated. Though thoroughly bored, he continued to show up for work every day. At the same time, he reluctantly initiated a job search. He came to work one morning to find his desk occupied by somebody else. He was assigned to a work station in the middle of the foyer—a foyer through which, to his dismay, all the employees had to pass on entering or exiting the office. There were no desks near Jon's; aside from a plant, he was alone in the foyer—except when the other employees walked by his desk on their way into work, when they went out to lunch, when they came back from lunch, when they left for home, and when they visited the foyer to remind themselves that their own work situations weren't so bad. After enduring two weeks of humiliation, Jon quit.

Taking a Risk

If you have a professional dream, this is probably the time to make a go at it. Your first couple of years out of school are a great time to take risks. If you don't have anybody else dependent on you financially, you're in a good position to take a gamble; you have nothing to lose. If you botch things up, you'll be back at square one, exactly where you are now. (And the fact that you've taken a risk may appeal to a prospective employer.) Once you get on a career track, it's very difficult to get off and try something different. You grow accustomed to a certain lifestyle and have a whole lot more to lose if things don't work out. And if you fail, you might have to start over at the bottom of the ladder. Also, it usually doesn't seem quite as appealing to potential employers when an established professional chucks everything to pursue a dream and returns dragging tail as it does when a young—read, "idealistic"—person takes the initiative to do something unusual.

Depending on your particular dream, you should consider: (1) looking for a job that somehow relates to it while enhancing your skills during your off-hours (e.g., if you want to be an opera singer, work at the opera house and take classes at night), or (2) working on your goals during the day and getting a job to make money at night (e.g., work on your book from nine to five and wait tables at night), or (3) volunteering in the field of your dreams and getting a money-making job on the side. For ways to support yourself while you pursue your goals, see the next chapter.

A few months after graduating from college, Scott started a monthly alternative music/arts magazine in Seattle together with a few friends. They all worked full-time at unfulfilling jobs and worked on the magazine in their spare time. Because Seattle's music scene was burgeoning, the magazine outlasted the "one-year rule" of most start-ups, and continued to be published for two years before it finally fizzled. Scott never considered the venture a failure; neither did he think of it as particularly successful. It had been a good experience and a great deal of fun. Much to his surprise, the magazine became the primary topic of discussion whenever he went for a job interview, whether in the publishing world or the academic world (Scott's a teacher now). Some potential employers were interested in the small-scale publishing business, others in his writing experience, and still others merely in the chutzpah it took to found a magazine.

This is the best time in your life to take chances. If you don't go for it now, you may never find out whether you have what it takes to make your dream a reality. And if it isn't meant to be, or your dream doesn't turn out to be so dreamy after all, you'll have something unusual to talk about at a job interview—and, who knows, perhaps also the time and will to dream a new dream.

REAL-WORLD PRESSURE

9. Dollars and Sense: Making It on an Entry-Level Salary

It was the best of times, it was the worst of times. I had eagerly anticipated my first paycheck from the moment I accepted my first postcollege job. (Actually, I had been anticipating my first paycheck from the moment I donned my cap and gown, but now the anticipation had an exact dollar figure attached to it.) I was preoccupied during the first weeks of work with two conflicting notions: On the one hand, the money I was going to get was earmarked for paying my father back for the money he had shelled out to cover my first month's rent and security deposit, the initiation fee for the gym my roommates had already joined, a couple of outfits I had on hold at the Limited, and my sister's thirtieth birthday present. Oh, and plane fare to visit my college roommate in San Diego. On the other hand, I had calculated—down to the hour—the precise amount I was earning and I knew that there was a modest discrepancy between the payment I would receive for my first two weeks of work and how I intended to spend it.

A "modest" discrepancy? Try not even on the same abacus. My paycheck was so far off from the amount I had calculated that I was tempted to sign up for a continuing-education math class. Deductions were taken for acronyms I'd never even heard of, and the amount left over had more in common with the hourly wage I had calculated than with the lump sum I was expecting. Suffice it to say that my father received a lovely Hallmark thank-you card, and I bought a couple of nifty pairs of socks at the Limited.

Your first year out of college may very well be the first time you experience the jubilation of finding a paycheck on your desk or in your mailbox once or twice or even four times a month. Neither piddly part-time remuneration nor the earnings of a short-lived summer job, these checks may seem, at first, to be the Midas-like salary of a Donald Trump-in-the-making. Very many graduates feel that earning a regular paycheck is the thing they like best about their first year out of college. Be proud of the fact that you are supporting yourself for the first time in your life—even if you do still have to turn to your parents for the security deposit on your apartment.

I wish that were all that wanted saying about money matters. It would be wonderful if the only thing you need to consider about your finances is whether to vacation in Wyoming or Hawaii, whether to buy a Porsche or a Jaguar—or even to choose between a Geo and an Escort. But back to the Real World: You'll soon find that the harsh realities of rent, insurance, food, entertainment, and utility bills will temper the elation you initially feel about earning a regular paycheck.

There's a cruel irony in the fact that just when you (presumably*) begin to support yourself for the first time, life suddenly becomes much more expensive. The cost of housing soars when you move out of a college town, Levi's and sweats no longer suffice for a wardrobe, and your social life—more or less free in college, where simply walking down the street is a social experience—is suddenly a major expense. This phenomenon might be considered merely an irony (and not cruel) if you could expect to earn a salary sufficient to cover your suddenly inflated expenses. But alas, it might not be so. The reality is that most new graduates are hired for entry-level jobs and earn entry-level salaries. (Which, in most professions, isn't a whole lot.) Furthermore, after state taxes, federal taxes, social security, insurance, and diverse other deductions are subtracted from your

---

*I am presuming that you are part of the vast majority of people who has to work for a living and has no other source of significant income. If you have a lucrative income and/or if you are free from the financial constraints that most of your peers are facing, you may want to skip over sections of this chapter. Likewise, if you put yourself through college or have been supporting yourself for a significant period of time, you probably know all about budgeting and saving.

salary, the amount you take home in your paycheck is significantly less than the amount you earn.

So: How can you establish a livable budget to ensure that your paycheck lasts until the end of the month? (And is it hoping for too much to have a few dollars left over to start a savings plan?) If you don't have a job yet, how do you figure out how much money you realistically need to get by? How can you cut costs? How can you make extra money if you are simply unable to get by on your regular salary? And how do your organize your finances and maintain financial responsibility?

Read on.

How Much Money Do You Need?

Everybody wants a higher salary. I would like a higher salary; my sister, whose salary is triple mine, would too; I've read that even Demi Moore and Jim Carrey, who respectively earn twelve and twenty million dollars per movie, negotiate for higher salaries. The question, obviously, is not how much money you'd like to earn. (We all know the answer to that one: "More.") The question, at least at this stage of your life, is how much money you *need* to earn. Your particular needs might include going to the bar three times a week, buying two new outfits a month, joining a pricey health club—that's fine. I don't presume to suggest which needs are legitimate and which ones are extravagant. What I do suggest is that you figure out exactly how much money you spend and where you spend it, so that you can figure out how much money you need to get by on a monthly basis. This knowledge is important for a few reasons:

- If you don't yet have a job, you'll get a general idea of the salary you'll need to earn in order to make ends meet.
- If you have a job and find that your paycheck always seems to "disappear" before the following payday, you'll get a sense of where your money is going and be able to strategically plan to make your money last longer.
- If you have a job, have no trouble covering your expenses, and are comfortable with your lifestyle, you'll determine in which areas your spending is highest so that you know where to focus your efforts when you initiate a savings plan.

To begin, make a list of your fixed costs—expenses that will not change throughout the year. These might include any of the following:

1. Rent/mortgage
2. Tuition loans
3. Car payments
4. Insurance (automobile, health, renter's)

Next, compile a list of regular monthly expenses, estimating the average monthly expenditure. (If you have just moved into a new residence and aren't sure about some of the monthly housing costs, talk to another tenant in the building.) These include the following:

1. Electricity
2. Gas (heat)
3. Phone
4. Trash
5. Groceries
6. Newspaper/magazine subscriptions
7. Cable TV
8. Transportation (gasoline, parking, public transportation costs)
9. Pet care
10. Birth control
11. Health club

Add to this list miscellaneous expenses. These are more than the obvious costs of entertainment, recreation, and eating out. Consider the following:

1. Haircuts
2. Gifts
3. Cosmetics
4. Postage
5. Computer accessories
6. Laundry/dry cleaning
7. Credit-card payments
8. Medical care (if you're uninsured)
9. Charitable donations

Note: Miscellaneous expenses, which are the hardest to quantify, are not merely optional add-ons to your regular budget. I've included on the miscellaneous list nonregular expenditures. Some of these are trivial; others can be of major importance.

I've taken a quick survey of some of my co-workers and learned that almost everyone has made a withdrawal at the ATM at least twice during the week. Not one person was able to recall where that money was spent. What's worse, a few people couldn't even remember the amount they had withdrawn. Try keeping a record for one week of every penny (nickels, dimes, quarters, and dollars, too) that you spend. This exercise will not only help you determine the amount of your miscellaneous spending, it will also give you insight into your spending habits. (If, for example, at the end of the week you realize that you spent fifty dollars on food while at work, you might want to think about bringing snacks from home.)

The last item in your list of expenses, unless you have money set aside already, should be your emergency fund. Decide how much money you want/can put away each month for unexpected expenses. Consider the following: What are you going to do when your car breaks down and you need to pay for repairs? What are you going to do when three of your friends ask you to be in their weddings next summer (and you're forced to spend money not only on plane fare, gifts, showers/bachelor parties, but also on ugly clothes that you'll never wear again)? What are you going to do when your siblings suggest that you throw a gala party for your parents' twenty-fifth wedding anniversary—suggest a backyard barbecue instead?

The point is that there are expenses that you cannot anticipate and budget for in advance. If you are taking home the exact amount of money you need to make ends meet or spending all of your money because, what the heck, you worked for it, you're going to be in trouble when unforeseen events (and—may you be protected from them— emergencies) require money. The bottom line is that you need to include a regular deduction in your budget for the unforeseen.

The following chart can be used to organize your spending. Once you have an idea of your miscellaneous expenses, decide whether you want to list them separately or group them together. It's useful to separate anticipated expenditure from actual expenditure so you can see where you're miscalculating expenses. If you're going to err, it's better to overestimate costs about which you're uncertain. (Keep this

Month of _____

Item	Anticipated Expenditure	Actual Expenditure	Date of Expenditure	% of Total
Emergency Fund				

TOTAL:

chart as a reference. Once you start implementing some of the savings ideas listed later in the chapter, fill out a new chart and see how much money you've saved. Developing a budget is an ongoing process. You'll continue to refine your chart as you alter your spending habits.)

After you've completed the chart, compare your total expenditure to the amount you earn at work on a monthly basis. (As mentioned above, if you don't yet have a job, the chart will help you determine a starting salary to shoot for.) The ultimate goal is to figure out a way for your salary to cover your expenses; money that you have in savings, CDs, mutual funds, etc. doesn't figure into the equation. Compare your take-home pay to your total expenses. If your expenses come out higher than your income, you're going to have to make some changes. Lower your expenses or increase your income. (We'll discuss both of these strategies.) If your income is *greater* than your expenses, you might want to make some changes. Increase your expenses or start a savings plan. (These options are not necessarily mutually exclusive. If you choose the former, do yourself a favor and start a savings plan as well. Later in the chapter you'll learn why and how.)

I Interrupt This Chapter to Bring You a Warning: Credit Cards

Put a little kid alone in a candy store and what happens? He will likely gobble up everything in sight, have a fantastic time, and spend the entire night sick to his stomach. Think of your credit cards as your personal candy store and don't overeat. Better yet: Do not think of your credit card as your personal candy store; think of it instead as the fearsome loan officer at your bank. Every time you use your credit card you are borrowing money. You will have to pay it, and then some, back.

You pay interest—typically, outrageously high interest—on the amount that you charge. Some banks charge interest only on the amount that you don't pay within the billing period but there are some that charge from the day you make your purchase. In either case, if you can't pay your monthly balance, you are going to be charged interest. That's the first problem with credit-card spending.

The second, and more serious problem, is the temptation to buy more than you can afford. Buy now; pay later. Only when it comes time to pay, you don't have the money. When you buy something with your credit card, that something is not free. You will have to pay for it sooner or later. And the longer you wait, the more it will end up costing you.

Also be aware that it is to the credit card company's advantage for you not to pay your bill on time so that it can earn interest. That's how it makes its money. For this reason, credit card companies conduct an enormous amount of research to identify those buyers who will pay the bill eventually but probably not pay the entire amount each month. Guess what? Recent college graduates fit that profile perfectly. You'll probably be besieged by offers to receive "low-interest" credit cards (I still get several a week). The catch is usually in the fine print where you'll see (if you squint) that the low interest rate is guaranteed for only a few months, or a year, after which time the rates may rise. There is no good reason to own more than one credit card.

Be aware that your payment activity—this means not only your general credit card payments and purchases, but also any individual store credit cards you have, along with bank loans (including your student loans)—are all available to credit bureaus. (Big brother, in short, is watching.) When you apply for a loan, the credit bureau will provide a detailed history to your lender. If you seem like someone who is unable to repay a loan in timely fashion, you are going to have trouble when you *need* to make a purchase that requires a loan.

One way to keep track of your credit card purchases and ensure that you have the means to pay for them is to deduct the amount you charge from your checkbook balance. Another trick is to limit your credit card spending to one category of spending, such as clothing or travel.

All this may sound so obvious as to require no comment, or may sound too scolding, a drizzle on your parade to a life of riches. And anyway, ours is a credit card society, so what's the big deal? The big deal is exactly this: There is no more certain way to get yourself into a truly serious financial pickle, and a sour pickle at that, than via that innocent piece of plastic in your wallet. Over and over again, I've had friends who've started down the slippery slope with the best of intentions, resolved to exercise real self-discipline in the use of their credit cards, only to find months and even years—sometimes several years—later that they're mired in debt from which they cannot extricate themselves. The vacation charged to your VISA, the one you couldn't really afford but that you'd be able to pay off within, say six months, continues to drain your monthly budget sixty months later. No kidding. So learn to live within your means, use your credit card judiciously, and be sure to pay off your credit card bill every month.

Cutting Costs

If your expenses are higher than your income, you're going to *have* to make some adjustments in your lifestyle. But even if you're getting by on your salary, it makes sense to get in the habit of lowering expenses when it's relatively easy to do so. The ideas listed below will help you save money either on a daily basis or in the long run. Some may seem obvious, some tedious, and some irrelevant. Pick a few ideas that seem reasonable to you and ignore those that don't. You don't have to change your lifestyle dramatically; I am not suggesting that you live like a monk/nun (unless of course you are a monk/nun). Try focusing on those areas that came out high when you filled out your chart and keep track of your savings so you can revise your budget.

51 Ways to Cut Your Expenses and Save Money

At the Table . . .

1. *Bring your lunch to work.* If you go out to lunch every day, you can expect to spend at least five dollars a day, twenty-five dollars a week. Start bringing your lunch with you; even if it costs you two dollars a day, you'll still have saved almost seven hundred dollars by the end of the year. (That calculation includes ten days off for holidays and ten days off for vacation.)
2. *Eat breakfast at home.* Buy a muffin and juice every morning on your way to work and you'll spend almost five hundred dollars by the end of the year. It's cheaper to wake up a few minutes earlier and eat at home.
3. *Prepare meals in advance.* Coming home from work and popping a frozen dinner into the microwave is a tempting convenience. It's also expensive. Instead, take some time on

the weekend to cook and freeze your own meals. The frozen dinners you buy in the store are a waste of money, and anyway, they don't taste nearly as good as home-cooked meals. (If frozen meals taste better than *your* home-cooked meals, consider investing some of your saved money in a cookbook.)

4. *Clip coupons.* If you use them regularly, coupons can save you quite a bit of money. The trick is to use them to buy only those items that you would buy anyway. Look for coupons in your mailbox, in the newspaper, and in the grocery store circular.

5. *Shop at convenience stores only when it's completely inconvenient to shop elsewhere.* There's no mystery about it—the raison d'être of convenience stores is that they are convenient. They rely on the fact that when you need to pop in for a cup of coffee, you'll stock up on other goods as well. They don't make their money on volume, they make it on markup. And that costs you.

6. *Buy generic or supermarket brands.* By spending less on advertising and fancy packaging, manufacturers keep the prices of generic and supermarket brands much lower. Check the ingredients; you'll often get the exact same thing for a whole lot less.

7. *Shop for groceries at a food co-op.* Food co-ops, like all co-ops, are owned and run by members. Food co-ops generally buy food in bulk and pass the savings on to their members. Some co-ops extend shopping privileges to members only, others serve nonmembers as well. Becoming a member usually involves donating a few hours of work (e.g., working the cash register, stocking merchandise) each week, or paying a membership fee.

8. *Shop in a warehouse buying club.* Warehouse buying clubs buy products in bulk and sell items at or near wholesale price. You can save quite a bit of money, but you may need to pay an annual fee (generally thirty-five to fifty dollars). To join some clubs you need to have certain credentials (e.g., participating employer, community association, etc.). The negative side to warehouse shopping and buying in bulk is that you might not have space to store what you buy. (Fifty rolls of toilet paper do not make an attractive living-room

sculpture, although they might make a comfortable couch.)
If you are shopping just for yourself, you may also find that
you are not able to eat all of the food that you buy before it
goes bad. Some of the major warehouse buying clubs are
Costco, BJ's Wholesale Club, Price Club, PACE. Call the
chamber of commerce to find out which ones are located in
your neighborhood.

9. *Buy groceries in a grocery store and stay away from the other
products.* Ever notice that nongrocery items in a grocery store
(e.g., plants, greeting cards) are in the front of the store?
There is a philosophy—more accurately, a strategy—behind
the way items in a grocery store are displayed. Chances are
you don't go to the grocery store to buy a plant; the store marketing gurus are hoping that you'll be swayed into purchasing
one when you pass the display, even though the price is
higher than you'd find elsewhere. Likewise, the cost of cosmetics, drugs, and other nonfood items will be inflated in a
grocery store.

10. *Look beyond the obvious in a grocery store.* Remember
there's a design to the way items are displayed in the grocery
store. The most expensive goods are placed at eye level, so do
some stretching (or squatting) to find the lower-priced items.

11. *Don't buy more than you can eat.* This is one trick I can't
seem to master. Every time I go to the grocery store I buy a
couple bags of fruit and vegetables, thinking about how
healthy I'm going to be. Then when I get home, before I unload the bags, I empty out the fruit and vegetable drawers in
my refrigerator and throw out all the produce that's gone bad
since the last time I decided to be healthy. Don't buy more
perishable items than you can possibly eat. You don't get
healthy by having healthy food rotting away in the refrigerator. (Unless, of course, looking at all that mold ruins your
appetite.)

12. *Buy day-old bakery products.* Stores that sell freshly baked
foods have no use for the food that is left over at the end of
the day. Most stores will sell these foods for a vastly reduced
price. (Some stores even give the leftovers away for free, so
do some investigating.) Since you probably don't eat the entire loaf the day you bring it home anyway, you're no worse

off buying one-day old. And day-old food from a specialty
shop might be fresher than the food you'd purchase at the
supermarket—which makes the bargain doubly delicious.

13. *If you live with roommates, establish an economical food
arrangement.* If you and your roommate(s) have different eating habits, consider buying your food separately. On the other
hand, there are some items that make sense to purchase together (e.g., milk, butter, toilet paper), so talk it over and figure
out a plan that is mutually beneficial.

On the Road . . .

14. *Take public transportation instead of driving to work.* Not
only will you save on gas, parking, and wear on your car,
you'll also be helping the environment. Think of it as a good
time to get some reading done and go public.

15. *Buy a monthly public transportation pass.* In Boston, for example, buying a T-pass saves a regular commuter nearly one
hundred dollars a year (not to mention the time it saves by
not having to scrounge around for change every morning and
afternoon).

16. *If you must drive to work, join a car pool.* When you join a
car pool you reduce your gas, parking, and car-wear costs.
You may also save time if you drive on a highway with car
pool lanes. And let's not forget the environment.

17. *Serve yourself at gas stations.* Why pay to have somebody
else do what you can almost as easily do yourself?

18. *Pay in cash at gas stations.* Some gas stations charge extra if
you pay with a credit card. Also be aware that those gas stations that advertise "same price cash and credit" may in fact
be bumping up the price across the board.

19. *Keep your car tires properly inflated.* Invest in a tire-pressure
gauge (available at auto-supply stores and gas stations). Check
the tire pressure once a month. Driving with underinflated
tires increases friction between the tires and the road and uses
more gas.

20. *Keep your car healthy.* Avoid serious car problems by changing your car's oil, oil filter, and air filter regularly, all of
which help it operate more efficiently.

21. *Invest in jumper cables—and learn how to use them.* The first time your battery dies you'll be glad you made the investment.
22. *Ride a bike.* Save on gas, save on parking, save on public transportation costs, save on a health-club membership, help save the environment.

On the Phone . . .

23. *Let your fingers do the walking.* Use your telephone book instead of calling directory assistance, you'll save approximately thirty-five cents each time.
24. *Shop around for the most economical phone service.* Second to my rent, I spent more on phone bills my first couple of years out of school than on any other single item. Keeping in touch with my family and college friends cost me hundreds of dollars each month. Make sure you have the long-distance service that saves you the most money. Plans differ and policies change fairly frequently so take the time to do the research. You can reach the major long distance phone companies at the following numbers: AT&T: (800) 222-0300, MCI: (800) 444-3333, Sprint: (800) 877-4646, Allnet: (800) 881-8860.
25. *Make calls during off-peak hours and share the financial burden of phone calls.* Try to avoid calling during peak hours when rates are higher. It's easy to lose track of time when you're having a juicy conversation, so decide in advance how long you're going to talk on the phone and time your call. If you talk to a close friend frequently, split the expense by trading off calling or switching callers half-way through the conversation. If all else fails, write.

In the Bank . . .

26. *Compare banks.* Visit several local banks and compare the fees for checking and saving accounts, ATM, and other services that you'll use. Bank charges vary depending on the types of accounts you have and the fees can add up to a substantial monthly sum.
27. *Use your own bank's ATM machine.* Some banks charge for all ATM transactions, while others charge you only if you use

another bank's machine. (Some don't charge you for using any ATM, but that's generally if you keep a significant minimum in your account.) The fees add up quickly and may explain why your checkbook never seems to balance exactly.

28. *Get rid of all annual-fee charge/credit cards.* Why pay approximately fifty-five dollars a year to have the privilege of spending even more money?

29. *Get a piggy bank.* If you put all of your pocket change in one place every day, the coins may soon add up to a significant sum. One of my roommates saved her change for three months and accumulated three hundred dollars.

30. *Keep warranties.* File all merchandise warranties in one place so that when something breaks you don't have to wonder if there was a warranty and where it might be.

Time Off . . .

31. *Check the local Y or community center for discounts on health clubs.* Many centers offer low-income memberships for fitness centers. It's worth looking into if you think you might qualify.

32. *Take advantage of happy hour.* During my first year out of school there was not a single Friday on which I paid for dinner. Happy hour was a ritual for my roommates and me, mainly because we were celebrating the start of a two-day respite from the tedium of our jobs. We'd meet at the bar, have some cheap drinks, and eat more than our fair share of the free food. Though some bars no longer discount drinks, you can definitely find free munchies at numerous establishments in the early evening hours.

33. *Drink at home.* I wouldn't advise anything that might infringe on your social life, but if you meet your friends for drinks at someone's home instead of the bar, you'll save money and you won't have to deal with annoying strangers trying to pick you up. (On the other hand, if you're hoping to be picked up, ignore this tip.)

34. *Check the newspaper for free local events.* Many communities sponsor free concert series and free outdoor movies. Book readings are generally free and many museums are free

all of the time or offer one free admission day a week. Get in the habit of checking out the "Calendar of Events" section of the newspaper to find out what's going on around town.

35. *Become an usher.* If you enjoy theater or concerts, find out about ushering opportunities. In exchange for a few hours of work, you get to see the show for free.

36. *Buy an Entertainment® Book.* Discount-coupon books have allowed me to eat at restaurants and stay at hotels that I would have never been able to afford otherwise. My favorite is the Entertainment® Book, which is available in regional editions. Each book has hundreds of discount coupons for local restaurants, movie theaters, cultural and sports events, lodging, and more. The book costs thirty to fifty-one dollars (depending on the region) and pays for itself with just one or two uses. To purchase a book, call (800) 374-4464.

37. *See the early show.* As the cost of seeing a movie in the evening continues to rise, it makes sense to get to the theater before 6:00 P.M. and save close to half the ticket price. (You can use the money you save to buy the overpriced popcorn.)

Going Shopping . . .

38. *Buy quality merchandise even if it costs more.* When my third answering machine broke, my father advised me to invest in a hundred-dollar machine. I thought that was absurd and I ignored the advice; there were plenty of machines on the market that were significantly cheaper and I didn't feel I could justify spending such a sum on something I couldn't wear or drive. Shortly thereafter, when I had purchased my fifth answering machine, I felt differently.

39. *Buy and sell clothes at a consignment shop.* Consignment stores operate as brokers for people who want to sell used merchandise. If you have some clothes or furniture that are in good shape and that you'd like to sell, set up an appointment at a shop in your city. If the store agrees to display your wares, you and the owner determine asking prices for each item and they are put on the floor for a certain number of days. If an item sells, you and the owner each get a preagreed-upon percentage. Or, if you prefer, you can usually get a

higher percentage of the sale price in store credit. Consignment stores tend to be very discriminating about the items they sell, so they're also a good place to shop for quality merchandise at a discount.

40. *Negotiate.* If you shop at owner-managed or smaller stores, you may very well be able to negotiate the price of an item. If, for example, you plan to pay cash or buy more than one of an item, the owner will often be willing to discount the merchandise. It's worth asking. This obviously won't work in Bloomingdale's or Macy's, but even in those stores you might be able to get a discount on merchandise that's slightly damaged or has been on display.

When at Home . . .

41. *Use fans instead of air-conditioning.* Your electric bill will soar during those months that you use air-conditioners. If you can bear it, use a fan instead.

42. *If you're making changes to your apartment, find out if your landlord will pay.* If you decide to make permanent changes in your apartment (e.g., painting, wallpapering), you'll need to discuss them with your landlord anyway. Position the changes as an apartment improvement and ask if s/he'll fund them.

43. *Cut costs in the kitchen.* Run your dishwasher only when full, don't leave the refrigerator door open for long periods while you blankly gaze into it, use sponges instead of paper towels, recycle grocery bags as trash bags, don't overcrowd the freezer, cook several items in the oven at the same time.

44. *Buy a bottle of white distilled vinegar and a box of baking soda.* There's no need to buy distinct cleaners for your windows, sinks, floors, counters, refrigerator, and oven. Instead, purchase some vinegar and use it for all your cleaning needs. Mix it with water and pour in a little bit of lemon juice so the smell doesn't make you nauseous. After cleaning, wipe the surface with water to get rid of any lingering odor. Baking soda is another multipurpose product. Use it to clean your sink, deodorize your refrigerator, and even to brush your teeth.

45. *Ignore the recommended dosage directions when you use detergent.* Your clothes and dishes will get just as clean if you use one-half the recommended amount of detergent. (Manufacturers obviously want you to use more, run out faster, and purchase more frequently.) You can also cut your dishwashing liquid with water and get your dishes just as sparkly clean.

For Your Reading Pleasure . . .

46. *Share a newspaper with your co-workers.* If you read the paper at work, split a subscription with your colleagues and save a few dollars a month.

47. *Share magazine subscriptions with your neighbors or friends.* I use the fact that I work in publishing to justify my six magazine subscriptions. My sister loves it; she gets all of them when I'm through. Instead of throwing away periodicals you've read, pass them along to your friends and split the subscription price.

48. *Use the library.* When I first got out of school, the thought of going into a library made me break out in hives. I immediately got the "I hate research" pit in my stomach if I even stood in a library doorway. After a year, however, I summoned the courage to venture into a small neighborhood library. I started slowly, just browsing the magazines, and worked my way up to checking out one book at a time. Before long I was hooked. I realized that using a library for pleasure is an entirely different exercise than using it for study and I began to appreciate that libraries are one of the truly great free services of our communities. P.S.: I saved the not-insignificant monthly sum I had previously spent at the bookstore.

49. *Start a book-trading club with your friends.* Here's how it works: Each person brings at least two good books from home to a meeting and chooses two books from the lot that he or she wants to take home and read. The group gets together again in about a month and continues trading. It's a great way to access new books on a regular basis without spending a dime.

Miscellaneous

50. *Return cans and bottles and collect the deposit.* Ideally you're recycling anyway, but if you live in a state that charges a deposit for bottles and cans, you'll make a few cents when you turn them in.

51. *Forgo the dry cleaner when possible.* This is another one that I can't seem to make work. When my clothes get wrinkled, I take them straight to the dry cleaner. A huge waste of money, I know, so don't be as lazy about ironing as I am. I'm also guilty of toting bags of sweaters to the dry cleaners every fall when a bottle of Woolite could just as successfully and far more cheaply do the trick.

Supplementing Your Income

Once you start cutting your expenses, you should have an easier time making ends meet. But if (1) you're still coming up short at the end of the month, or (2) you want to earn extra money to cover a major expense, or (3) you just want to bring home a few extra dollars each month, consider supplementing your income with additional work. What you need to think about is work that can be done in the hours you're not at your regular job (probably evenings and weekends). The ideal situation is to find something you enjoy doing enough so that you won't resent having to do it in your "off" hours. If you think creatively, most hobbies and interests can be turned into a means of earning a few extra dollars. Consider the following:

- *Become a tutor.* One-on-one instruction generally has several advantages: flexible hours, flexible meeting place, good pay. The pay tends to be quite high; approximately twenty-five dollars an hour (compared to the fifteen dollars an hour you can expect for teaching a whole class in adult education programs). Call local schools to let them know that you're available, advertise in the newspaper, or post signs in community centers.
- *Work for a catering company.* Regardless of the hours you normally work, you should be able to fit catering work into your schedule. Catered events take place morning, noon, and night,

seven days a week. And though it's hard work physically, the benefits are great. In contrast to waiting tables, you make a good hourly wage, you have a virtually pressure-free relationship with the people whom you serve (since they're not the ones paying you), and the event at which you're serving might actually be fun. You generally get a free meal (and sometimes get to take home leftovers). To find out about catering opportunities, contact companies listed under "Caterers" in the phone book. Be prepared to be flexible; if you can be called upon at the last minute to fill in for a regular who doesn't show, you increase your chances of getting regular work. Christmas is the busiest season, so call in October or November to get the most work. You might have to supply your own tuxedo; if so, check out local thrift stores.

- *Exploit your talents.* Whatever your talent is, there is probably a way to make money expressing it. I know a photographer who takes pictures at weddings, an opera singer who sings in church every Sunday, an artist who arranges flowers for formal functions. And even if you don't have a talent, there's probably something you don't mind doing that someone else will pay not to have to do. I know a person who irons someone else's clothes on a weekly basis. I even know someone who gets paid for preparing a homemade lunch for a co-worker five days a week. Think about it and be creative. If you don't know someone who will pay for the service you're offering, advertise in the "Classified" section of the newspaper or put up signs around your community.

- *House-Sit.* Many people are uneasy about leaving their house vacant when they're away, and are prepared to pay for their peace of mind. The benefits of house-sitting are obvious: You get paid *and* you get to stay in a house that's nice enough for someone to hire a house-sitter. The hardest part about house-sitting is getting your first job. People generally entrust their home only to someone they know or someone who knows someone they know, so spread the word to people *you* know that you're interested in opportunities. Once you complete your first job (presuming nothing is lost, broken, soiled, burned, flooded, shattered, etc.) you may get hired again through word of mouth. (People will also pay for someone to stop by their

house and take care of their home chores while they're away—
water the plants, take in the newspaper and mail, feed the cat.)

- *Do for others what they cannot do for themselves.* Yard work,
  shoveling snow, walking dogs, even grocery shopping, pose serious problems for some people. Whether you choose to help
  one person with an array of chores or a number of people with a
  specific task, you have the potential to make some extra cash in
  the hours when you're not at work. Think about what jobs
  you're able/willing to do and advertise your services. Don't forget to post notices in places that older people or sick people
  might frequent (e.g., medical office buildings, rehabilitation
  centers, physical therapy offices).
- *Plan parties.* If you're creative, extremely organized, and like
  working with people, think about becoming a party planner.
  There are numerous details associated with parties and other
  functions: venue, food, invitations, music, program, flowers, fa-
  vors, and so forth. There are plenty of people that have neither
  the time nor the inclination to think about such things, so if you
  do, you can make some money. You'll have to make a lot of
  phone calls, mostly during business hours, so if that's incom-
  patible with your full-time job, party planning probably isn't for
  you. This is another field that's hard to break into. Since professional events are organized by professional planners, your work
  will probably be in the form of private functions. You just need
  one party to get started (you'll then have experience and refer-
  rals), so consider doing the first one free of charge. Spread the
  word that you're available and advertise within the community.
- *Tend bar.* If you don't like dealing with people, even when
  they're sober, forget about becoming a bartender. But if you
  like a good party and late hours don't faze you, consider en-
  rolling in a mixology course. Whether you work in a restaurant,
  bar, or at private parties, you'll be able to make quite a bit of
  money. And the fringe benefit is that you'll acquire a skill that
  can come in handy in your off-hours as well.
- *Wait tables.* If you've given any thought to ways to earn extra
  money, you've probably considered waiting tables. Restaurants
  are busiest in the evenings and during the weekends, the times
  that you're probably not at your regular job. Waiting tables can
  be quite lucrative and you usually get to eat for free. You can

save money on your gym membership because you'll get a great workout. But if you've done it before, you know that waiting tables isn't only hard physical work, it can be stressful to your psyche as well. If you have the stamina, give it a try. Realize, though, that it can be competitive to get hired and the best shifts (weekends and evenings) go to those with seniority. Apply at a variety of restaurants and if you have no experience, be prepared to start as a host/ess or table busser.

- *Sell, sell, sell.* Since retail stores are open on weekends, you might think about getting a job as a salesperson. If you can get hired to work for a store that pays commission, you might even make good money. Apply to stores that sell merchandise that interests you; it's easier to get people to buy if your pitch is genuine, and you'll be able to take advantage of the employee discount.

For more money-making ideas, check out *555 Ways to Earn Extra Money: Revised For the 90's,* by Jay Conrad Levinson (New York: Henry Holt, 1991).

A Penny Saved . . .

Saving money may not seem important to you now. After all, you probably have no one to support but yourself and chances are you don't have to worry about major expenses such as a home or children.

Which is exactly why now is the perfect time to begin saving. If you wait until you're supporting a family and financing a home to start saving, you'll realize very quickly that more of the money you earn is earmarked for specific expenses and it's much harder to isolate funds for saving. You'll also find that it gets progressively harder to develop a saving habit. Perhaps most important, the money you save tomorrow will never be worth as much as the money you save today.

Compound interest means that the interest on the money you save in the first year of your savings earns you additional interest in the second year. By the tenth year of saving, then, you're earning interest not only on the principal—that goes without saying—but on the first nine years of interest as well. (Assume an average interest rate of just five percent: one hundred dollars saved at age twenty-two, for example, becomes $815 by age sixty-five. If you put away just one hundred dollars every year, you'll have over *$15,000* when you're sixty-five.) And if saving for retirement seems too preposterous a notion to you right now, think about a goal that is more enticing, like buying a home or traveling around the world.

Clearly it makes sense to start saving early. But that doesn't mean that saving is easy. It's much more fun to spend money than to stash it, which means that unless you get off on watching the zeros multiply on your bank statement, you're going to need to make a plan to save on a regular basis. Here's how:

The Ten Percent Rule (or Maybe, in Your Case, the Five Percent Rule). "You spend what you earn," as the saying goes—and whoever said it was right. People spend money because they're happy, because they're depressed, because they have a hot date, because they're dateless, because they have a job interview, because they just got a new job, because they were fired. Spending money is one of the easiest things to do; it's a hobby at which even a novice can excel. Which is why, without a savings plan, the tendency is to spend all of the money you earn, and then some. The solution? Set aside a percentage of every paycheck for your savings plan and adjust your thinking to believe that you earn less than you actually do.

Every book on fiscal planning gives the same advice: "Pay yourself first." (I know it sounds weird.) What the financial wizards advise is to take ten percent of every paycheck and put it into savings. Ideally, the money will be directly deposited by your employer into your savings account so you never even see it. (Some employers don't have direct deposit plans; in that case deposit the money into savings yourself when you deposit the bulk of your check into your regular bank account.) The idea is that you don't miss what you never had in the first place. If you rely on your own thrifty intentions, the money will probably never make it into savings. If you wait until the end of the month and vow to put whatever you have left over from your paycheck into savings, you'll be surprised how often you have nothing left at the end of the month. And the strange thing is that even if you get a raise, you'll still manage to spend your entire salary by month's end.

As the director of communications for a nonprofit based in Seattle, I was earning a reasonably comfortable salary. The cost of living in Seattle is relatively low. Still, I managed to spend my bimonthly paycheck with ease. One day, I had a conversation with a co-worker about banking. We were talking about interest rates and different kinds of bank accounts—boring stuff—and I told him that I keep all of my money in a checking account. He suggested I open a savings account as well, and deposit into my checking account only enough money to cover my expenses. The rest, he said, should be put into a savings account. I knew that from the amount I was earning, I should have managed to save at least a bit, and since I hadn't, I decided to give his idea a try. Within a few months, I had saved enough to buy a used car, and when I left Seattle a year later, I had accumulated enough to cover the costs of my relocation. Not much, but enough, and a world of difference it made. Even though I had previously been spending my entire paycheck, I found that I was able to live just as well on quite a bit less. Where had the extra money been going? No idea. I never missed it.

The amount you save will depend on the amount you earn and on your expenses. You might experiment with different amounts in order to learn how much (or little) you really *need* to pay your bills and live comfortably. Eventually you'll want to save at least ten percent of your salary. For now, however, don't pressure yourself to save the magic ten percent; figure out the amount that's right for you. Getting into the habit of saving a fixed amount—any amount, really—every month is what matters. Another strategy is to work toward having three months salary put away in your savings account. That way, you'll have money that you can readily access in time of need—such as, for example, between jobs.

The Games People Play. Putting money into savings right when you get your paycheck is the best way to make sure the money actually makes it into your savings account. But how can you ensure that the money stays there? It's hard to stick to a budget or to resist impulse buying if you know you have money in the bank. That's why it's important to know yourself and your spending habits; that way you can develop a system that's realistic for you. Here's how some people do it:

- Jillian lives in New York but keeps her savings in a checking account in Boston. To make a withdrawal, she needs to write a check from her Boston account, deposit it into her New York account, and wait five days for it to clear. "I know it sounds ridiculous," she says, "but if I want money, I really have to think about it and plan in advance. It solves the problem of impulse spending."
- Tina keeps an ATM card for her checking account only. "If I want to withdraw money from my savings account I have to go into the bank," she says. "I know myself well enough to know that I wouldn't save a dime if I could easily access my savings. And this way, I can't withdraw money during the weekend when my spending is highest."
- Tom withdraws a set amount of money from the bank at the beginning of the week. "That money has to last for the entire week," he explains. "If I spend it by Tuesday, I'm out of luck. But I find that what happens is I think about my spending much more. The whole thing becomes a kind of game; the point is to have enough money left for the weekend. So far, I haven't lost.

Different Kinds of Savings

Once you reconcile yourself to saving money on a regular basis, the question becomes where to put the money that you're saving. (No, your sock drawer will not work just fine.) There are different reasons to save money (e.g., creating a safety net, saving for your future goals, saving for your immediate goals, saving for retirement—yes, retirement), and the purpose of your saving prescribes the method that makes the most sense. If you are saving for retirement, for example, you'll want to take advantage of your employer's 401K plan (a system in which part of your salary is deducted, tax deferred,* and invested in a retirement account) or open an IRA (Individual

---

*Tax deferred means that you postpone paying taxes on your earnings until you begin making withdrawals; in the case of a 401K plan, that's when you're 59½ or if you become permanently disabled.

Retirement Account). There are myriad accounts, investments, and other options of places to put your money, and figuring out what makes sense for you can be confusing enough to make you want to forego the entire endeavor altogether.

Many banks have specialists who will be happy to meet with you free of charge to discuss your finances. (You should take their advice with a grain of salt because they are not exactly neutral advisors; they'll most likely recommend that you use the services offered by their bank.) I recommend you check out the following books to help you make sense of your personal finances:

- *The Wall Street Journal Guide to Understanding Personal Finance,* by Kenneth M. Morris and Alan M. Siegel (Lightbulb, 1994). Self-touted as "An easy-to-understand, easy-to-use primer that helps take the mystery out of personal finance," this guide presents loads of factual information (with fascinating historical trivia sprinkled throughout), in an extremely visual and user-friendly manner. A handy resource for those who break out in hives at the mere mention of "escrow" or "risk ratio," it covers everything from what a check is to the benefits of a Unite Investment Trust. Invaluable.
- *Personal Finance for Dummies,* by Eric Tyson (IDG Books, 1994). This book covers a wide range of finance issues including managing your finances, saving, and investing. It includes tips, information, and advice, and provides a thorough overview of the subject. If the shoe fits, read it.

Taxes, or Why to Dread the Month of April

My television debut was on the evening news, April 14, my first year out of college. The segment was called something like, "Morons Who Wait Until the Last Minute to File Tax Returns"; it was filmed at H&R block and it wasn't exactly how I had envisioned my fifteen minutes of fame.

From this point on, chances are you'll be filing a tax return every year. Chances are also that your tax return will get progressively more complicated as you start a family, purchase a home, and in other ways develop a more complicated financial portfolio. The best

thing to do is to get into the habit now (just in case there's any confusion, "now" does not mean next year) of keeping your records organized and filing your taxes in timely fashion.

Why Bother? It's really very simple. If you don't file your taxes
you are breaking a federal law. Taxes may be, as Justice Oliver
Wendell Holmes, Jr. said, "what we pay for civilized society," but
you can bet that if the payment were optional, very many people
would opt for the jungle. Think of the process as the way to settle
your account with the government. Throughout the year, taxes are
taken from your paycheck. You fill out tax returns to make sure that
the amount deducted wasn't too high or too low. Then, to make the
process just a little more complicated, you add in to the equation
other monies you have—like bank accounts and investments—on
which you also must pay taxes. Finally—this is where it gets complex and sometimes even creative—there are deductions you can
take (that means you lower the amount of income on which you have
to pay taxes) for a whole host of things, including charitable donations and dependents.

Nuts and Bolts. The United States has a progressive tax structure, which means that people who earn more money are taxed at a
higher rate than those with lower incomes.

Taxes must be filed by midnight on April 15. (If April 15 falls on
a Saturday or Sunday, taxes are due on the Monday following.) If
you don't earn the minimum taxable amount, you don't have to pay
taxes. So if you worked for only part of the year or made a very, very
small salary, it's worth looking into. (Check the 1040 Tax Brochure
or call the IRS.) If you do not fall into that category, you'll need to
pay federal taxes—and unless you live in Alaska, Florida, Nevada,
South Dakota, Texas, Washington, or Wyoming, you'll have to pay
state taxes as well. (New Hampshire and Tennessee require taxes on
unearned income only.)

Sometime in January, you'll receive an official-looking form in
the mail from your employer(s). This is the W-2 form, a copy of
which your employer will also be filing. It is the principle basis for
your tax returns, and you need to submit part of this form with your
tax return, so *do not throw it out*. Check to see that your name and
social security number are correct, and file the W-2 away in your tax

folder. You may also be getting forms from your bank or other institutions where you have savings or investments. Make sure to file these with the rest of your tax information.

You'll get your IRS tax forms in the mail; if you don't, you can pick them up at the local post office, library, or at the town hall. If you're having trouble finding the forms, call the IRS at (800) TAX FORM [829-3676]. And be patient; in season, it usually takes approximately forever for the IRS to pick up, and that's after you've spent absurd amounts of time winding your way though their recorded menu of choices. Your state tax form, too, should arrive in the mail. If you don't get it, go look for it. Remember, the burden is on you.

There are three versions of the federal form for people with different filing status, earnings, deductions, and credits.

1. *1040EZ.* If you are single and earn less than $50,000, you're in luck (in respect to taxes, anyway). You can fill out the 1040EZ, which is a simple one-page, double-sided form with just nine questions. (But remember, don't feel bad if even this form stumps you. It was for none other than the 1040EZ that I sought relief at H&R Block in the final hour.)

2. *1040A.* This is a slightly more complicated form than the 1040EZ and should be used if you earn less than $50,000 but have to report income from several sources and/or take IRA deductions.

3. *1040.* A majority of taxpayers fill out a 1040 form, which is the most complex version and contains sixty plus items. This form allows the taxpayer to take advantage of all the deductions and adjustments the law allows. My feeling is that if you're just out of school and you're earning enough money to require a 1040 form, you're earning enough money to pay somebody to help you with your taxes. If you can do it alone, more power to you. (You may want to invest in a computer program that prepares your taxes for you. You feed it the information, it does all the calculations and actually prints out your return. No, it does not sign your check to the IRS. Check out the various programs at your local software store.)

The Process

1. After you have all your W-2 forms, your filing forms, any other receipts or financial information you're going to use for filing your taxes, and your calculator, you're ready to complete this exercise. While you're at it, get a few extra forms in case you make a mistake. The instructions contained in the tax booklets will lead you through the forms.

2. If you don't understand the instructions, seek help. The IRS has many free booklets to help you with tax issues; you can get these at your local IRS office or by calling the IRS. You might want to ask a parent or friend who has filled out taxes before to help you. You can also walk into your local IRS office (find the address in the phone book under "Government Agencies") and ask for an "assistor." If all else fails, consider paying a professional tax preparer, whether a national agency like H&R Block or an accountant.

3. When your returns are complete, proofread them carefully and recalculate your arithmetic. (Here's where a computer tax program comes in especially handy.)

I have a friend who asked her sister, a Department of Revenue employee, to fill out her tax forms for her. The sisters' social security numbers differed by just one numeral and the sister accidentally filled in her own social security number instead of that of the tax filer. The IRS, therefore, received two tax forms with the same social security number and no tax form with my friend's social security number, which led to a series of problems that took a year for the sisters to straighten out. Go over your tax forms carefully to prevent trivial errors. In the eyes of the IRS, nothing is trivial.

4. Tax booklets come with preaddressed envelopes to make submitting your form a little easier. If the envelope is missing, you can put the form in a regular envelope and address it to the IRS office indicated in the tax booklet. You also have the option of filing your taxes electronically. For a fee, a professional tax preparer can file your taxes directly from a computer to the IRS. You get your refund quicker when you file electronically, so if you are

getting a refund and you need the money in less than the four to eight weeks it usually takes, you might want to think about electronic filing. Otherwise, mail in your taxes and save the fee.

5. If you can't file your taxes on time, you do have the option of filing for a four-month automatic extension. You'll need to fill out an *Application for Automatic Extension of Time to File U.S. Individual Income Tax Return* by April 15. But note: The extra time is just for filing the return, not for paying the money you owe. Delay sending the money and you'll owe hefty interest. Unless there are extenuating circumstances, if you're going to go through the effort of finding the necessary form and figuring out how to fill it out correctly—which is the only way you'll know how much you'll have to pay—why not file the return at the same time?

6. Don't flip out. If you make an honest mistake on your tax returns, you're not going to end up in jail. People end up in jail for committing tax fraud, not for committing tax mistakes. (In my second year out of school, I was determined to fill out my own returns and not risk the humiliation of being on the news a second time. My returns were a little bit tricky since I had been a part-year resident in two different states, and I made a mathematical error. In the end, the mistake caused a slight delay and an adjustment in my refund.)

Getting—and Staying—Organized

All tax mistakes, however, are not created equally. Sure the IRS didn't care much about my mistake; I was only off by about twenty-five dollars. But when the IRS suspects that you've significantly miscalculated (innocently or not-so) your tax return, they can ask you to produce your records for closer examination. That examination is called an audit. In 1990, for example, approximately one percent of individual tax returns were audited.*

That's probably not going to happen to you now, but you're required to keep your records for three years just in case. It's also a good idea to get in the habit of keeping your financial paperwork,

*Kenneth M. Morris and Alan M. Siegel, *The Wall Street Journal Guide to Understanding Personal Finance* (Lightbulb, 1992), p. 171.

because your chances of being audited increase as your financial portfolio becomes more complicated. Still not convinced? Think about the following:

- Though we'd like to believe that computers are incapable of erring (especially when we're 35,000 feet above the ground), the fact is that nobody, not even a computer, is perfect. If you get a bank statement that doesn't correlate with the amount of money you think you have in your account, you'll have a much better case if you have the records (e.g., canceled checks, receipts) to back it up.
- As you earn more money and—these two always go hand in hand—spend more money and diversify your investments, it ought to be of some interest to you to be able to look back over your accounts and analyze where your money is coming from and where it's going.

Keeping your records, however, won't do you much good if you can't find them. You'll want to organize all your paperwork in one place. Taking the time now to do this will save time (otherwise spent searching for receipts, warranties, bank statements), money (otherwise spent buying new products when you've lost warranties and receipts), and energy (otherwise spent castigating yourself for not being organized) in the future.

Buy a few file folders or one accordion-style folder and label it "Finances." You should have separate folders for warranties, unpaid bills, paid bills, receipts, bank statements, bank withdrawal slips, and canceled checks. Put your files in a desk drawer or some other accessible place and make a commitment to file your records as you acquire them so that they don't get thrown out, used as scratch paper, or buried under a six-foot-high pile of newspapers that you have every intention of recycling.

If you choose to file unpaid bills instead of paying them immediately upon receipt, designate a date as the monthly day to pay bills. You might want to schedule the day to coincide with the time of month you pay rent or around the time you receive your paycheck. Since most bills provide a one-month "grace" period before payment is due, it doesn't make much difference exactly when you pay them, as long as it's within the billing cycle.

What is critical, though, is that you pay your bills on time. Tardy payment can result in penalties far more severe than having your phone or gas service temporarily shut off. If you pay bills late, you run the risk of developing bad credit, and that can hound you far into the future. Banks look at credit history very closely to determine whether or not to extend a loan and on what terms to charge interest. Not only will you have difficulty getting a loan if you have a bad credit history (which could hinder your ability to purchase a house or a car), you might even run into trouble renting your next apartment. (Most landlords run a credit check before agreeing to rent.)

You're probably not going to earn—at first—the amount you'd like to or think you deserve to earn. (Most people never do.) But if, after the initial shock of your take-home salary subsides, you start to develop good budgeting, saving, and organizational habits, you'll find that your paycheck lasts longer and that your savings are fruitful and multiply.

10. One More Piece to Put in Place: You

The first few months after college are typically spent attending to the dizzying array of details that accompany your transition—finding an apartment, roommates, furniture, a job, friends, and so forth. You're so busy running from job interview to real-estate agent to Goodwill that you haven't the time nor the energy to consider the emotional aspects of your move. Then, when the practical elements finally begin to fall into place, you're ready to sit back and breathe a huge sigh of relief. Designing a pattern for your new life was undoubtedly stressful and confusing; now you should be able to relax.

Unfortunately, your sigh of relief is usually followed—within a few minutes or a few months—by an equally deep sigh of despair. Because now that you've stitched together the pieces of your new life, you have to put it on and wear it . . . and just as it takes a while for your new jeans to fit perfectly, it will be some time before your new life feels cozy. You may even need to make a few alterations before it fits properly, feels right. And in the meantime, you may experience some minor (or even not so minor) discomfort.

Once upon a time, life was less complicated. You knew what was expected of you and you were given grades to let you know how well you were doing. Your friends were all pretty much moving along at the same pace as you and your parents' aspirations for you matched your own. You had enough time in the day to accomplish everything you had to, and then some.

Now you're in the Real World, where life isn't quite so simple. Here, you can do virtually anything you want to do (within the law and within your means), which means you have to figure out *what* you want to do. Here, lacking a formal structure of evaluation, you may find yourself measuring your own progress in life against that of your friends. Here, your friends do their thing and you do yours. Here, you may want to go in one direction and feel yourself pulled in another by your parents. Here, different facets of your life compete for your time, and the competition is sometimes stiff. Here, you will find myriad sources of pressure and stress.

Many of the issues you'll struggle with as you find your place in the world have no simple solution. If it were as easy to give instructions for coping with parental expectations, self-doubt, disconnectedness, and so forth, as it is for, say, painting a room, there would be a huge number of psychotherapists out of work. But just because there's no easy solution doesn't mean there's no way to lessen the negative impact of stressful situations. What follows, first, is an exploration of some of the different kinds of pressure you're likely to encounter, and then, some strategies for coping with them (You'll find general stress-management techniques at the end of the chapter, so don't get discouraged that some pressures don't have ready solutions.)

Staying Afloat

In college, you knew what was expected of you; you knew the rules of the game. Now, the very same things that make your transition exciting—freedom, independence, responsibility, and so forth, are likely as well to be the cause of considerable anxiety. Forget about not knowing the rules; you may not even be clear about what game you're suddenly playing.

"I have no life," my friend Lara lamented when my sister, Nomi, answered the phone. I was a year or two out of college, home for the weekend to visit my family. Mistaking my sister's voice for mine, Lara jumped right in to one of our typical conversations. Though most of us under normal circumstances would find Lara's comment at least mildly worrisome, my sister calmly handed me the phone. She was a survivor of post-college angst and therefore understood Lara's lament perfectly. Our dialogue was, as usual, a debate about which one of us had less of a life than the other. (We had had loads of practice with this form of argument in college, when the subject was which one of us had more work to do and, inevitably, which one had in fact done less.)

> "At least you're not answering phones eight hours a day."
> "That's true, I'm not. I'm not even answering phones once a day because not one of the one hundred people who received my resume last week has called me."
> "Okay, but at least you have a boyfriend to hang out with while you're not working. I'd much rather be doing that than going in to my ridiculous office every day."
> "Great, so Jon and I can starve together. If one of us had a job, we'd be able to go out to dinner once in a while instead of eating with five roommates every night, no offense."

The situation we were in, though not unusual, was frustrating and stressful, but "no life"? What was that all about?

Up until that point, our lives had been structured for us. We knew when classes started, when they finished, and what assignments were due when. We were students, most of our friends were students, and that was a very major part of how we defined ourselves. College was a contained structure and as dutiful cogs in that structure, we knew what we were about. It is an immense and potentially disabling frustration suddenly to lose the structure and to have to figure out for yourself what you're about.

> My friend Eli graduated from college with a degree in philosophy. "What does one do with a degree in philosophy," he asks, "sit around and think?" But he wasn't really concerned with career issues because he planned to travel to Israel and live on a kibbutz for a while. A friend and fellow philosophy major was speaking

with Eli a couple of months before graduation. "I think I'll go to the kibbutz with you," said the friend. "What do you mean?" Eli asked. "You don't have any interest in living on a kibbutz." "I know," the friend replied, "but I'm just so jealous that you know what you're going to do."

To complicate matters, just as this process of self-evaluation is beginning, it seems that everybody you bump into wants to know how you plan to spend the rest of your life. And if you don't have a quick and acceptable response, be prepared to get some advice. As in, "Plastics." (If you haven't yet seen *The Graduate*, rent it.) It's amazing how so many people know the key to your happiness, even if they hardly know *you*, when you graduate.

Societal Expectations

When Douglas Coupland coined the phrase Generation X in his book of the same name, he became a reluctant voice of our generation, and sociologists and writers and other people who spend their time thinking about such things seized on the term. Our generation became characterized as generally lazy, indifferent, and self-involved. We are, we were told, "slackers" and "twenty-nothings." These days, if you don't start working in a "respectable" field the day after graduation, you have the feeling that society's censors are turning up their noses in disdain and saying something like "Hmm, typical. Young people today really are so apathetic."

My friend Mo decided to spend the summer after graduation waitressing and taking some time to figure out what her next move in life might be. Though she was personally content with the decision, she felt she needed to offer an explanation to her customers. "When I ask my customers if they want fries with their burger, I feel like adding the fact that I graduated from B.U. and that I'm considering going to culinary school," she told me. "I feel like people make assumptions about me based solely on the fact that I'm waitressing right now. It's embarrassing."

I worked at the Gap when I first moved to Seattle. I figured that the evening and weekend work would allow me the time I needed for a job search. (See? I'm still making excuses.) I often found myself getting into lengthy discussions with the customers about my job search and giving them far more information than they cared to have about my educational background. At the time, I thought it was a great way to network. Everybody shops at the Gap. Maybe I'd meet a future employer. Looking back, however, I realize that part of my need to overshare came from my desire to let people know that I was a serious person, not "just" a salesperson. I wanted people to know that I knew a whole lot more than just the difference between Slim Fit, Classic Fit, and Loose Fit.

Parental Expectations

If you don't feel pressured enough by society, how about some parental pressure? Many parents (most?) have high expectations for their kids. Maybe it's because they want your life to be easier than theirs was. Maybe they want to know that you'll continue to live in the lifestyle in which you were raised. Maybe they feel that after all of the money they've invested in your education you ought to be using it for something "productive." Maybe they expect that you'll follow the sterling examples of your older sisters and brothers. Who knows? Who cares?

More interesting, for our purposes, is how those expectations make you feel and how they affect the choices that you make. Your parents have presumably been your major source of support (financial and otherwise) for the better part of your life. Now, your more or less conscious disposition may well be to follow a course that will make them proud—even if that means not following a path of your own choosing. All the more so if you don't really have a path of your own choosing. For many of us, moving on in the direction we think our parents prefer is the path of least resistance. "I didn't just feel obligated to my parents for paying sixty grand for me to attend a private high school and another one hundred thousand so I could go to an exclusive college," a friend of mine says. "I felt obligated to them for giving me life." You may feel that the least you can do in return for all they've done for you is live up to their expectations (in terms of the career that you choose, where you choose to settle, who you choose to spend your time with, and/or any other aspirations they have for you).

Sometimes it's not easy to distinguish between our own choices and our parents'. After all, their expectations—sometimes made explicit, often left implicit—have been with us for a very long time. Early on, before we were able to distinguish between what we want and what is expected of us, they became part of our way of looking at the world and at our own place in it.

You know people who in the third grade said they were going to be doctors or lawyers when they grew up, just like their parents. You run into them thirteen years later and sure enough, they're premed or studying for the LSAT. In some cases, they go on to pursue medical or legal careers, become immensely successful, and are professionally fulfilled. But some—in all likelihood more—realize, whether through an epiphany or through the grappling with a persistent sense of discomfort, that they do not in fact want to be doctors or lawyers. Accepting that realization and acting upon its implications can be painful for both the child (that's you) and the parents.

My friend Ethan says he had general levels of accomplishment and clear professional expectations set out before him by his parents, as he tells it, "from the time I was old enough to understand what an expectation was." He silently and unquestioningly absorbed the expectations throughout his childhood. Programmed to become an attorney, he took the LSAT during his senior year of college. His first year out of college, while he completed law school applications, he took a job teaching at a private high school. "My parents viewed teaching as a time out—something nice for me to do before I got a real job. I loved it, but I felt like my familial obligation was to become a lawyer, so while I was teaching I took the Princeton Review to improve my LSAT scores. I hired somebody to help me on my application essay and I paid another person to type all of the applications. I applied to thirteen schools and I didn't get accepted to one. In the meantime, I was physically ill throughout the entire application process. I must have sabotaged my applications, because I scored in the 56th percentile on the LSAT. I was at the ninety-sixth percentile on the GRE; I know how to take a standardized test. I immersed myself in teaching. My parents decided to send me to a private vocational counselor where I was given twenty hours of career assessment tests. I answered each and every question the way I thought someone inclined toward law would answer it; the results all said I should be a social studies teacher." Ethan's been teaching for a few years now and has absolutely no professional complaints. "I guess at that time I wasn't prepared emotionally to make my own decision. I couldn't be a disappointment; I couldn't be a rebel. Then I got married and my priorities and my loyalties changed. Now, I couldn't be happier."

I could probably fill an entire chapter with the stories of friends of mine whose parents pressured them to pursue a legal career. And that's only the beginning. I know people who became teachers, accountants, and doctors to please their parents. I know people who are living in a city that their parents approve of even though they'd prefer to be somewhere else. Sometimes things work out, and the course that makes your parents happy turns out to be the course that makes you happy, too. But when you have little interest in your parents' ambitions for you, there's no quick and easy solution. Some of my friends endured years of therapy in order to find the courage to stand up to their parents. Some people I know distanced themselves (physically and/or emotionally) from their parents, and a couple of my friends spent some time following their parents' dream before changing direction. And yes, there are those I know who remain in situations that they don't like because their parents want them to.

I couldn't possibly give you advice about how to deal with your particular case. But at the risk of oversimplifying, ask yourself if the path you are choosing is a road *you've* chosen or if it's been staked out by somebody else. How does it relate to your interests, your values, your goals? Ultimately, you are the one that has to live your life; you should be the one to direct its course.

Self-Expectations

Just to make your life a little more complicated, you may also be struggling with fulfilling your own expectations of yourself. What happens when you have an idea of where you think you ought to be by now, whether in your career or personal life—and you aren't quite (or even nearly) there? "I always wanted to go on to graduate school after college," a friend of mine says, "but my grades weren't high enough for me to be accepted into the programs that interested me. Now I'm working to get practical experience to strengthen my applications. My self-esteem has definitely suffered from the setback."

You may feel that after investing so much time and money in your education, you ought to be prepared for a highly skilled job. The truth, though, is that many majors do a better job of teaching you how to think or reason or write than they do in preparing you with the practical skills you'll likely need in the world of work. You may, therefore, find yourself in a job that you feel you could have done just as well without a college education. Or you may not even find a job for a few months, and that will be demoralizing. We've all had fantasies about what our lives would be like postcollege (I'll be running my own advertising agency and I'll meet Brad Pitt on a photo shoot and we'll have a wild, passionate affair.) Most of us had realistic expectations as well. (I'll get a copy-writing job in an advertising agency and I'll start dating someone who didn't go to my school.) If the reality doesn't match the expectations (I'm answering phones in an advertising agency and the closest I've come to a date is having lunch with my cousin David), you may feel that you've let yourself down.

Failure to fulfill your expectations of yourself is completely different from failure to fulfill the expectations of others. When the expectations are your own, you can presume that fulfilling them is something that interests you. Ask yourself, then, were your expectations realistic in the first place or were they confused with your fantasies? (Fantasies are wonderful until they obscure realistic expectations.) Have your expectations changed along with your interests or goals? Are the expectations you've set for yourself still valid—that is, still what you really want for yourself, or are they hangovers from an earlier time? If they still describe what, upon reflection, you want, what steps do you need to take in order to get closer to their fulfillment? In many cases, it will simply be a matter of time before you get there. (You'll be promoted from answering phones to assistant copywriter and your cousin David will introduce you to his roommate, who didn't go to your school, and with whom you'll fall madly in love.)

Will Somebody Please Let Me Know How I'm Doing?

Without the structure of finishing one grade and moving on to the next, you may well find yourself gauging your own advancement against that of your friends. It starts when you're still looking for a job and your friends, one by one, call to tell you they've been hired. Then, when you're still making fifteen thousand dollars annually and your friends are making three or four times that, watch out. If you're all playing the dating game together and your two best friends find seemingly perfect mates, you probably aren't going to feel one hundred percent elated for them. For the first time, your friends' success may actually make you feel miserable about yourself. It's not (I hope) that you begrudge your friends their success, but you want to be succeeding at the same pace as they. Your feelings can be especially troubled if your friends and you are pursuing the same kinds of things.

"When I graduated," says Beth, "I temped for several months. I would talk to my friends who had all of these cool environmental jobs—exactly what I was looking for—and I felt like such a loser for being unemployed. They told me to take advantage of my freedom, but I couldn't really enjoy that time because I was just so focused on getting a job."

"When my friends who are in different fields from mine call to tell me about their promotions or raises," says Joe, "it's the greatest feeling. I'm genuinely happy for them. But when friends of mine in the finance world [Joe's field] get promoted, it's a different story. Of course I want them to get promoted, but I want to be getting promoted along with them. I grit my teeth and tell them how cool it is—and then I hang up the phone and go to the bar. I

know I sound like a horrible friend, but I think I'm just being honest. It's hard to be completely happy for somebody who gets what
you want. When my friend from college who now works in the
film industry gets hired on new movies, all the friends in our
group get totally depressed. None of us is pursuing a film career,
but it makes us feel like our lives are boring."

My friend Donna had planned to return to her college for a re-
union the year after she graduated. "All of my friends were going
to get together; we'd been talking about it since our graduation,"
Donna explains. "I started dreading it about two months earlier. I
knew that most of my friends had great jobs, but I hadn't yet
found what I wanted to do. I felt as if everybody expected me to
be doing something interesting, but the truth was that I was a secretary. In the end I went and had a great time. We didn't even talk
about our new lives; we were too busy reminiscing about our old
ones. Two months of worry—for nothing."

I've been on both the receiving and the giving end of this phenomenon, and neither is much fun. During my three-month tenure at
the Gap, it was hard to talk to my friends about their "real" jobs. The
fact that I sold the most tee shirts and was chosen employee of the
week somehow didn't quite compare to my friend's three-thousand-
dollar bonus. But later, when I was the one getting the bonuses in
my publishing jobs, I knew there were certain friends with whom
it would be wise—and kind—to talk about other things. The friends
who were unhappy in their own careers, and the ones who subtly
(they thought) changed the subject when I began to talk about something positive at work didn't need to hear about my bonus.

One way to avoid bad feelings is not to talk about salary with your
friends. When you feel the need to boast about your raise or bonus,
call your parents; they'll be genuinely happy for you. If you need
more, call your grandparents. Under no circumstances may you call
the parents of your friends.

But that doesn't resolve the fundamental issue: You and your
friends are no longer going to enter and exit life's major phases on
the same schedule. Not only will you have to confront the fact that
your friends might find a job or a beloved before you do (or vice

versa), but that when they do, their priorities and interests may change. You may find quite simply, but painfully as well, that you have less in common with them. One solution, obviously, is for you to get a job of which you're proud, or to become involved in a relationship. But in the meantime, it might make it easier if you:

- Remember that the grass always seems greener on the other side of the fence. You might be envious of your friend's promotion but she might have been working eighty-hour weeks while you've been out meeting new friends and becoming involved in your community. Would you want her promotion if it meant giving up a personal life?
- Enjoy each phase to the fullest. Beth's friends were right when they told her to enjoy her freedom during the job search. Rest assured that you will find a job, you will get a promotion, you will meet a lover. And when you do, you'll probably miss aspects of your pre-job (freedom), pre-promotion (less work), pre-lover (independence) life. As long as you're stuck, you might as well take advantage of the fact that you can go to a matinee or spontaneously take off for the weekend.
- Expand your social circle and get involved in new activities. When you're happy personally, it's much easier to be happy for your friends. You'll have friends who are in many different phases of life and that will make your own life more interesting. If you have only one friend in your new city and he becomes involved with somebody, you're going to be less than enthusiastic. But when you have different friends and a rich personal life, you'll find that you're genuinely happy for your friend.

Learning to Balance

Time is the least thing we have of.
—Ernest Hemingway

In college, having more than two classes on the same day was perceived as a heavy schedule. When you didn't see your friends for the entire day you felt out of touch. Now you're going to be working eight hours a day (at least). Tack on pre- and post-work commutes, grocery shopping and other errands, and you aren't left with much free time. Finding enough hours in the day to exercise, meet new friends (and see them once they're met), keep in touch with old friends, and do whatever else you like to do when you have the time to do it, is, to put it mildly, challenging and potentially stressful. But unless you figure out a way to fit a social life and personal time into your regular schedule, work will be the sole focus of your week. And even if you love your job, a one-dimensional existence is, by definition, flat. You want curves, valleys, pinnacles, arches, contours—you want a life with a stimulating shape. Now, all those ups and downs and ins and outs can easily reflect utter chaos, which is no big improvement over life in the rut. The place to start—whether you're starting from wild disorder or from absolute flatness—is with a balanced core.

You don't want to wake up a year or two from now and realize that though you've advanced four levels on your career path, you haven't met a single person since college—and you've gained fifteen pounds to boot. You probably also don't want to find yourself two years out of college with a tight group of friends but still looking for an entry-level job. The idea is to find a balance between your personal, professional, and social life, giving each the attention it deserves.

If life were as simple as doing laundry, there would be a big "out of balance" signal that would flash in front of us when warranted. There are ways, though not quite as manifest, to recognize life's out-of-balance signals. How can you tell when you need to shake things up?

- When you feel like your entire life is about work, you work overtime, and think about work even when you're not there, you need to put some effort into your personal and social life. (Other warning signals: you work most weekends, you turn down social invitations because you have work to do, you keep a pillow and blanket at work for nights when you work late, you haven't done your laundry in three months because you're always working.)
- When you go out six or seven nights a week, stumble into work bleary-eyed and jeopardize your work performance, you need to restore some balance. (Other warning signals: You can't remember your parents' or siblings' names because who has time to keep in touch with family?; you keep a pillow and blanket at

work in case you can sneak in a nap; you haven't done your laundry in three months because you're too busy partying.)

- When you go to work, come home and sit in front of the television five nights a week, and go to the video rental store during your lunch break on Friday to make sure that you get the best pick of weekend rentals, you probably need to invest in some other aspects of your life. (Other warning signals: you look forward to *Saved by the Bell* reruns; you're on a first-name basis with the pizza delivery man; you only own three pairs of underwear because who needs more now that you do your laundry so frequently.)

When you feel generally blah about one or more dimension(s) of your life, you need to rethink what you are doing to achieve your personal goals in that area. If you're stressed out much of the time because you feel you simply can't get everything done, it's time to get some balance.

Here are some general ideas to get you started:

- *Love the weekend but don't live for it.* When you spend the entire week counting the hours until 5:00 P.M. Friday, you're wasting 104 hours of the week. You also put so much pressure on the weekend that unless it's perfect, you end up disappointed. Moreover, you become susceptible to a serious case of Sunday Night Blues, the depression that comes with knowing the weekend's over and that you have a whole week of work ahead of you before the next one. To avoid this dismal scenario, try to schedule something that's fun to do a couple of nights during the week so you have something to look forward to before the weekend arrives. If it's possible, meet friends for lunch during the week so you have something social to do during the day, too. Make your work week more interesting; it is, after all, five days.
- *Leave your work at work.* The major advantage of being in an entry-level position is that you are unlikely to have work-related responsibilities after hours. (As you advance in your career, you may well find that you're either working or thinking

about your work virtually all the time.) Enjoy your freedom; don't worry about work when you're not there. And if you find that you're frequently bringing home work, perhaps you need to rethink your productivity level at the workplace.

- *Take care of personal things during the workday so you have less you "have" to take care of during your off hours.* The development (and success) of service companies that do people's errands for them proves how difficult it can be to get personal things done when working full-time. Since you probably can't afford to hire one of those companies, however, you need to figure out the most efficient and least invasive way to get your personal errands done. If you work in the city, you can take advantage of your lunch hour to get quite a bit accomplished. I have one friend who drives to work and brings a cooler with her so she can do her grocery shopping during lunch. If you commute via public transportation, pay your bills and write letters to friends while riding. (It's said that Toni Morrison wrote *Beloved* during her daily commute.) If you work in a remote area and you drive to work, you won't be able to take care of as many personal things during the workday, so consider designating one night a week for grocery shopping, laundry, and other tasks you need to do. The idea is to have a regular time to get things done so you don't always feel like you have a huge "to do" list hanging around your neck.

- *Make a concerted effort to see your local friends and to keep in touch with your long-distance ones.* It's hard to get used to the idea of having to make an effort to see friends. In school, you had to make an effort to get away from them. It's great if you can find friends who live in your building or work in your office; you might actually have a chance of seeing them once in a while. But when your friends are working and living miles away, working different hours, dating people you don't know, it can be difficult to schedule time to see each other. Try to find a way to work friends into your regular schedule: work out together, do errands together, go to the laundromat together. These are all things you have to do anyway—why not catch up with your friends at the same time? It will be even more difficult to coordinate schedules with your long-distance friends, and you'll probably find that (notwithstanding your vows of eternal friendship) you lose touch with some. With luck, they're the ones you don't feel are worth the effort. Get into a routine for keeping in touch with the others. Whether you talk every Tuesday night or the first of every month or write to one person a week, find a system that works for you and stick to it. Your friends can provide invaluable support during your transition.

- *Treat yourself; you deserve it.* So you're sticking to your budget and you're saving money and you can't remember what a menu looks like or that the smell of department stores nauseates you. Once in a while, it's important to reward yourself. Go out for an expensive meal or buy five new CDs or spend the weekend in a romantic inn with your new girlfriend. It's important to splurge once in a while, to reward yourself for working hard and saving money. After all, you probably don't have to account to anybody but yourself right now for how you spend your money. So go ahead and indulge.

But don't make a habit out of it.

- *Don't rely on work as your sole source of intellectual stimulation.* In college, one of the principal purposes of your day was, presumably, intellectual stimulation. You were surrounded by people who were involved in intellectual pursuits and you had books and professors to help foster your intellectual development. Now you're answering phones in a dentist's office. Or typing memos or writing copy for advertisements or programming computers or whatever. Think of your mind as a muscle; don't let it atrophy. Read the newspaper, read books, keep your mind involved in things other than your work. Even if you find your work to be the most intellectually challenging activity in which you've ever engaged, it's still important to stay involved in other intellectual pursuits as well. Because even if through your work you discover the cure for cancer, chances are that your friends will want to discuss other things once in a while, and it would be nice if you were able to contribute to the conversation.
- *Make a personal pact to develop non-work-related aspects of your life.* While at school, your work was graded. At work, too, you'll be graded, with good grades taking the form of praise, a

bonus and/or promotion. In both settings, it's taken for granted that the "grading system" works as an incentive for people to do their best. You tried hard in class because you wanted to get an A; you push yourself at work because you want to advance. There you were given a syllabus, here you're given a job description; both are intended to let you know what you need to accomplish in order to succeed. But there is no comparable system to measure your achievement in other arenas. You don't get an A for joining a reading group and nobody's going to give you a bonus for joining a soccer team or meeting a new group of friends. Nor is anyone is going to hand you guidelines for your successful personal development. You have to take the initiative to expand the nonwork areas of your life, but with the energy that you're going to be putting into your new job, and the energy you're going to expend getting used to the new routine of your life, you might not have much energy left over for personal growth. Ignoring the development of new activities and friendships is one of the easiest ways to fall into a rut.

One way to ensure that each aspect of your life gets equal attention is to set personal non-work-related goals. Your life is not going to become interesting and diverse on its own; you have to put some thought and spirit into it. Think about personal goals you'd like to accomplish and try to come up with three short-term (three to six months) and one long-term (one year) goal in each part of your life. The exercise will force you to give some thought to what you'd like to accomplish over the next year.

Whether or not you successfully fulfill all your personal goals is irrelevant. You might decide that you hate writing in a journal or that you would rather learn to speak Italian than play soccer. The point is to give some thought to developing new dimensions to your life. We're conditioned to think about work before we can even read (e.g., "What do you want to be when you grow up?") and the pressure continues as we mature (e.g., "What on earth do you plan to do with a major in anthropology?" or "What are you going to do after college?" or "How's the job hunt going?"). Nobody ever asks us what new hobbies we've developed or how the friend hunt is going, so once is a while you have to ask yourself. Remember: You work to live and your life is about much more than work.

Physical Health

When your body doesn't feel up to snuff, it's much harder to deal with the pressure in your life. Feeling sick or tired can itself be a source of stress. The first time you get the stomach flu or strep throat after you've moved to your new city is not the time to realize that the student health service is located on the other side of the country and your family doctor is in the same state as your family—a thousand miles away from where you are. You need to find a doctor and a dentist in your new city and you should do so *before* you get sick. The day that you wake up with a 104-degree temperature is not the day to try to find a new local physician to see you. And the day that you have debilitating stomach cramps is not the day that you want to explain to the local doctor who has agreed to squeeze you in that you have a history of gastrointestinal trouble. Establishing rapport with a local doctor means: (1) you'll know whom to call when you get sick; (2) the doctor will have seen you in a healthy state and will therefore have a better gauge of the severity of your symptoms; and (3) the doctor will already have copies of all your medical records. And if you think that you'll be able to get your doctor from back home to prescribe medication over the phone, think again. Many states don't accept out-of-state prescriptions.

Establishing a relationship with a physician involves transferring copies of your medical records (easily taken care of with a fax or letter of authorization) and scheduling regular checkups. There's no universal standard for how often healthy people should have comprehensive medical evaluations, but the general thinking is every two to three years. Healthy women should schedule a gynecological exam once a year and men and women—sorry—should have a dental cleaning every six months.

Though I lived in Michigan for four years, D.C. for one, and Seattle for two, I never found local medical care. My old doctor was just fine, thank you, and the fact that she lived and practiced in Boston only meant that I had to schedule my visits home around my biannual doctor appointments. But when I had a questionable result from a medical exam and needed to schedule an immediate follow-up appointment, it would have been considerably more convenient to walk around the corner to a local doctor than to cough up six hundred dollars for a round-trip plane ticket. It's neither practical, nor cost-effective, nor responsible to be without local medical care.

So: How do you find a primary-care physician and a gynecologist and a dentist in a new city? The first thing to consider is whether or not you have medical insurance and if so, what kind. Your employee benefits administrator should be able to answer any questions you have about your medical insurance options. If you have medical insurance, you'll want to make sure that the doctors you're considering are covered by your plan. You can find out simply by asking the doctor's office or by requesting from your insurance company or employee benefits administrator a list of authorized medical providers.

The best way to find a doctor is through word of mouth. If you have a friend in your new city or a co-worker with whom you feel comfortable, ask if s/he could recommend doctors to you. You can also call your doctor from home and ask for a recommendation of a doctor in your new city. If those approaches fail, call the local hospital and inquire whether it has a referral service. (Most big hospitals do.) A referral service will conduct a short intake interview over the phone, asking you a series of questions along the lines of what kind of insurance you have and if you'd prefer a male or female doctor. The referral agent will find a doctor whose qualifications match your preferences and might even take care of setting up an appointment for you.

However you find the doctor, what's important is that you feel comfortable with him/her. It's perfectly acceptable to schedule a preliminary interview in which you ask all your questions (medical and ethical). You might want to know where the doctor studied medicine or how long s/he's been practicing (why do they call it practicing?) or what his/her feelings are about abortion. Most physicians will meet with you free of charge. (A physician who refuses an initial meeting is not a doctor you want to consider. Look elsewhere.) You should get the feeling that as you get to know the physician, you'll be able to confide in him/her (obviously less important with a dentist than with a general practitioner or gynecologist).

Establishing a personal medical-care system is one of the most important steps in taking responsibility for your health. But let's face it, aside from your regular checkups, you want to visit these new doctors as infrequently as possible. How can you take responsibility for your health—as distinguished from your medical care—on a day-to-day basis?

An Apple a Day . . .

In the Real World, it takes more thought and planning to lead a healthy lifestyle than it did in college. There are two reasons for that: (1) in college you weren't sitting on your butt for eight-plus hours a day—you had more time to be active; (2) in college, you had more time to plan your meals and were probably able to eat more meals at home; you might even have been on a meal plan. In college, you had the time, energy, and inclination to focus on your health and appearance. Now you're going to spend most of your waking hours at a job that may very well be sedentary. If you have to schedule time just to see your best friend, where are you going to find the time to work out and go grocery shopping?

Regular exercise is an essential ingredient to overall general health. It seems as though there's a new study every day proving just how important exercise is and suggesting how much of it is necessary. Exercise not only helps you control your weight, it strengthens your cardiovascular system, fortifies your bones (especially important for women), increases flexibility and strength, and helps relieve stress and lethargy. There are also emotional benefits to exercise, such as increased self-esteem and relaxation.

So why isn't everybody doing it? Two of the most common reasons (excuses) for not exercising are lack of time and lack of energy. After a full day's work, chances are you want to crawl home and sack out on the couch or, alternatively, you need to rush home to get ready for a night out. So how can you fit exercise into your schedule and how can you make the process more enjoyable?

Try scheduling exercise into your day so that it doesn't infringe on your free time. If possible, walk or bike to and from work. If you're an early bird by nature, set your alarm for one hour earlier than usual a few times a week and get your exercise done before you go to work. If there's a gym near your office, try working out during lunch. And if the only realistic time for you to work out is after work, try to draft a friend into becoming your workout buddy. It's somehow less burdensome to work out when you have a friend with whom to do it (and with whom to blow it off on those days when it's just not meant to be).

My first couple of months out of college, I loved being home by 5:30 and not having any work to worry about until 9:00 the following morning. The only problem was, I would get home at 5:30 and be utterly bored until my roommates got home from the gym at 7:00. I decided to check out the gym for purely social reasons. Since all my roommates and most of our other friends belonged to the same gym, it was actually a great place to go after work— except, of course, for the exercise part of it. The only exercise I had done in college was walking to and from class (which was not trivial on a campus the size of the University of Michigan). So I wasn't quite sure what to do at the gym the first several times I went (exercise by osmosis?), but I had the incentive of seeing friends to keep me going. I quickly learned the ropes (which seems, I know, a suspiciously low-tech form of exercise when everybody else was on the treadmill or Stairmaster). Lo and behold, after just a couple of months I felt stronger physically—and I've been working out ever since.

Try to find a form of exercise that you enjoy; you're more likely to stick to the program if you like the activity. The benefits to joining a health club are the social potential it offers (I have three friends who met their girlfriends/boyfriends at the gym), the variety it provides, and the pressure you feel to actually use the gym for which you've paid membership dues. If, however, the thought of other people seeing you in your leotard makes you shudder, you'll probably want to find a more private form of exercise. You might want to consider the cost/benefit of jogging or walking as compared to the cost/benefit of paying fees at a health club. It's also worthwhile to compare the costs of purchasing your own equipment to the cost of a club membership. If the only machine you ever use at the gym is the rowing machine, find out how much it would cost to buy a machine of your own. You may find that you'd pay for it in the equivalent of four months of membership dues.

Clear any home exercise equipment with your roommates first, though. Exercise equipment takes up quite a bit of space. Also, if you live in an apartment building, consider the floor on which you live. My friend Dana invested in a treadmill, planning to work out at 5:30 A.M. each morning before work. Complaints about the noise of the machine from the neighbors in the apartment below hers forced her to stop using it just weeks after she bought it. (You may remember Dana from Chapter 4. She's the one who bought the couch that wouldn't fit through her apartment's narrow door.) Above all, remember that owning a machine doesn't make you healthy; only using it does. This is a point so often overlooked that the collection of used never-used rowing machines, exercycles, treadmills "out there" is well beyond vast. Accordingly, you might ask around and check the classified advertisements before buying a piece of new equipment. Often enough, people will be glad to have you take their stuff off their hands—or, if they still harbor the fantasy that they may end up using it, they may well be prepared to "lend" it to you permanently.

Aside from regular workouts, try to incorporate more physical activity into your standard daily routine. Get into the habit of taking the stairs instead of the elevator at work and at home. Don't automatically jump into your car when you're traveling around your neighborhood, consider a brisk walk instead.

Whatever form of exercise you choose, don't be overly ambitious. If you decide you're going to run ten miles a day or work out five days a week when you're just starting out, you're going to become discouraged very quickly and likely give up the entire endeavor. Set realistic goals both in terms of frequency and activity; increase your activity as your body gets stronger.

As for the "not enough energy to exercise" argument, guess what? Part of the reason you don't have enough energy is that you aren't currently exercising. (Life does have a sense of humor after all, even if we can't always appreciate it.) One thing that all the exercise studies agree on is that physical activity gives you more energy. Just like the idea that you need to spend money to make money (but with a greater guarantee), the fact is that if you expend energy by exercising, you'll feel more energetic. It's the getting started part that's the hardest. Once you get over the hump, you'll be fine, and you'll find yourself thinking of exercise as an integral part of your day.

Eating well is the second essential ingredient in overall health. When you're working full-time, the easiest thing to do is to eat on the run. Pick up a croissant on the way to work, grab some fast food for lunch, and eat whatever you can scrounge up in your refrigerator (leftover pizza?) or pasta for the twelfth night in a row. Popping a couple of "One-A-Day" vitamins whenever you happen to think of it won't compensate for this kind of diet. Nor will three-hour workouts every single day.

Most of my friends are so wiped out when they get home from work that their sole requirement for dinner is that it take minimal energy to prepare, perhaps even to eat. My friend John, a professional chef, has a regular dinner of a peanut-butter sandwich and a bowl of cereal.

By now we all know that saturated fats are bad, fiber is good. But down with fat, up with fiber isn't the only key to a nutritional diet. Eating well means eating a balanced diet (and that doesn't mean balancing pizza with fish and chips). You should eat a variety of foods every day, with an emphasis on fruits, vegetable, grains, and legumes (e.g., peas, beans, etc.). I know, I know—you already know all this. You learned it in second grade, and then again in sixth and ninth. You read it once a week in the newspaper. It's tedious in the extreme, and here I am, repeating it. But it turns out there's a huge gap between knowing and doing.

When you have a busy schedule that includes full-time work, eating well usually means planning meals in advance. If you start thinking about what you're going to have for dinner when you get home from the gym at 7:00 P.M., chances are you're going to wind up in a restaurant or, like John, having a second breakfast for dinner. Get in the habit of buying food for the week every weekend. Cook some meals on Sunday that you can put in the freezer for weeknight dinners. If you eat with roommates, have a different person be responsible for dinner preparation each night. Healthy eating is in vogue now, and you'll find shelves of cookbooks with easy and healthy recipes in any bookstore. Check out *Quick and Healthy Recipes and Ideas*, by Brenda Ponchitera, to get started.

Eating a healthy lunch requires less forethought than dinner. Salad bars are everywhere now, even in most fast-food restaurants. (But remember to hold the french fries.) If you take a short lunch break, consider bringing a sandwich and salad to work. You'll save money, too. Bring some fruit or vegetables to snack on if you get hungry while you're working and keep healthy foods around your apartment; it's more convenient to eat what's there than to bother with a trip to the store. Finally, if you're having trouble establishing a healthy diet, consider scheduling a consultation with a professional nutritionist.

All Stressed Out and Nowhere to Go

If you've survived college, stress is nothing new to you. You've already adapted to a new environment, been through final exams, term papers, finding a date for a formal at the last minute—you've probably dealt with your fair share of stress. Maybe even your unfair share.

But as you've read in this chapter, your life is now likely to become considerably more stressful. It's therefore more important than ever to learn to recognize stress and figure out how to manage it. Many people assume that stress is just a normal part of life and don't, therefore, do anything to contain or contend with it. While it's true that stress is something that everyone experiences, left unmanaged it can become emotionally debilitating and even manifest itself physically. Physical reactions to stress can include headaches, chest pain, abdominal pain, heart palpitations, insomnia, irritability, loss of concentration, and abnormal eating patterns. Many people experience these symptoms and don't recognize them as responses to stress. They either ignore them entirely or fear they're sick, which only exacerbates the situation.

According to Dr. David Chodirker, a family physician in Newton, Massachusetts, stress and the anxiety that often accompanies it are among the most common reasons people seek medical care. Dr. Chodirker says that nearly half the patients he sees each day are there directly or indirectly due to stress and its myriad manifestations.

The best way to reduce stress is to incorporate stress reduction methods into your daily life; exercise and a balanced lifestyle are the most effective of these. A balanced lifestyle lends perspective when any one path of life gets rocky. (If they all get rocky at the same time, forget it.)

But even if you work out regularly and have a great professional, personal, *and* social life, you're going to run into situations that cause you to feel exceptionally stressed or anxious. What's the best way to handle those situations?

1. *Identify the stressor.* It's very common to feel stressed out or anxious and not know why. Sometimes we don't even realize we're stressed; we're just irritable or particularly sensitive. Next time you're feeling unusually tense, take some time and try to figure out what could be causing it. Are you going through a major change in any area of your life? Are you nervous about something you're experiencing at work? Are you experiencing strain with your roommate(s)?

2. *Once you've identified it, deal with it.* Sure, you can ignore it, ride it out, and there's a decent chance it will eventually go away on its own. But that could take a while. Why not fight back instead? If you can identify exactly what it is that's making you feel agitated, you can take control of the situation, dispel the stress, and try to avoid similar triggers in the future. I've spent hours and hours on the phone with friends who were having problems with their roommates. Fearing that a confrontation with their roommate might lead to an exacerbation of the problem, they chose to gripe to others about the situation. One friend of mine suffered in silence over tensions with her roommates until she finally couldn't take it any longer and moved out. She never let her roommates know what was bothering her. When friends tell me that they're annoyed with their roommate's boyfriend living in their apartment or that they wish their roommate wouldn't eat all their food, they get a sympathetic ear—but that brings their problem no closer to a solution. Left to fester, such conflicts usually end with a blowout over something minor or with the roommates splitting up. (I usually go to the opposite extreme: I confront a problem at the first hint of a conflict, and often

make an issue over something that just isn't worth it. Balance, please.)

Dealing with stress situations at work might be a little more tricky. You can't tell your boss you think he's an unreasonable boor just because he's making you feel stressed. But if you feel anxious about work on a regular basis and you have no way to improve the situation, you might want to reevaluate your position. Remember, it is not healthy—literally—to live with unmanaged stress for extended periods of time.

3. *Try new stress-management techniques.* Aerobic exercise, yoga, massage, aromatherapy, meditation, biofeedback, tai chi, sensory deprivation tanks, hobbies, relaxation and visualization exercises are all touted as stress reducers. Do some experimenting and find out what works for you.

4. *Indulge yourself.* When you are in the midst of a particularly stressful time, it's important to treat yourself well. Get a professional massage or take a weekend trip. (Shopping usually works for me, but if that's your method, make sure you don't do it so often that what you owe on your VISA becomes a new source of stress.) If you know the situation is temporary (finishing a major project at work, surviving your roommate's parents' visit), schedule some personal activities that make you happy and take your mind off the problem. Remember though, if the situation is ongoing, you need to confront it. Going shopping won't get rid of your roommate's boyfriend.

5. *Seek medical attention* with your primary-care physician or visit a counselor if the stress causes major dysfunction in any aspect of your life. Some stress is normal, but debilitating stress is not.

Whether or not you face the specific pressures that I've outlined in this chapter, it's a virtual certainty that you will encounter pressures of one sort or another. After all, you are engaged in a major life transition. And transitions, even those that are rich in promise, are never easy. The upside to all this is that there are ways to deal effectively with stress; you've already begun by reading this book.

* * *

Finally:

It may not be much consolation that tens of thousand of others are going through the same transition as you. But remember: Hundreds of thousands more have already survived it. You'll make it, too.

I hope that earlier chapters in this book will help make your transition smoother. But the gnawing pit in your stomach will permanently go away only when you begin to plant roots in your city. You've embarked on an adventure, and if you think of it that way, if you open yourself to surprise and keep a sense of humor (and irony, too), you'll be fine. Even if you only end up staying for a year or two, you'll always know that you've transformed a strange city into a home. Sweet home.

"How Does It Feel to Be on Your Own?"

LIZ: What I liked best was feeling independent, having the freedom to be able to do anything I wanted to do. What I liked least was realizing that I had to pay for those things.

LARA: What I liked best was having so much unstructured time. What I liked least was having nothing to do.

ANDY: I liked the fact that I was moving on. The hardest thing was not knowing the rules of the game.

DANA: The best thing was that I was no longer a student. The hardest thing was becoming independent from my family.

KIM: Knowing that I had an education and feeling free to do whatever I wanted to do were the best things. Being broke and having to pay off the loans that I had incurred was the worst.

LESLIE: I had money coming out of my ears, financial freedom, and I could do anything I wanted to—those were the best things. The worst was the insecurity of a new job. I didn't feel like I belonged; I felt like I was playing dress-up in business clothes.

ROB: The thing I liked best was living alone and feeling that I could do anything I wanted. The hardest thing was people in the job market telling me that I couldn't do what I wanted to do.

SARAH W.: The best thing was having an income; I liked getting a regular paycheck, being able to pay my bills, having money to have fun with and money to save, health benefits, and a 401(k) plan. The hardest part was knowing that I was in the real world and I was never going home again.

PETER: The best thing was having a salary; the worst was the realization that I was going to be working for the rest of my life.

KIRK: The best thing was simply being out of college; I was anxious to move on. The worst thing was living in poverty.

KARA: The best things about life after college were meeting and hanging out with new friends, exploring a new city, not having homework constantly hanging over my head, feeling more of a sense of freedom, and feeling more responsible. The hardest thing was the way relationships changed: Making the transition in a romantic relationship from college to the real world; making the shift from dealing with professors to dealing with bosses.

SARAH L.: I loved being completely anonymous and having a fresh start. The worst things were being so far away from my family, and realizing that I was not going to make a career out of what I had studied in college.

JEN: The best thing was the excitement of starting new and having a clean slate. The worst was the uncertainty of my future.

STEWART: Moving to New York to try a new job was the best thing. The worst was getting my first paycheck—how staggeringly low it was. I had always been told that you were doing okay if you earned your age. My salary was far below how old I was, and I figured that if I got a thousand-dollar raise a year, I'd be in poverty for the rest of my life.

MICHAEL: The best thing was getting a paycheck; the worst was that I had no idea what to do with the rest of my life.

KAREN: The best things for me were getting a paycheck, setting up my apartment, learning my way around a new neighborhood, and moving by myself across the country—feeling independent. The hardest part was feeling insecure at work and not having a formal structure to let me know how I was doing. As a teacher, I had to rely on myself to know how I was doing and I was very self-critical.

SCOTT: The best thing was making my own money and spending it however I chose. The hardest thing was having to cook after a long day and not being able to simply stomp into the school dining hall.

BETSY: Being anonymous in a new, big city was the best thing. Having to find a job without any contacts or local network was the worst.

WILL: The best thing was not having extracurricular activities tying me down; I had the freedom to explore new things. The worst thing was sharing costs with unemployed roommates.

CHARLES: The best thing was that I never had to pick up another book that I didn't choose. The worst thing was knowing I didn't prepare myself for the future I wanted, because I didn't know what I wanted for my future.

WENDY: The best thing was not having to go to classes, study, write papers—not being a student. The hardest thing was not having any friends and having no structure to meet them. I dreaded the weekend because I didn't have to go to work and I had nothing to do.

KEN: The thing I liked best was living with my high-school friends. The worst was that I felt like I had come out of the womb and been dropped on a cold floor. I was staring at the future and was obsessed with questions of success and failure.

Appendix:
How to Paint a Room

1. Take a rough measurement of the area you need to paint so that you'll have an idea of how much paint to buy. Don't forget to include the window frames and doors, if you're going to paint them. And think twice and then a third time before you decide not to. While they'll take much more time than the walls, freshly painted walls will call attention to nonfreshly painted frames.

2. The color(s) you choose will color not only your walls but also your life. And, if you find that formulation a bit too dramatic, let's settle for this: They will set the tone for your living space. Keep in mind that dark colors tend to shrink a room and light ones to expand it, so if you want to stray from the standard variations of white (and you don't want to decrease the perceived size of your apartment), opt for bright yellows, light blues, and so forth, over dark reds and browns. You'll want to buy water-based (latex) paint. You can buy flat, eggshell (a relative newcomer to the world of interior paint, that combines elements of both the semigloss and flat), semigloss (frequently recommended for baseboards, door frames, and window frames, because it's the most durable), or high gloss. Be sure to buy interior paint.

3. Pick up a small or medium-sized soft paintbrush as well as a roller, paint pan, paint-pan liner, and roller covers (thick matte is preferable, 1/4 inch or so). Be careful not to get the cheapest brush available, as the bristles will certainly fall out into your paint job, leaving the walls looking sloppy and hair-covered. (Hairy walls? Ick!) Also, pick up a small can of Goof-Off,™ which will come in handy when you drip paint on the carpet or on your clothes.

4. If possible, have the paint mixed at the store. If not, mix it in the can when you get home with a flat mixing stick, which should be included with the paint. Mix the paint in a figure-eight motion, periodically reversing the mixing direction.

5. Now you're ready to start. Almost. Do yourself a favor and give the apartment a quick cleaning job first. The most important areas to focus on are dust-collecting surfaces such as windowsills, shelves, and baseboards. Painting directly over dust might seem to be an easy alternative to the drudgery of cleaning, but the dust will ruin the paintbrush and make the paint job unsmooth. You'll wind up with walls that look as though they have a mild case of acne. (If you're not going to take the time to clean, you might as well buy the cheap paintbrush. Acne goes better with hairy walls.)

6. Unscrew and remove switch plates, light fixtures, and outlet covers to avoid painting over them. If they're already painted, you can remove the paint by chipping or with a paint-remover solution. This is a relatively easy trick that will give your paint job a more professional appearance.

7. If your landlord hasn't already done so, fill any nail holes or small cracks in the walls and ceiling with a patching compound (available at hardware and home stores), either one that's premixed or a "just add water" brand. These compounds can be easily applied with a putty knife (and will come in handy a second time when you move out and want to avoid being charged for any holes you put in the walls). A "water putty" compound can also be used to fill gaps in wood floors, but for this purpose be sure to get one that will flex without cracking. (This should be indicated on the back of the package. If not, ask a service person.)

8. If your belongings are already in the room you're painting,

move them to another room or to the center of the room where they can all be easily protected with a drop cloth. If the floor is carpeted, cover it entirely with a drop cloth (fabric or plastic), trash bags, or newspapers. Tape around windows and doorknobs to keep them free from paint. It's also a good idea to tape down the drop cloth or newspaper to the floor where it meets the walls. 3M makes a blue masking tape referred to as "painter's tape" which, while more expensive than standard masking tape, will neither strip off previous paint nor hurt wood floors.

9. If you're painting a lighter color than the current one, cover the dark paint with a primer so it doesn't show through. (Primer can also be used in spots if there are dark smudges or pen or pencil marks on the walls.)

10. When you're ready to paint, pour a small amount (approximately one cup) of paint into the lined paint pan or a small, clean bucket. (Children's plastic beach buckets work well.) Any areas you may have difficulty painting with a roller (e.g., windowsills, corners) should be done with the brush, and it's best to do those areas first. Dip the brush about an inch or so into the paint, and wipe off any excess along the rim of the bucket or pan. This will help curtail the inevitable drips that accompany an oversoaked brush.

11. Paint the trim of the apartment first, with even, delicate strokes. Remember that the trim includes all corners, windowsills, and the area around electrical outlets. Be careful not to paint windows or doors closed. Start with the highest areas of the walls and ceilings and work your way down, to avoid dripping on any spots you've already covered. When the trim is finished, or at any time you take a break for longer than a few minutes, rinse the brush carefully in water. (That's one of the reasons you want a water-based rather than an oil-based paint.) Keep in mind that if you've held it upside down, paint has probably run backward into the upper portions of the bristles, so clean the entire brush thoroughly. If you've used a bucket, pour the unused portion back into the paint can and either rinse it out or wait until the paint dries, at which point (with eggshell or semigloss) you can easily peel it out.

12. After you finish the trim, you're ready to use the roller. Pour a few cups of paint into the lined paint pan, and put the roller cover on the roller. Spin the roller in the paint until the cover has paint evenly dispersed over it, then roll it up and down the sloped area of the pan to rid it of excess paint. Roll the paint onto the wall or ceiling with long, even strokes. Again, start with the ceiling so you don't drip paint on walls you've already painted. When you're finished with the roller, it's generally a good idea to toss the used cover and liner; it's no fun rinsing the paint out of them.

13. In a couple of hours, after everything is dry, take stock of the job you've done. If there are areas that clearly need more paint, in which paint is uneven or brush strokes are apparent, you'll need to put on a second coat. Many paints on the market are touted as "one coat," but unfortunately this isn't always the case.

14. Strip excess paint off windows with a razor knife or with your putty knife. Semigloss or eggshell paint will actually peel right off without scraping.

INDEX

PLUME

PEOPLE GUIDES

☐ **HOW TO ATTRACT ANYONE, ANYTIME, ANYPLACE** *The Smart Guide to Flirting* **by Susan Rabin with Barbara Lagowski.** This indispensable, step-by-step guide gives you effective strategies for attracting that special someone . . . from places to meet people to advice on body language and sure-fire conversation openers, this book will take the mystery out of meeting people and turn you into the success you always wanted to be.   (270863—$8.95)

☐ **GUERRILLA DATING TACTICS** *Strategies, Tips, and Secrets for Finding Romance* **by Sharyn Wolf.** "Plucky, commonsensical guide for finding people, getting past the first date, and proceeding to romance."—*Publishers Weekly*   (271304—$11.95)

☐ **WHEN OPPOSITES ATTRACT by Rebecca Cutter.** With cogent examples and illuminating analysis based on her years of experience in counseling couples, the author calls a cease-fire in the gender wars and offers new insight into the "art and science" of loving. "Excellent strategies for resolving conflicts when partners see the world differently."—Lonnie Barbach, co-author of *Going the Distance*   (271142—$12.95)

Prices slightly higher in Canada.